# Paul E. Cannon

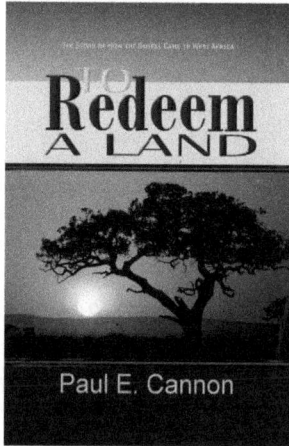

# To Redeem A Land

*The Story of How The Gospel Came to West Africa*

**Contact Information**

To purchase books please email Publishers of New Hope:
pecmlc@gmail.com

**Publishers of New Hope.**

Copyright © 2012, Paul E. Cannon – All Rights Reserved Under International Copyright Law. Contents and/ or cover may not be reproduced *in whole or in part, in any form, by any means – electronic, mechanical, photocopy, recording, or any other* – except for short excerpts for printed reviews, without the express written consent of the author.

ISBN: 978-0-9885074-7-0

Cover: Stock Photo © Copyrighted. Used by permission. All rights reserved.

# To Redeem A Land

*The Story of How The Gospel Came to West Africa*

## CONTENTS

# Introduction

By Charles Green
Founder, Word of Faith Church
New Orleans, Louisiana

Many people can put words on the page, but not many can make the words come alive with knowledge and excitement as Paul Cannon does.

I know many of the people Paul wrote about, but when I finished reading his story about these people and his own ministry, I wanted to go back in time and meet them all over again.

Paul Cannon's story is about the power of God in action with normal, ordinary people. It is the story of God's glory, God's healing power, but it also the story of sacrifice and hard work.

Having known Thomas Wyatt, his son Max Wyatt and many others Paul mentions, I was excited once again to read about their powerful miracle ministry. When young preachers ask me about starting a church, they go straight to the point, "How is the best way to start a church?" I go right to the point with my answer, "Start working miracles, and you will have no trouble building a church."

In his book, Paul makes the working of miracles come alive as he tells the story of blinded eyes and deaf ears being opened, leprosy vanishing instantly, crippled people running and dancing with joy and the power of the Gospel bringing many thousands to the knowledge of God's Salvation and to the Baptism in the Holy Spirit.

Do yourself a favor, buy Paul Cannon's book as soon as possible. You will thank me for introducing you to Paul ... and his book.

**Charles Green**
Founder, Word of Faith Church
New Orleans, Louisiana
Charlesgreen777@gmail.com

# Preface
## The Reason for Writing this Book! Please Read First!

Luke begins his gospel with these words: *"Inasmuch as many have taken in hand to set in order a narrative of those things which have been fulfilled among us, just as those who from the beginning were eyewitnesses and ministers of the word delivered them to us, it seemed good to me also, having had perfect understanding of all things from the very first, to write to you an orderly account, most excellent Theophilus, that you may know the certainty of those things in which you were instructed."* Luke 1:1-4.

I kind of feel like Luke may have felt when he penned these words. Many have tried to capture the illusive history of the Church in Africa, especially Ghana and Nigeria. Having been in on the beginning of the phenomenal growth of the church in Ghana and Nigeria, I felt it necessary to record the events which have been such a vital part of my life and a part of their lives.

The events recorded in this book are not taken from memory because memory is too faulty. There is a tendency to enlarge and make them bigger than what they were. These are taken from a detailed, hand-written diary (we call it a journal today) which had been stored away but couldn't be found for years. I haven't tried to enhance anything in this account, but have simply tried to put it in a readable format. I was able to salvage a few of the pictures and newspaper articles which are included in this work.

We spent a little over five months in Nigeria and Ghana but they were filled with unbelievable activity. Very few in this day and time could carry the schedule that was handed to us and live in the primitive conditions we had to live in.

I've not tried to paint a glorious picture without any problems but have tried to tell the story as it happened on a daily basis. This is done purposefully so that the reader could experience the joys of the mighty workings of our Lord when thousands were saved and healed. Yet along with it, you need to feel the boredom, the difficulties, and pain of things going wrong. What was accomplished in our meetings could not have happened had it not been for other missionaries and nationals without which we could not have done what was done. They are the real unsung heroes who laid the foundation for those happenings. We are eternally grateful for all the work they have done.

## Results of Many Laborers!

In Missions, the outcome is the result of many people's labor. They are never the results of one or two people even though we like to pinpoint it to them. This is always true whether it is Hudson Taylor in

China, William Carey in India, Patrick in Ireland or any of the other great Missionaries. No one does it alone. However there are times when many people are laboring, but there doesn't seem to be many results. Then along comes a person or several people that just seem to be the spark that is needed to see the thing really go. It's kind of like an automobile engine. You can have the perfect engine but until you get the spark from the spark plug, it won't work. The spark plug is not of much value by itself. In fact its worth is only a tiny fraction of the overall engine but the engine is of little value without the spark plug.

That is the way I feel about the meetings we had in Africa in 1953-4. The results of the last fifty years in both Ghana and Nigeria have been astounding. Many groups have labored incessantly as well as many individuals. That work is a result of all the combined labors of everyone that put their hand to the plow and didn't look back. Many of the pieces of the machinery were already there when we arrived. They just needed the spark that we brash, young men had to offer.

These are days of celebrity ministers with high powerful advertising and PR people that can make whatever kind of image they want of a person. Huge crowds possibly will assemble as a result. Video cameras, it seems, are almost as visible in such religious gathering as trees in a forest. Yet with all that machinery, we have to ask, "What is really accomplished when viewed from the perspective of time and distance?"

## Days of Simplicity!

The middle of the 1950's were days of simplicity. Life wasn't very complicated, especially in the land of Africa. Just to live was a big task because of so many killer tropical diseases. For our meetings, we basically had no advertisement. In fact, our advertisement often was nothing more than the sound of the village gong, ordered by the chief. Sometimes the word went out to other places by people telling it to others. Sometimes it was by nothing more than messages sent by log drums. Our sound system often was nothing more than an old amplifier, if we had one, that seemed to have a mind of its own and two of the old brassy trumpet speakers. Yet huge crowds gathered to hear the gospel of Jesus Christ. At other times, we just went out on the main street and stood preaching the gospel and people would gather around to see what these "white guys" were propagating. At first the crowd might be small and be very unreceptive but they would grow, especially when they saw miracles happen.

We never tried to focus the attention on ourselves, or on our prayers but upon the Risen Christ. He was the Fountain of living water that would flow out to meet their desperate needs. We were only a tiny instrument in His wonderful hand. We often said that God did it, not because of us, but in spite of us. At the time, we didn't know it would accomplish all that it has because it was only a dream and a vision in our hearts. We knew we were living in desperate days when the Colonial Empires would come crashing down. We had the sense of being people of destiny. Live, die, sink or swim, we had to help prepare this people to stand on their own two feet and become a great force in the Kingdom of God. To us the mandate was "do or die."

Our understanding was that the future of the Church very well could depend on them carrying the gospel to the ends of the earth. This had to be done with real miracles to demonstrate the glorious benefits of that kingdom and to bring the people into a vital, living relationship with the Lord Jesus Christ. The signs and wonders surely got their attention and it opened their hearts to receiving the Lord as their personal Savior and being filled with the Holy Spirit. This would, in turn, empower them to continue doing what we were doing and to carry it on without us. We deliberately were trying to work ourselves out of a job. This is always the true test of real leadership and revival. What happens when you are gone, whether you are a pastor, teacher, or superintendent? Can the people you have ministered to carry it on when you are removed from the scene?

### Time Tells the Tale!

To see the real results of meetings or revival, it must be looked at over the period of a long time. There are often little upswings that grab the attention of many people but when you look at them several years later, they didn't make much difference, if any, in the advance of the Kingdom of God. Instead of being a ground swell as we thought, they were nothing more than a small ripple over a small pond. There are many "works" we get involved in that we think are the greatest. We give ourselves to them unreservedly but in just a few years they become obsolete and are gone and didn't amount to "a hill of beans."

My purpose in writing this historical account is first of all to glorify our Lord and Savior, Jesus Christ. He was the one who opened the way and provided the funds and called us to go. We only responded to Him and His calling. Therefore all glory must go to Him, who gave Himself a ransom for us. It was He that allowed us to experience this wonderful visitation though it was not without many hardships and difficulties.

My second reason for writing this is so that the wonderful people of Nigeria and Ghana who have come to a saving knowledge of our Risen Lord and built local churches as a result of what the Lord did in those days might know a little of their own history. They need to know how and when their churches began. This is a story that hasn't been told much, if at all.

The third reason I wanted to write this book is so that it might inspire others to arise and accomplish great things in their day, especially young people. They need to know that one doesn't have to be an older, well-seasoned minister to see people met by their loving Lord. When I consider the fact that I was only 22 years of age at the time and just graduated from Bible School a few months before. When I entered Bible School and was asked about my calling, my answer was that I did not feel called to the ministry. In fact, my pastor had told me before leaving for Bible School that I would never make it in the ministry. I replied that I didn't want to be in the ministry, I just wanted to be a better soulwinner. Evangelism was high on my list of priorities & still is.

## Not Much Going On!

Considering the religious climate in those days, there wasn't much going on revival wise. Most mission groups were only sending people on 4 year stints on the field where they would first learn the language and slowly build their works of teaching and training. The works were always dependent upon the missionaries as the overseers. When one would go home, another was sent to take their place. We were considered radicals because we wanted to empower the Africans to the extent that they could complete what we were starting. Our ultimate vision was to see them raised up and boldly carry the gospel into regions we could never go into. We honestly believed that they could do the job as well if not better than we could. Underlying all of that was a deep compassion to bring all the benefits of the Kingdom of God to a very needy people. There were thousands of lepers and cripples plus multitudes of very sick people. Children had a hard time of surviving because of so many tropical diseases. We had such a deep love for them and they did likewise for us. Love indeed breaks down many barriers. It was so manifested that it made the headlines of many newspapers wherever they had one.

## Miracles Had to Be Real!

When it came to healing and miracles, we were insistent that they be real. We used no gimmicks whatsoever. If a person was healed of blindness, we didn't hold up our fingers to prove they could see or excite the crowd. It was our firm belief that if they were healed they would let us know as one would be surprised with an unexpected gift. If they were deaf, we didn't clap our hands or snap our fingers to see if they could hear. They shouted out excitedly, "I can hear, I can hear!" We didn't help cripples walk to show that they were healed. They leaped to their feet and danced up and down on their own. Only in small meetings would we lay hands upon people and pray for them individually. Most of the time, it was much better to pray one prayer enmasse for the whole crowd once their faith was built up to believe the Lord. Often we would pray and take a half step back with our head bowed and wait for the Lord to work. At times it seemed like a half hour, when in reality it was only a minute or so. Then miracles began to happen as the Lord met a people He dearly loved.

May this book encourage you and strengthen your faith to believe for the impossible. We pray that the Lord will use it to further His Kingdom by stirring the hearts of His people to *"go into all the world and preach the gospel to every creature."* He is still the same yesterday, today and forever.

**- Paul E. Cannon**

# Unforgettable Meetings
# Chapter 1

### Christmas in Africa!

It was Christmas morning in 1953 and I was standing before an enormous crowd of people in the town of Wiamoase, Gold Coast, (name changed later to Ghana) West Africa. There were no signs of Christmas anywhere or decorations of the season. It seemed to me we were right in the heart of the jungles of Africa, some ten thousand or more miles from my home in Baton Rouge, Louisiana. It was a day I would never forget!

### A Heart Breaking Scene!

I thought that my heart would break as I looked out across that sea of black and brown faces. There was such a cry of desperation on the face of each one of them. In those days and in that area, there was almost no health care available except in some of the major cities. Very few Medical Missionaries were on the field as well.

As usual in all of our meetings, the African Ministers that came with us had roped off a large area right in front of the improvised platform and podium. This was so the sick and needy could gather in close to the speaker. Usually it was put right in front of the pulpit and platform so as you looked out over the vast crowd you saw the neediest ones of all. They did this out of compassion for the sick and the maimed. Sometimes I felt it was an intimidation factor with all those hopeless and suffering people looking at you with such longings in their eyes.

There were easily more than 600 people assembled in that roped off area. It was filled to overflowing with people with every kind of sickness that you can imagine. There were the, all too familiar, lepers with various body parts missing, the running sores of yaws, the huge legs and arms of elephantiasis, the hopelessly crippled with their distorted bodies and the blind with their clouded, milky looking eyes, the deaf and the mute. These were the ones that caught your attention but there were many others just as desperate. Heart trouble was a major problem as well as lung trouble which they called consumption. There were the epileptics, tumors and kidney problems besides the horribly distended stomachs and ruptured navels that were not included. On top of that, were untold numbers of people who said they had "snakes in their bellies" from a curse placed on them by a witch doctor and were literally starving to death. Hundreds of little naked babies were there with their legs and arms just hanging dead and useless. Many of them were blind, deaf and mute. Thousands of all ages packed together, covering acres of ground. Add to this, almost everyone had a fever as malaria was running rampant in those days. The mortality rate of children was so enormous.

We were told it was running seven out of ten dying before they reached the age of ten. I don't know if that was true as we had no way to check it out.

I remember one fellow who had some horrible disease that had eaten his nose and lips off. His teeth were gone and you could look right down into his throat. The needs were so pressing that it broke my heart and I couldn't hold back the tears. It seemed that my whole being was filled with the compassion of Calvary as I stood there openly weeping. At the same time there was such confidence that our crucified and Risen Lord was well able to minister to this hurting mass as individuals and do it on a large scale.

Max Wyatt

## My Colleague and Companion!

With me in this city of Wiamoase, Gold Coast was my teacher and my friend, Max Wyatt of Salem, Oregon. Max was the son of Dr. Thomas Wyatt, who was the President and Founder of the Wings of Healing International Radio Broadcast and Pastor and Founder of the Wings of Healing Temple in Portland, Oregon as well as Founder and President of Bethesda Bible Institute. The Wings of Healing Broadcast was the largest religious radio broadcast in the world at this time and had a hundred voice choir that was one of the best. If you had a radio, there was no place on earth that you couldn't hear the program as it blanketed the globe. Dr. Wyatt in earlier years had founded many churches in Iowa and Nebraska as well as held great healing meetings throughout the Midwest. We were told it was in one of his tent meetings in Oklahoma that Oral Roberts was healed as a young man and he would later enter into the healing ministry. Whether this was actually true, I cannot say.

Max was a teacher in the Bethesda Bible Institute; an auxiliary speaker on the Wings of Healing broadcast and was the founder and pastor of Faith Tabernacle in Salem Oregon. He was one of the finest preachers I have ever known and a tremendous man of God with a marvelous prophetic mantle. He was so easy to get along with & found great joy in seeing young ministers excel.

## A Big Brush Arbor

We were gathered under a huge canopy that had been erected in a big vacant area near the center of town. These canopies were similar to the old American brush arbor. Hundreds of bamboo poles were placed erect, with others placed horizontally on top of these. This provided a skeleton roof on which they placed many palm branches. It wouldn't be of any value in the rain but it did provide shelter from the scorching rays of the tropical sun.

What seats they had were nothing but rough planks placed on cement blocks or stones. The boards averaged about six to eight inches in width with no backrest. Some of these canopies would seat as many as fifteen thousand people. Regardless of how many they could seat, there would be far more people standing than seated. They would stand for hours packed close together in the stifling heat without any sign of discomfort or weariness. It wasn't unusual for some to walk six or eight miles to the meetings. They would stand for three or four hours in the services and then walk back home. The crowd was so enormous, running into the multiplied thousands. I have no idea how many were assembled as that didn't seem to cross our minds. They were even standing way beyond the dirt street because there were no hard surfaced roads in this vicinity and very little traffic.

## A Wave of Prophetic Healing!

Our plans this Christmas morning were that Max would teach for a while and then I was supposed to preach the main message. As usual, things were changed as most of the time we "flew by the seat of our pants." By that I mean, we did our best to do exactly what we sensed the Holy Spirit directing immediately. I spoke several minutes on the birth of our Lord Jesus Christ and the reason He came. I was dealing with the fact Jesus had come to deal with sin and bring people to God. This was the good news the angelic host brought to the shepherds. All of a sudden, I had such a sense that Max should finish the message. So I turned and said to him, "Max, the Lord wants you to finish the message." Instantly, He sprang to his feet and presented the story from that point on. He dealt with the purpose of our Lord's coming to earth and giving His life a ransom for all who would believe. Apparently it inspired him as he was so excited. He always was such a "spark plug" anyway.

Right on the spur of the moment with such a powerful anointing of the Holy Spirit, he ran off the platform right down among the sick, taking one of the interpreters with him. At the same time I grabbed a mike and took the other interpreter with me and went down the other side. Max had asked Paintsil and Sackey, our interpreters, not to wait to interpret but just explain what we were saying to them as we ministered to the desperately sick before us. There was such a prophetic anointing that came on both of us that we began prophesying to each one of the blind, sick, lepers and cripples in that roped off area. Our interpreters didn't say anything to anyone the whole time. They simply were praying with us as both of us were speaking to the people in their own language. Actually, we were speaking in tongues but it was a prophecy to them because we didn't know any of their languages. It didn't matter what their language was, the prophetic word was in that language.

After about two and a half hours of doing this, Max turned to Paintsil, our lead interpreter, and asked him what happened when we spoke to the various sick people. Paintsil about fell over backwards as he was so completely astonished by this question. He could hardly answer because he was stuttering so. Instantly he began pointing to different people around us in amazement that were healed and said, "What do you mean 'What happened?' For two and a half hours you were speaking to these people in their own language and you ask me what happened? Just look at all the people that are healed."

## Hundreds Came to Testify

By this time hundreds of people were lined up at the microphone to tell what the Lord had done for them. This was handled completely by our African brethren. The first man up was the first one that we spoke to. At the microphone he said he was born blind and had never seen anything in his whole life. I remember him vividly as his eyes were covered with thick white cataracts. He said the young American told him to "stand up and look." So when he heard those words in his own language, he just stood up and looked and for the first time in his life he could see. His clouded eyes had become crystal clear with beautiful pupils. The crowd roared with applause and praise to the Lord, saying Hallelujah repeatedly.

People had been set free right and left. It was the most amazing thing. I have never seen it done in this manner, either before or since, but everyone we prophesied to was instantly healed regardless of what was wrong. This only shows what can be done by the Holy Spirit working. He can do more in five minutes than we can do in a lifetime. Hundreds more testified of major miracles and impossible things they were healed of. There was such a healing wave that morning. The miracles were too numerous to mention them one by one. According to the testimonies, they were healed of every kind of thing imaginable, such as blindness, leprosy, yaws, paraplegics, "snakes in the stomach," deafness, epilepsy and heart trouble plus many others. The paralyzed and cripples were on their feet dancing and shouting. Many of them had been carried in by their family or friends. It was so wonderful to see them hugging one another, dancing around and shouting praises to the Lord. Needless to say, it was a noisy place. They were demonstrating the fact that they were healed and set free in every way imaginable. Everyone we laid hands upon that morning that did what we said to them to do, the Lord Jesus met instantly. The Word of the Lord is sure! What a tremendous visitation of God it was on that Christmas morning!

## A Side Trip

In the afternoon a brother took us up in the mountains to a little town in his car just to look around. We traveled up a dirt road almost encompassed with jungle growth. It was thrilling because when the people saw us, they would come up and say "Praise the Lord" or "Hallelujah." We used the word, Hallelujah, so much in the meetings that we became known as the Hallelujahs wherever we went. There was such joy on their faces and together they would begin singing some of the songs we sang at the meetings. No doubt many of them had attended the meetings in Wiamoase because they would come from many miles all around. What a wonderful people and they seemed so glad to have us. We loved every minute of it. We took some pictures of them and also the jungle and sent them to Portland later when we got to a big city.

## A Mighty Deluge of the Holy Spirit!

Most of the time in the meetings, one of us would get up and exhort for about ten to fifteen minutes and the other one would preach the main message. Max was supposed to preach in the evening meeting but while I was exhorting, there was such a sense that we should call for those who wanted to receive the Holy Spirit to come up to the front. Without trying to size the crowd, I figured there were well more than 250 people that came forward expectantly. However in talking with Max later, he insisted there were more than 400 people that came forward on the first call. It didn't matter to me because my idea was that we had all we had and not one less. We had them stand in rows where the sick had been placed in the morning so we could get between the rows to pray with them. It was now empty because no sick were there that evening after the great meeting in the morning. We really weren't concerned with numbers anyway. Max took a few minutes at the time to instruct the ministers first on what to do when we prayed for the people to receive the Holy Spirit. We needed their help in the laying on of hands with so many assembled. He specifically told them not to "tarry" or linger in praying with any of them. He then told the ministers that the Lord said all that came forward were going to receive the Holy Spirit tonight. Wow! This almost overwhelmed our African brethren. Of course we were absolutely sure that the Lord would meet the people when they came. There wasn't a doubt on our part it would happen.

In everything, we included our African Brethren because we wanted to plant the work of the Lord and they would be the ones to carry it on. It was never the big us and the little them. We wanted them to feel like they were our equals in every sense of the word. So we encouraged all the ministers with us to be in the Spirit, themselves, if they were expecting others to be filled. We had the seekers to line up in rows of fifties so the ministers and us could move among them. They were many rows deep and filled that whole area. Then Max gave a few instructions to the people and led them in a prayer of repentance and acceptance of Jesus as their Savior.

As they began to call on the Lord and before we could lay hands on any of them, the Holy Spirit began to fall upon them. Most of them were already so anointed with the Holy Spirit and were worshiping the Lord with their hands upraised and tears streaming down their faces. Max and I began praying and laying our hands on the first row to our left as the African pastors split up by twos and took other rows.

The Holy Spirit was one person ahead of all of us. As we would lay hands on one, the next one down the row would begin speaking in tongues as the Spirit gave them utterance. An interpreter was always right with us as we went down each row laying our hands upon them and making sure they had received. However we found that we could tell more about it by the anointing of the Holy Spirit. All of them but about 20 had been wonderfully filled with the Holy Spirit in that first group.

### Another Wave!

We had all of those who had received to sit down, and then we gave another invitation for people to come and be filled. To our amazement, more than 400 more came forward the second time. However, this group of people looked entirely different from the first group. We realized that many of these were sinners as they had so many fetishes on their arms and around their necks and waists to ward off evil spirits. Some were not dressed as the others were dressed, but rather unclothed to say the least.

Some of the ministers were greatly concerned about the fact of them being unsaved. So they wanted us to just deal with them in regard to salvation rather than the Holy Spirit. They reminded us that Max had said that all who came would be filled with the Holy Spirit. They didn't think they were ready for that as they needed to be cleaned up outside and get rid of the fetishes and put clothes on their bodies. By this time we had learned that people could accept the Lord and be filled with the Holy Spirit all at one time and then go home and do their own cleanup.

So in our instructions we included a short time of how to accept the Lord as their Savior and led them in a prayer of confession and repentance first. It was amazing to watch the tears begin to flow down their cheeks. You knew they were in earnest. In just a few minutes it was exactly like before when we laid our hands on them. Every one of them received the Holy Spirit except one lady. In my thinking, this made more than 500 people who were filled with the Holy Spirit.

In talking with Max afterwards, he insisted there were more than 850 people filled with Holy Spirit that Christmas evening. He was probably right as he had more experience with crowds than I did. It always seemed that I underestimated numbers as that didn't concern me at all. Sometimes I would actually try to count people in a group and found I was always way short numerically.

## What About the One Who Didn't Receive?

Before all of this wound down, some of the ministers brought a lady up front to us. They were deeply concerned because Max had said everyone would receive and they wanted to remind him of that again. Their problem was that no one knew the language of this one lady even with all of the various dialects they did know. They wondered why in the world she came forward without knowing what it was all about. So all of us gathered around her and prayed for her together. The Presence of the Holy Spirit was so great upon her that we were positive she had received, though no one could verify it by the speaking in tongues. So we continued praying with her because of the great respect we had for our fellow African brethren and we wanted them to be satisfied. Suddenly, she began to speak in clear English without any accent. With

Sakki, Paul, Paintsil

great joy she was praising the Lord, and making a declaration of His great mercy and grace. That absolutely electrified the ministers and the whole mass of people began shouting and praising the Lord for His mighty works. In trying to talk with the lady afterwards, we found that she not only didn't understand us in English but she didn't understand any of the other languages spoken there either. It's still a great puzzle to me, how she was able to receive the Holy Spirit not knowing any of the language spoken. But I vouch for it that it was real. I know the things I've spoken about sounds like exaggeration, but the things we saw and heard would be very difficult to exaggerate.

## Preach After All of That?

After all that, the African Ministers wanted me to preach a little. They said to me, "We've got to have the Word so preach to us a little." I tried but it was hard to create interest in the Word at the time. They just wanted to frolic and praise the Lord because He had been so good to them. Nevertheless many sick people were healed that evening as well even though none had been in the roped off area. These were mixed in with the great crowd, unbeknown to us.

When it came to dancing and singing loudly, how can anyone tell them not to do that when the Lord had done such extraordinary things among them and for them? There's no way you could, especially when you're a part of the ministry that has brought such fantastic benefits to a suffering and needy people. If you were the one receiving, there's no way you would stop it. You would be like the cripple at the Gate called

Beautiful in the Book of Acts when he was healed. He went leaping and jumping and praising the Lord.

I have learned a marvelous thing about the Lord Jesus and it is this. If you'll walk close to Him and seek His face earnestly, you'll come to fully realize that He is indeed the God He claims to be. When that takes place, He will definitely manifest Himself to you and through you. For my part, I couldn't help but be overcome with amazement that the Lord should use someone such as me. It was wonderful the way the Lord had worked. His grace is still so amazing! We knew down deep within our heart that we really didn't have much to do with all the things happening around us. We were so impressed that we were nothing more than weak instruments in the hands of a Sovereign God. This was my happiest day in Africa and my greatest Christmas!

### Reminiscing!

Looking back over this wonderful day, I realize that it was nothing but the gentle grace of our Risen Lord that prompted each of our actions in these meetings. It was His concern for this needy people and His delight to use us that made it all possible. We didn't orchestrate any of it nor did we try to work up anything. We didn't know what to do most of the time but we tried to be sensitive to the Holy Spirit as we felt He was there orchestrating it all. No doubt there are many times when each of us misses out on bringing in the spiritual harvest when it should be gathered, simply because we fail to respond to the leading of the Holy Spirit. We are prompted to act but we don't respond to it. I'm convinced the Lord wants to lead us by His Spirit more than we want to be led and it's not some spooky, weird thing. Just think! If all of us did this, it would bring into His Kingdom a far greater harvest than we could ever imagine.

### The Start of the Meeting!

We had come to Wiamoase two days earlier on the twenty-third of December, having finished up a morning meeting in the big city of Kumasi in Central Ghana. Wiamoase was about 31 miles off the beaten road, down an old dirt road, way up in the hills, in what seemed to be the heart of the jungle. We had gotten there by riding a "Lorrie" which is a small pickup truck made into a public bus like vehicle. They had rooms for us in the government rest house that the English had built for their governmental staff to stay in while traveling.

That evening was our first meeting and we had what we thought was a very good crowd out. I have no idea of how large the crowd was but it was huge by any standards. It was amazing since there had been no advertisement whatsoever on our part nor our African brethren.

Max seemed so tired and asked me to preach, so I did. After all he was the leader. It was close to the meeting time when he asked. So it was, an on the spur of the moment thing, without any planned notes. In those days, we did a lot of things on the spur of the moment. Before I could finish preaching and without any warning, the people came up and just swarmed all around me. I really didn't know what caused it as I was just delivering the Word. Suddenly, a wave of healing from the presence of the Lord flowed among them. A great many people were healed right then but we didn't take a lot of time to have them come and testify since it was our first night. There seemed to be an awful lot of heart failure and epilepsy in these parts. I guess that certain diseases run more in certain areas than in others. However, the Lord was setting them free and it seemed to be a sovereign act.

### The Best Interpreters

Wherever we went in Ghana, we used two interpreters most of the time and though we were in "Ashanti" land we still used both. They were absolutely the best that I have ever used through all the years of ministry and I have had some excellent ones in many nations. A young man by the name of J. Egyir Paintsil interpreted into the "Twi" or "Fanti" language while another young man by the name of Sakki interpreted into the "Ga" language. These two young men would get into the same anointing as we had. The one could hardly wait for the other one to get through at times. They both would get so excited about a truth being preached that they would jump up and down waiting for us to finish the sentence or thought so they could give it. Without them we would have been helpless. They truly were mighty men of God! There is no doubt that a lot of our success came as a result of their translating.

A Missionary friend, James McKeown, had set up our meetings in conjunction with the small Church in the area on the invitation of the King or Chief of the area. However James McKeown was not with us in Wiamoase but was with our other team, Erskine Holt and Paul Shaver. James McKeown and several Gold Coast brethren had recently formed, the Gold Coast Apostolic Church with its headquarters in Accra. Later they would change their name to The Church of Pentecost and J. Egyir Paintsil would eventually become President of the group. In those days, you never called anyone by a title or their first names. You always used their last names. So we were Cannon, Wyatt, Paintsil, Sakki, McKeown, etc. to each other.

### A Lonesome Christmas Eve

The next day was Christmas Eve and there was a huge crowd out for the morning meeting. Max finally consented to speak and preached a wonderful sermon. I really loved to listen to him preach. There were quite a few that were healed and delivered, mostly of heart trouble and epilepsy. Max preached again in the night meeting and a good number again were healed. To me the people didn't seem to respond to faith very much as we had been seeing in other places. They move but there didn't seem to be the exuberance of faith at first. This disappointed us but God still seemed to meet them regardless.

Being human and missing our families, when we got back to the Rest House, Max and I grew very lonesome as darkness crept over the jungle and you could hear so many strange sounds. You can't even imagine what it was like unless you have been there. It was cloudy and so dark that you couldn't even see your hand in front of your face and that seemed to magnify the loneliness. So we sat around, just the two of us, talking about Christmas and home. We tried to remember the Christmas poem, "The Night Before Christmas." We used what we could remember of it as the basis and made up our own poem about Christmas Eve and what we were experiencing.

### Our Poem

'Twas the night before Christmas when all through the rest house,
The mosquitoes were buzzing and the ants crawling about.
Our stockings were hung by the window to dry,
And hoping the Bowiea would not begin his cry.
Under the nets that were tattered and torn
From fighting the mosquitoes they were pretty well worn.
While Paul and Max were tucked in their beds
And visions of sweet home danced in their heads.
When out in the jungle there arose such a chatter,
We flung off the nets to see what was the matter.
We grabbed up our pants and sprang to the floor.
Made a great clatter but got to the door.
The light of the moon then shown on the ground
Showed us a mammy Lorrie coming from town.
From the bottom of the hill and over they went,
For they journeyed along as the night was far spent.
And I heard them say, ere they drove out of sight,
Thanks for coming to deliver us from our plight.

After finishing it we both closed our weary eyes as we fell onto our army type cots wondering how things were back home with our loved ones and what the morrow would bring us.

### Christmas in an Unreached City

In America, we are so used to the colorful lights and decorations for the Christmas season. This was not so in this particular part of the world at least in this city at this time. I can't remember a single sign that said anything about Christmas. There were no decorations, no Santa Claus, no carols being sung, no dreams of a white Christmas, no chestnuts roasting on an open fire or anything that we Westerners associate with Christmas. If you didn't know it was Christmas day, there wouldn't be anything to let you know it had arrived. Christmas day in the jungle was no different from any other day. Of course there was a very good reason for this. How could they celebrate the birth of Jesus when they had never heard that there was a Jesus that had come to save them? If you said that the Bible said, they didn't know what a bible was as most of them had never seen a bible.

In some places they were still doing the human sacrifice thing to their gods. The British government had outlawed it a couple years before but by no means had they fully extinguished it at that time, so we were told. Animal sacrifice was still the religion of the populous being headed up by the Juju Priests (Witch Doctors). Even with all of that, Max and I couldn't help but rejoice in the fact that God had sent His one and only son, born of a virgin, into our world in order to redeem mankind from sin and its consequences. This Christmas was different from all the rest because no one was giving out any gifts to each other. To us it seemed like God was the one that was doing the giving and He gave out the most spectacular and marvelous gifts that anyone could ever desire.

### The Day after Christmas

We arose early and had our usual breakfast of porridge (oatmeal) with evaporated milk diluted with boiled and filtered water along with eggs and toast. This was all cooked over an open wood fire. We then went to the morning meeting where another large crowd was in attendance. I preached on Hosea 10:12, *"Sow to yourselves in righteousness, reap in mercy; break up your fallow ground: for it is time to seek the LORD, till he come and rain righteousness upon you."* I pitched the message along the lines of consecration and our need of seeking the Lord and doing so till He comes to us individually. We had those that wanted to really dedicate their lives to the Lord to come forward and kneel at the platform. Many, many of them came forward and kneeled. Ministers and laymen, young and old began to seek the Lord with a real cry coming from their hearts. Most of them were weeping and sobbing as they called upon His name, dedicating and rededicating themselves to His service. The Lord really met them. His presence was so mightily in our midst. These were occasions when you could sense the Sovereign hand of God in meeting people and bringing them into the Kingdom of God. It was not something that was done by a "high powered" evangelist with slick advertisement and a highly orchestrated program. Our meetings were totally un-regimented. Our African brethren ran all the services, with us doing the preaching or teaching. This was the beginning of a glorious revival in that nation and it has been going on ever since.

Jesus would never have given the command to His disciples to go into all the world and preach the gospel to every creature, if it wasn't possible for it to be fulfilled. We've found that when a Child of God sees the Lord's purpose and His intention to reach the unreached multitudes, then it becomes real to them. At that moment, they become equal to the task by the Spirit of God because He divinely enables them to accomplish His task. It is still as true today as it was when the word of the LORD came to the prophet Zechariah saying unto Zerubbabel, *"Not by might, nor by power, but by my spirit, saith the LORD of hosts."* Zech. 4:6.

While in Wiamoase, we received official word from Dr. Wyatt and the Wings of Healing in Portland that they wanted to start a Bible Training School right away in Accra, the capital city of Ghana and the funds were available. We would look into buying land and a building our next time in Accra. Max then told the congregation about starting a Bible school in Accra. That really excited them, especially the young people and ministers. Many of them said they wanted to be in it.

### A Walk in the Jungle

In the afternoon I was very bored as there was nothing to do. That's an understatement to say the least. After such high moments, there is always a big letdown emotionally especially if there isn't anything different to do. So I told Max that I was going to go for a walk as I had read my Bible and prayed all that I felt I could and needed some exercise and a change of pace. Max jumped up and said that was a good idea and he would go with me. We began to walk down this jungle trail that led past the Rest House and down a big hill to only God knows where. This was all new country to us and so different from anything we had ever seen. We poked along the trail enjoying the African jungle with its huge, colorful trees, and vines. It was a tropical paradise! There were all kinds of gorgeous flowers and beautiful birds along with the little animals. Everything seemed so lush and beautiful so we walked much farther than we had intended or even realized. As we rounded a curve in the trail, we were, suddenly, in the courtyard of about six or eight mud huts with thatched roofs. The whole area didn't have a single sprig of grass or vegetation on it, and was swept entirely clean.

### Surrounded by Children and Adults

Almost immediately, we were surrounded by a dozen boys and girls, just jabbering and laughing. They didn't have a stitch of clothing on any of them. When they saw our whitish, tan looking skin, they wanted to touch our arms and hands so badly. Not wanting to disappoint them, we held our arms out so they could. Then we realized what an oddity we were to them. When they touched us, they would just laugh and giggle, jabbering in a language we didn't have any experience with. Then the older people came up to us. They seemed to be very friendly and smiling for which we were very thankful. At first we were just a little apprehensive and hoped that they wouldn't mind us being there. Immediately our minds went to some of the horrible Missionary stories we had heard or read about. We couldn't communicate with them as they spoke no English and of course we didn't know their language. All we could do was use hand gestures and smile.

Suddenly both of us noticed a baby boy sitting on the bare ground just a couple yards away and that he was very sick. He didn't seem to have any energy or enthusiasm at all. His stomach was terribly bloated, his eyes were watery and his face was drawn in pain. You just knew that this baby was terribly ill. Without giving any thought to it, both of us at the same time stepped over to the child and knelt with one knee on the ground by him. As we knelt there, such an overwhelming sense of compassion swept over each of us for this little boy. The two of us laid our hands on him and began to pray. We knew this situation was hopeless because he was just "burning up" with fever. The instant we finished praying, he vomited and passed some fluid. He was healed sitting right there. The fever had completely left him. In just a few minutes he was smiling and began to play with the smaller kids. He seemed so happy and alert with absolutely no sign of pain or illness.

### The Whole Village Follows Us Out

By this time, it was getting late and we had to leave to go back up the hill because we had to minister in the service in an hour or so. We hadn't gone far when we realized we were being followed. The entire village was walking right behind us. We wondered what in the world they could want. They came right up to the rest house where the people in charge explained to them who we were and that we were having large outdoor meetings in the center of town. They came to the meeting that evening where all of them accepted the Lord that night. Our Interpreter told us that the child had been very sick and when they saw the child healed, they wanted to find out what had happened to make him well. So they simply followed us up the trail to find out more. They had never heard the gospel of Jesus Christ in their lives. Though the meeting wasn't far from their village, they hadn't been in it. It's strange because others had come in from many miles away yet these weren't over a mile or two away in the jungle and knew nothing about the meetings.

Many times I've thought about that lonely trail and the small village of people in that clearing in the jungle and the presence of God coming to heal that baby. Without any sermon being preached, even without us understanding their language nor them understanding ours and without any faith on the part of the parents, Jesus healed him. It was just the love and compassion of the Lord Jesus as He sovereignly moved through us to meet that little boy. Perhaps in our Western churches we have a tendency to put too much emphasis on the things that we can do and forget what the Lord can do. We use these things as props for our religious services when really what we need is a fresh out pouring of the love and presence of the Lord among us.

Max preached in the service that evening. He was having trouble with his throat so I stepped out and got him a portello (soft drink) so that he could continue. What a wonderful sermon he preached that night. Quite a large number of people were healed but the crowd of sick was getting quite low because of all that had been met by the Lord in healing and deliverance up to this point.

### Fever Broken Through Prayer

We moved from place to place quite often in meetings. Sometimes we were from two days to a week in a city or village with meetings usually twice a day. We always tried to stay in a British "Rest House" whenever it was possible. In America it would be kind of like a small Motel or a Bed and Breakfast Inn. After being here a couple of days, we couldn't help but notice something was wrong with the couple who took care of the Rest House. Looking at their faces, they seemed to be so sad and down cast. Their actions really showed it. So Max asked them if anything was wrong. They told us their eight-year-old daughter who was their only child was extremely sick and wasn't expected to live. We asked them if we could see her and they took us to her room. When we saw she was running a high fever and her eyes seemed to be sunken in her head, compassion again filled our hearts. Instantly there was an inner peace in both of us that the Lord was going to minister to her need. So we began to pray and even while we were praying, the fever broke. That evening the parents brought their daughter to the meeting, completely healed. Both of them accepted the Lord and were filled with the Holy Spirit. Oh, the wonders of our God never cease!

I have often wondered from that day to this, how much we miss and how much the work of the Lord suffers because we're not aware of the people around us in everyday life. So many times, we're not very concerned about the welfare of those we come in contact with. Even those who serve us in stores, restaurants, gas stations and even in Church, we pay little attention too. We tend to tune them out and consider it none of our business. May the Lord constantly make us aware of everyone around us so we can be used to finish His wonderful work.

### The Final Day Here

It was a relatively cool morning on the twenty-seventh of December, so we put on our sport coats for warmth. This would be our final day of meetings among these wonderful people. So we gathered at the canopy and I preached in the morning meeting. The pastor wanted us to dedicate his newly constructed church building, so we didn't linger at the canopy very long. This was the only Church in town and it was extremely small.

We were there in meetings because the King of the area had invited us through the pastor. There seemed to be an unusual excitement among the people, as all of us walked down the main street. It reminded me, in a small way, of when the Lord Jesus rode into Jerusalem on Palm Sunday. We had come to cut the ribbon and enter the little church building and dedicate it to the Lord as a place of worship.

Max spoke a few words outside the building then the King came up in his royal procession with his gold crown and purple and gold robe on. He and Max officially cut the ribbon and the pastor opened the door. I was too busy taking pictures of the crowd with them opening the door to have a part. Many thousands of people filled the yard but only a small portion of them could get in. The new building could only hold about a hundred people as it was about twenty-four feet square and was soon jam packed. I declare, that about five hundred people squeezed into it. We were like sardines in a can as it seemed that all of us had to breathe at different times to have enough room. It was the biggest thing that this city had ever seen. When inside, we sang a song and there was a good word of prophecy. The King then said a few words and gave them ten Guineas ($30 dollars) in West African currency for their church.

This was a time of such thrilling fulfillment for the local pastor. As we left the building to return to the canopy, the pastor asked us a startling question which Max and I had already talked about. What was he going to do with the hundreds and thousands of people that had been saved and filled with the Holy Spirit? His church building was too small and he was living in a very small mud hut with a packed earthen floor and a thatch roof, with his wife and three children. He had come to this town a couple years earlier in order to start a Church and introduce the gospel but had not been very successful in reaching the city. We suggested that he build a large canopy in the yard of the church and that he and his family should move into the church building. After we left, this was exactly what happened. They built a canopy for several thousand people, and it was filled with rejoicing Christians. What a tremendous beginning for a local church!

### Back to the Canopy

We walked back to the canopy with the crowd following us. An African pastor led us in some singing and worship. My, how the people rejoiced and danced before the Lord. Reluctantly the Ministers allowed us to take an offering. They kept saying the people were too poor to give. Our argument was on scriptural principles that to give is to be blessed. We must give them an opportunity to give with no pressure on them.

The Lord would use this as a channel to bless them. Finally they agreed and were greatly surprised when they got 55 pounds ($170) in the offering. It would have been wrong for us not to allow them to give. Of course none of the money went to us as we paid our own way and our own upkeep. All the money was handled by our African Brothers and they paid the bills and gave some to the African ministers and put the rest on the church.

The afternoon was very busy as we had to pack our belongings so we could leave early the next morning. Max had to be in Kumasi at 8:20 to catch the train for Accra as he was scheduled to leave on the thirtieth. The railroad from Accra to Kumasi was said to have cost a "white man's life" for every mile to build mainly because of the deadly disease of malaria.

The night service was another great time of the Lord giving out Christmas presents. Max preached his final sermon in Africa and it was indeed a great one. He was truly a tremendous preacher! I could listen to him all day. We made another call for those that wanted to be filled with the Holy Spirit and over two-hundred more came. Every last one of them received that wonderful experience. The brethren told us that on Christmas night there were more than 500 that received rather than 400 that I had thought. Max still insisted there were 850 that night. They did pack very close to each other so that most of the time you would underestimate the number greatly. That made more than 1,000 people who were filled with the Holy Spirit in those six days. Many of the people had to leave before the service was dismissed as they had quite a ways to go. We can truly say that the witness of the gospel of the kingdom had been preached and demonstrated in this West African city. They would never be the same again and neither would we.

Max and I arose at 5:00 that morning, December 28, and had breakfast (the proverbial oatmeal and coffee) then we loaded a Lorrie and left from Wiamoase at 6:00 a.m. Typical of our African problems, the Lorrie ran out of gas near Kumasi but we made it in time for Max to catch the train.

### The Effects Are So Far Reaching

Max had an interesting trip riding back to Accra, the Capital City, on the train. I've heard him tell about it so many times. It seems that when you are in the spirit of revival, things just happen wherever you might be and many times it's very unexpected. In those days in Ghana, every "white person" was required to travel in the first class coach. You had no choice in the matter. You sat in a compartment that was just a small room with about six lounge chairs in it. There were four to six compartments to each coach. The conductor came by and started collecting the tickets at the front of the train as usual. According to Max, he was a very friendly and outgoing person. When he came to Max, he asked if he was Max Wyatt, and Max replied to the affirmative. He then began telling him how his sister and some friends had attended our meetings in Kumasi the week before and many of them had been healed and delivered. He had to hastily fulfill his duty of collecting the tickets from all the passengers and in a few minutes he returned. Along with him, about a dozen African people came from some of the other compartments who needed healing. After almost everyone in the first class coach had been in his room where he prayed for them, the passengers from other coaches began to come in as well and in a very orderly manner. Max talked, ministered and prayed for groups of people all the way to Accra. Of course the Max I knew was always so tender hearted. All of the people were so needy and the Lord was ever so gracious. Then to top it all off, when Max got off the train in Accra, the passengers all lined up outside the train to shake his hand and to thank him. They were all full of smiles and excitedly clapping their hands.

Things like this completely overwhelm me with emotion at times and fill my heart with such gratitude to the Lord Jesus for His Amazing Kindness. As I write about these things today, I can still see in my mind the many thousands of needy people being met by the Lord and it fills my heart with thanksgiving for His marvelous guidance and blessings. I'm so very thankful that He allowed me to have a part in a visitation like this. Such experiences as these really quicken a person's soul and causes them to keep pressing ever onward. You know beyond a shadow of a doubt that it was the Risen, Ascended Christ that was doing the work of healing and not yourself. To Him be all the praise and glory!

### The Two of Us - Paul and Paul Left Alone!

It sure was a funny feeling to see Max leave and I was left all alone in this foreign land not knowing a single soul. Brother Anaman, a leading African pastor, came later and took me to the Wilbin hotel in Kumasi where I waited for my close friend and colleague Paul Shaver to come from another area. Paul and I had been roommates all through Bible School and had traveled extensively together during the summers in the ministry. So in the hotel, I sat down and wrote a few letters and tried to sleep a little as I was so weary. Somehow, I over slept, so I had to hurry, as fast as I could, since I was supposed to meet the train at 5:00 that evening. Paul came in on the train all-right but he had to wait a while for me to get there. Of course I apologized to him and he was very gracious. He was like Santa Claus as he had a lot of mail for me (15 letters). Wow! At last I finally got some mail from home and it felt so great.

That evening we had the famous English meal of "steak and kidney pie" for supper at the hotel and we really enjoyed it. That was my first time ever to eat the renowned dinner. I had heard our Pastor tell about eating "Steak and Kidney Pie" while ministering in Canada. Where they stayed, the lady asked them if they liked "Steak and Kidney Pie." They said they loved it. So she fixed it the first night and they enjoyed it immensely. So she fixed it the next night and the next night for five or six nights. Finally they were so tired of it they couldn't eat any more and to this day couldn't.

## Loneliness Gets to You!

I can never forget how terribly lonesome I was till Paul came. This lonesomeness would plague us at times as there was nothing to do when you were not in the meetings but read our Bible and pray or go for a walk. We had no books or magazines to read. We couldn't speak the language so we couldn't talk much to the average person on the street. Sometimes when young men saw us on the street, they would prostrate themselves on the ground in abeyance. We would quickly reach down and help them up and try to tell them that they shouldn't do that to us as we were just ordinary men like themselves. We always felt bad when they would do that as we were on a mission with the gospel to lift a civilization into the glorious liberty of the Kingdom of God. So therefore we wanted them to know and understand that they were on the same level as us and there was no such thing as a Bwana (great white father).

## Now the Rubber Meets the Road

When Paul and I were left alone and Max and the others had all gone home, we knew that this was where the "rubber met the road." Dr. Wyatt's vision was to send out "Invasion Teams" to be as shock troops, demonstrating the power of the gospel with signs, wonders and miracles. This was to form a beachhead and get the attention of the nation. We would war a war of amazing kindness, demonstrating our love and concern for each member of the body of Christ. This would be done by sending out people two by two just as the Lord Jesus did in the Bible. To start, each team would be made up of one young minister and one older and seasoned minister with a proven record for a while then the young ones were to be put together to carry it on a month later. We believed that this is what the Apostle Paul did.

Our intent was to bring the nation, whether kicking or screaming, into the Kingdom of God, with all the benefits of the Kingdom flowing out to meet the needs of the people. In our hearts, we saw a nation of primitive and exploited people being brought into the glorious liberty of the children of God and would be used mightily by Him. The object was not to build or plant churches of our own but to work openhandedly with any and every Evangelical group that was there and let them build the churches. We knew that we could not do the job alone. However, we fully believed that if we could bring healing to the sick and hopeless that it would open doors to many unreached areas as Kings would come to the brightness of our rising. With the invitation of Kings, we would not be bound by the religious traditions of particular groups and they would be happy to go along when they saw it working in love. Later we would send "occupational forces" to drill water wells and put in schools and do whatever was necessary to help lift that nation of people.

Our motive was still not to have churches of our own but to work with the existing ones that preached and taught the true gospel with no strings attached. If there was no Church in the area, it then would become the responsibility of the existing churches from the closest area to plant one. Because we saw the vast need for more ministers, one of the first things we wanted to do was establish a Bible Training School to train and equip the Nationals on the fast track. This would be done under the auspices of whatever group or groups saw the vision.

We saw the day coming when the Colonial Empires were going to fall and the Africans needed to be prepared for that time. We knew the day would come when many doors would be closed to, so called, "white Americans, Canadians and Europeans" but they would be open to the Africans. They would take the gospel to places where we couldn't go. So we must prepare them and get them ready to carry it on.

Again, this was not for us but for them. Some of the Missionaries told us that it wouldn't work as they thought the people were incapable of doing it as many of them were just a half-step from the jungle. Our argument was that it didn't depend on the people but the Spirit of God and us teaching them. If we taught them properly, they could go forth and do it without our help or support. Time has proven us right.

That is why at this point it was so crucial for Paul and me to be able to continue the work with the same manifestation of God's power as it was with the older ministers. Could we pull it off or was this just "a pipe dream of ours and Dr. Wyatt?" We had already been in many meetings prior to these with the older ministers. Some of them were tremendous and some not very good. Would we go on to have even greater meetings in some places or would they not be very much? Before we go into any of those, let me bring you up to speed on how all of this came about and why we were there.

# Chapter 2

It was toward the end of January in 1953, just after my twenty-second birthday, when I became extremely ill. All of us Bible School students were at the Wings of Healing Temple helping to stuff letters for a mailing for the Wings of Healing Radio ministry. Once in a while they would call upon the students to help them get the letters out when they fell behind.

This was my final semester of Bible School at the Bethesda Bible Institute and I had been "burning the candle at both ends" by working and trying to finish school. Not realizing it, I was treading on some dangerous territory. I pushed myself, working long hours and not taking time to eat properly.

## A Life and Death Situation

It seemed that without notice, I suddenly began to have such excruciating pain in the center of my abdomen. The pain was almost unbearable, so some friends took me back to the Bible School dorm and I went to bed. The hurting never ceased but it seemed to intensify. Hilda, the school cook came in and thought that I had gotten some kind of food poisoning. So she proceeded to have me drink a lot of fluids which came right back up. This only made me worse.

After several hours & much prayer, they took me to the Emergency ward of Emanuel Hospital in Portland, Oregon. My dear friend John Warwick had taken me there as Joyce, his lovely wife was head nurse over the third floor. Joyce had come down to be with us as she had finished her day shift. It now was late in the evening with no let up whatsoever with the pain. An Internal Medicine specialist was on duty. He took one look at me and said that this young man needs a surgeon. Joyce called a noted Gastro-surgeon whom she knew, to come look at me and do the surgery if needed.

Dr. John McKinley Guise felt of my abdomen and immediately said that I had a perforated ulcer and must have surgery immediately. He told Erskine Holt, the Dean of the School to call my family with all possible haste as I was in a very dangerous condition. It had been eight hours from the onset of the pain and he said that a person could only live twelve hours with that condition. So they didn't have much time to do the surgery. Since I had already gone eight hours with it, he didn't understand why I wasn't already unconscious. After prayer, they quickly wheeled me into the operating room. Joyce Warwick went right along with me as she was a Registered Nurse, qualified for the operating room. How comforting it was to have a child of God and a dear friend with me all the way. They gave me a shot and I was out like a light.

## Out of Death a Vision

Hours later, I awakened and Joyce, along with her husband John, was with me in my room. She had watched over me through the whole process after working her shift all day. Along about two or three o'clock in the morning, with my eyes wide open, I saw this *"bony creature"* with a robe over his head and a sickle on his shoulder fly through the window and stand at the foot of my bed. He looked just like the classic figure of death and said, *"I have come for you."* Suddenly I felt such cold as I have never felt in all my life. It seemed to be coming from this "bony creature" as it started at my feet and radiated right up my legs. I knew it was death that had come for me and he was standing there laughing at me saying there was nothing I could do now. I knew I was ready to meet the Lord so that didn't bother me. So I cried out to the Lord with all my heart, saying, *"Jesus save me!"*

Instantly that creature sailed out the window and Jesus came and stood at my bedside to my right shoulder. He didn't say a word but was looking at the wall at the foot of my bed. Naturally I looked in the direction He was looking and He showed me a vision. It was like watching a giant full-wall, full color video screen. Television was just coming in at the time and they were very small and only black and white.

I saw a newspaper that was pasted together and shaped like the continent of Africa. Suddenly a hole burst outward toward me in the area of where Nigeria is on the map. I saw them clapping their hands in a beautiful rhythm I had never heard before. Then I saw myself preaching to multiplied thousands of Africans. How well I remember their dress and the clapping of their hands.

Immediately another hole opened to me in the area of where Ghana is located and the same thing happened. I saw multiplied thousands of Africans in bright and colorful clothes singing and dancing. I was again standing before a great multitude of people preaching the gospel to them. How well I remember the headdress of the women as well as the attire of both the men and women. I could hear the songs of joy and see them dancing as I had never seen anyone dance before.

In a few minutes that scene was gone and another map made of newspaper appeared. This time it was in the shape of India. Suddenly it burst in the center and out toward me and I was preaching to thousands of people in India. This was followed by another one. This time it was in the shape of China and again it exploded outward toward me and I was preaching to thousands of people there. This vision has never left me.

Joyce Warwick said that my blood pressure had dropped below 40, between two and three o'clock that morning. She knew I couldn't survive the night so she kept a prayerful vigil. All of a sudden it changed and it went back up too normal for no apparent reason. As far as I am concerned, the Lord Jesus was the reason it went up.

## Another Night, Another Vision!

The next night another vision came. This time I could see the whole Church was in a mighty war of survival. It seemed that retreat was the order of the day because no one wanted to fight. We had been pushed back to a beachhead. My friend, Paul Shaver, and I had been in the thick of the battle and had been sent to the coast to get some rest and relaxation as I had been wounded. It seemed that there was no one in leadership to lead an aggressive attack against the enemy and that was why we were taking such a beating. As we were lying on the beach with shells falling all around us, suddenly we heard this loud voice crying "Charge! Charge!" We would recognize that voice anywhere. It was Dr. Wyatt with a sword upraised leading the troops up a great valley and multitudes were coming out of the shadows to join him. We instantly jumped to our feet, running as fast as we could and worked our way right up by his side in hand to hand combat with the enemy.

You could see the fearlessness in the eyes of the troops and the determination on their faces. It seemed that the whole Church was rallying behind us and the enemy was in a rout. We worked our way up this great valley to the top of this huge mountain and we could sense a great victory was right at hand. Then for some reason, Dr. Wyatt took a small group of us up a side draw but there didn't seem to be any enemy present. We went on over the top of the mountain and suddenly the enemy attacked us with great numbers. They seemed to be coming out of nowhere as this was a trap. Paul and I along with some of the others were able to find a tunnel complex and we worked our way back to the main body of the army but the enemy had killed Doc along with many others.

The vision puzzled me to no end as I wondered what it could mean yet I knew that it had something to do with my immediate future. It gave me great courage and strength during my recovery period as I thought often of Doc with his sword raised and shouting, "Charge and many rallying behind him!" In the process of time I would come to understand more about it.

## A Miracle of Finances Yet Some Bad News

Very speedily I recovered from the surgery and in four days was out of the hospital and back at school. Nevertheless there was a huge problem as there was no way to pay the huge medical bills as I had no insurance. In those days hardly anyone had health insurance. However, the Lord had plans. Erskine Holt, the Dean of Students, got permission from Doctor and Mrs. Wyatt to take an offering at church to pay them. More came in than was needed for which I was so grateful to the Lord and to each of them.

Before Dr. Guise dismissed me, he said that during surgery he didn't have time to remove the ulcer as I was too far gone. So he could only sew up the hole and clean out my abdomen as much as they could and hope that I would live. Also when I had fully recuperated and regained my strength I would need surgery again to remove the ulcer as that was standard procedure of that day. In the meantime I had to be very careful about what I would eat. I had lost an immense amount of weight and would be plagued with stomach problems for months.

### The Trip That Started it All

About this time, Dr. Wyatt went to Gold Coast and Nigeria for a two-week meeting in each place. He had mammoth crowds with tremendous signs and wonders following. He came home with a glowing report and spoke about a thousand million heathen being awakened out of the darkness of superstition, poverty, disease and colonialism. As Joel the prophet said, there were multitudes, multitudes in the valley of decision. He declared that we must go with our hearts filled with love and wage a war of amazing kindness to sweep them into the kingdom of God. If we don't reach them, they would in turn rend us in pieces. If we will go, reach and train them, the day will come when they will be able to go where we could not go. They will be the missionaries of the future.

I could never forget him playing a tape of the crowds singing in Accra, Ghana. I wept openly with many others as we listened to the beautiful song that sounded something like this: "Ne dza a ye. Ne dza a ye. Ne comfo Yehowa, Ne dza a ye." In English the words went something like this: "We praise the Lord. We praise the Lord. We worship Jehovah. We praise the Lord." It was the same music that I heard when I saw them dancing in the first vision.

There wasn't a dry eye in that place with over a thousand people in attendance that Sunday morning. The Lord was opening our hearts to the plight of the unreached peoples and we could hear them calling. In those days when we used the term, "the heathen," it didn't carry the harsh overtones that it does today. We simply meant the unreached people groups of that day.

### Radical Plans Begin to Develop

Dr. Wyatt began to prayerfully form a plan that would radically affect the lives of so many people. In the next few months he began to articulate the plans of calling for five hundred recruits to be trained and sent forth to sweep whole nations into the Kingdom of God. He envisioned sending hundreds of teams to various countries of the world to bring the gospel of the Kingdom of God to them with all of its benefits.

Up to this point when asked if I would return to school for the next year, my reply was "definitely not" because I'd been through enough suffering & privations to get this far and was weary with going to school. But now the call of the unreached began filling my heart and mind.

## Graduation Banquet Becomes a Propelling Force

Bethesda Bible Institute's graduation was on April 17, 1953 where I graduated with honors. What a graduation banquet it was. As the student speaker, my message was on the words of David when Israel was confronted by the giant, Goliath. He went up and down the lines of discouraged and fearful warriors crying, *"Is there not a cause?"* His older brothers accused him of just coming to see the fight but he didn't understand them being fearful of the giant. His rallying cry seemed to permeate my heart and soul. To me, "The Cause" was a million heathen crying for release from their bondage and for the gospel to be preached to them. Goliath was the force that made it impossible.

What a tremendous response there was to that message from my fellow students and the huge crowd. Then Dr. Wyatt spoke on "From there to here and from here to there." He used the third verse of the old song, "Amazing Grace." He began by quoting the third verse of it, "Through many dangers, toils and snares, I have already come. Tis grace that brought me safe thus far and grace will lead me home." He spoke about many of the dangers that we have faced in life to this point and of the toils we have endured as well as the snares that the enemy laid for us. He told about how the Lord had taken him from the red, clay-sided hills of a poor Iowa farm and gave him the Wings of Healing International broadcast. Then he brought it down to the present with the tremendous doors that were opening for the gospel all over the world but especially in Africa. He closed with the fact that the same Lord that brought us from "there" to "here" will be faithful to lead us through countless dangers, toils and snares from "here" to "there," and eventually to the Heavenly City. What a stirring message it was! Everyone, it seemed, was ready to give their all for Jesus.

## The Launching Pad

This became the launching pad for a number of student teams to leave on ministry trips to carry this vision all over the nation. One team would cover the Southern part of the United States while another would cover the Midwest and another go into Northern Canada.

Immediately after graduation, Paul Shaver and I would begin a preaching tour of the United States and parts of Canada for the Wings of Healing. Multitudes of doors were opened to us as Doc began to speak of it on the radio broadcast. We preached in many churches in Edmonton,

Alberta, Canada and all over Wisconsin and Minnesota. Following those we ministered in Chicago, Illinois; many cities in Indiana, Ohio and Pennsylvania then all through New York from Buffalo to Watertown to Utica, Albany and New York City; New Jersey; Maine; Vermont; New Hampshire; Massachusetts; Rhode Island; Connecticut; Delaware; Virginia; North and South Carolina; Louisiana; Texas; Arkansas; Oklahoma and Idaho. We also ministered in dozens of churches in Ontario and Quebec. This trip took us over four months to complete. We had meetings almost every night and twice on Sundays. We covered about 18,000 miles that summer in ministry.

## A Quiet Talk with Dr. Wyatt!

Before any of us left on our tours, Dr. Wyatt called all of us to a meeting in the Wings of Healing Temple. All of us gathered and sat on the front and second rows of seats. Doc came in, always dressed in a suit, to talk with us about the ministry. To us, he was always a very humble man, quite shy around people unless he was preaching. Then he was as bold as a lion. He really put you off guard with his timidity and farm colloquialisms. His smile was as broad as his face that showed a genuine happiness. When he got serious, he would just turn his head from side to side gently in quick succession. He really had a heart for people, regardless of position in life or race. He gave us some pointers that have stayed with me all through life.

One of the first things he said was: "So you want to preach? If you can get out of it, do so; God hasn't called you. If you've got to preach, for God's sake spare the people." By this he meant not scolding them or condemning them from the pulpit. He continued, "If Jesus loved them enough to die for them, how can we do less? We must make a way for them some way," he said.

Other tidbits he dropped on our ear that day went like this:

"Don't use the pulpit to strike out at people or to intimidate them or rake them over the coals."

"Remember that faith only works in the brackets of the grace of God."

"Let your illustrations in preaching be limited in telling about yourself but try to use Biblical ones as they are more powerful since they are the inspired word of God."

"Always be faithful to the Word of God and don't use any tricks or gimmicks."

"Many preachers put the responsibility of having faith upon the sick. You are responsible for believing with them. Remember that faith comes by hearing the Word of God. If they are not healed, it is just as much your fault as theirs so don't allow condemnation to come to them. Keep encouraging them to believe the mighty promises of God."

"Don't go into a room or home alone to pray for a person of the opposite sex."

About traveling in the ministry, he had this to say:

"Don't go and get the finest hotel or motel but rather go to the less expensive ones."

"You must be thrifty in the ministry as it is the Lord's money and you must spend it wisely."

"Ministers' must not be extravagant."

Likewise with restaurants he said:

"Go to the cheaper ones as long as they are clean."

"Eat your larger meal at noon as most places have noon specials and it will cost you less."

"Try and eat where the local people eat."

In regard to meetings he said:

"Always be on time! Never be late if at all possible!"

"Don't be like some preachers that run in when it's their time to speak but do your best to be in the beginning of the worship service so you can get or have confirmed the direction of the meeting."

"Don't be late for appointments, be a little early."

"Never leave a phone bill charged to your room if the Church or someone is paying the bill."

"When you make a phone call from a church or a person's house, always pay for that phone call."

"Remember that you're a guest in their Church or home, so don't act like they owe you something."

In regard to personal dress he had this to say:

"Always be clean shaven when you have ministry to do."

"When ministering the Word of the Lord, always wear a shirt with a necktie. You represent the King."

"Always wear your suit or sport jacket to Church. If it's too warm, you may remove it then."

"Do your best to look successful. No one wants to listen to a failure."

"Always keep your person clean. Watch your breath that it is not offensive."

"Iron your clothes and keep a crease in your pants."

"Keep your shoes polished and looking good though they may be old."

"If you have holes in the bottom of your shoes, don't kneel with the bottom of your feet facing the congregation. It'll make people feel sorry for you."

In regard to young men dating young women, he said:

"Don't date a young lady in every place you minster. When you do date, go out with a group together as much as possible and keep it on a high level."

"Don't lead a young woman along, making her feel like she is the one for you if you are not serious."

"Remember that a rumor will destroy your ministry as quick as the outright sin. So shun the very appearance of evil."

With these words and many others, he admonished us then he prayed for us. Could that man pray? He brought heaven down to earth and you knew the Lord was there in answer to prayer. The next morning we would leave for our various destinations, feeling honored to be in the service of the Lord. These were not laws he handed down but advice to help make us successful in the ministry. Today we may laugh at some of these things but are we better off not doing them? I don't think so!

### Healing Comes Instantly

During this trip, we received word from Dr. Wyatt for us to meet him in Lima, New York at the annual Elim Camp Meeting as he was the evening speaker. We arranged our schedule accordingly and were there. The second night as he finished preaching such a magnificent message on faith, he began to say to the crowd that they should take a step of faith and begin to act like they were healed. Such joy filled the air as mighty miracles began to happen all around us. The presence of the Lord was mighty in our midst!

Up to this point my stomach was so sore from not eating properly for weeks that I could hardly stand my belt. With the Lord's presence mightily upon me, I turned to Paul and said, "Hit me in the stomach with your fist." Without hesitating, he did and about knocked the wind out of me. I certainly don't recommend anyone doing this and I don't know why I did it then, except I felt I had to do it to express my faith. In that moment I was completely healed of all stomach pain. Up to that point the ulcer had given me no end of trouble. After the service we went to the food stand and I ordered a hamburger with lettuce, tomatoes, ketchup and mustard with potato chips. All these things my doctor had told me not to eat and I felt wonderful afterwards.

The next morning when we had breakfast with Dr. Wyatt and Carlton Spencer, the head of the Elim Bible School and Fellowship, I ordered pancakes, eggs and bacon. Again these were things that I wasn't supposed to eat and felt wonderful again.

As Paul was driving up the mountainside near one of the Finger Lakes of New York, I rolled down the window and told Paul, "Here goes my Belladonna pills Dr. Guise had given me as I no longer need them."

From that time forth I have been free of stomach problems though eating sometimes eating such hot food, it would bring tears to our eyes, particularly in Africa.

## Many Miles Brings a Problem

We drove over 18,000 miles that summer in Paul and David Shaver's practically new 1952 Ford, wearing out a brand-new set of tires. In fact, on the last leg of our journey we had a flat tire as we were going up the Bannock Pass from Dillon, Montana on our way to Salmon, Idaho. It was a narrow, winding, partially graveled road across the vast region of the continental divide. I was driving and just got out of the car when I heard Paul say, "Yep, we have one on this side." I then saw that we also had one on the other side. Of course, we only had one spare and were 18 miles or so from Dillon and much farther to anything on the other side of the mountain pass in Idaho.

There was absolutely no traffic on that road. It was extremely hot and no water for miles. Paul took one of the tires and happened to catch a ride down the mountain in a log truck while I stayed with the car. Dillon, in those days, was a small town, and seemed nothing more than a wide place in the road. Since that size of a tire was relatively new, no one had any to fit. So Paul didn't know what to do but for some reason, he looked in a place where tires were thrown away and found one that would fit but all the tread was worn off of it. He had the fellow mount it anyway and hitched a ride back.

I had put the spare on already so we quickly put on "old baldy" and prayed that we could make it into Leadore, Idaho, which was across the Continental Divide and get one there. Of course, there was no such tire size in Leadore. We drove very slowly because we didn't want the sharp gravel to pierce the bald tire. We finally made it all the way into Salmon, Idaho to Paul's parent's home late that evening. The next day, we bought a new set of tires for the car and spent a few days with them. From there we journeyed on back to Portland where we received a hero's welcome.

## People Were Very Generous

That summer we raised about $15,000 in cash for the Wings of Healing to start their Missions program that eventually would send Paul and me to Africa. People and Churches had also pledged about $45,000 for the broadcast. While on the road, we didn't use a single dime of the money raised for the Wings of Healing as the churches also gave us money for our own expenses. Both of us returned to Bethesda Bible Institute in the fall of 1953 to do postgraduate work in Missions and teach. They made me the Registrar of the School and put me on the staff of Teachers as well. Doc Wyatt had issued the call for five hundred new students. He called them recruits.

One of my roommates, Paul Metcalf was dating a young lady who was a new recruit from Dallas, Oregon. Her closest friend, Mildred Akers, also came as a new recruit. I had met Mildred a year before when we ministered in Faith Tabernacle in Salem. I was on the platform when she and her sister Frances walked in a little late. I felt the Lord said to me, "That is your wife." I thought, "No, I don't think so" and left it with that. After I had ministered and the service was over, Max Wyatt, the pastor, wanted us to meet them and so he introduced us. Mildred was a little shy and nothing came of it. The next year, she was hired to work in the office of the Wings of Healing along with Paul Metcalf. So I asked Paul if he could get me a date with her. He did and this began a wonderful courtship that would be consummated in marriage the next year.

## Africa on the Horizon

A few weeks after school got under way the Wings of Healing began to send out teams to various places from which they had received invitations. One team was sent to Cuba and another would leave for the Peace River Country in the Northwest Territories of Canada. As yet, there was no word about Africa or who would go, though there was high expectancy it would be soon. All the students and teachers were hoping they would be among the ones chosen.

To everyone's joy, an invitation came to send teams to Nigeria and Gold Coast, West Africa. The Nigerian one came from Sidney Elton, a Missionary with The Apostolic Church of Wales of Bradford, England. Coinciding with that came the invitation to come to the Gold Coast from James McKeown who also had been with the Apostolics of Wales but was just forming the Gold Coast Apostolic Church with a number of African ministers. There was such a spirit of independence sweeping both nations at the time. The British Government had already begun the long process of giving the two nations their independence.

Quickly, Dr. Wyatt and his staff made plans for him to lead a team to both nations. Accompanying Doc was Raymond G. Hoekstra of little David fame who later became known as Chaplain Ray of the Prison Ministries. They had teamed up in great meetings many times before. A pastor friend of theirs from Denver, Colorado, Vernon Sanders was also invited to go along. Doc and Raymond Hoekstra would go for a week at each place. They were the spear head of the invasion teams. Along with them would be two older, proven ministries and two younger ministers. Then it was announced that Max Wyatt, Erskine Holt, Paul Shaver and Paul Cannon were to be the shock troops. Max and Erskine were to stay one month while Paul and I were to stay six months. The meetings were to be intense with services twice a day every day that it was possible. Later occupational forces (as we called them) would be sent to help build churches, establish schools and put down water wells.

## We Knew We Were Being Sent by the Lord

When we received word that we were to go, we had only two weeks to obtain our passports, visas, and get all the necessary "shots and inoculations." It took a lot of doing to get all this done but it all worked out well. When I received my passport, I could hardly believe it and the emotion of it all just overwhelmed me. In our final service at the Wings of Healing Temple, the place was packed out and there was great excitement filling the air. Hands would be laid upon us by the Presbytery with the Word of the Lord in prophecy going forth over us. It spoke about the signs, wonders and miracles that would be happening and that multitudes would be brought into the Kingdom of God and that kings would be inviting us to come to their places.

# The Journey Begins
# Chapter 3

We arose early on November 11, 1953 to finish packing after going to bed about 1:30 that morning. We had breakfast at the school for the last time for a good while. At 9:30 fellow students, Dean Burnett and Pat Murphy took Mildred and me to the airport. We had a little time but I was so nervous, I could hardly stand still. It was very difficult for me to believe that I was chosen as one to be on the first team to be sent and I was actually leaving for Africa. It still seemed like an impossible dream. This was the most exciting thing that I had ever been involved in. In fact all of the team was so excited and filled with such conflicting emotions that Max forgot to tell his family goodbye. He did finally phone them from Boston. It seemed like the entire Wings of Healing Temple and Bethesda Bible School came out to see us off at the Portland airport. What a send off!

As we were leaving, our hearts just burned within us. Our prayer was that we might be able to truly love the Lord and fully minister by His love effectively to the suffering multitudes who had never heard the gospel. Prior to this we had sought the Lord diligently and were now determined that we were not going to let the Heroes of Faith down, if the Lord would truly bless us. We believed that He would.

## The Beginning of Problems

When we checked in at United Airline, we were much concerned about being overweight with our luggage because we were taking a large wire recorder to James McKeown in the Gold Coast. However as we weighed in, another passenger weighed his suitcase with ours so they let us through without paying any extra. We boarded the plane at 10:55 on a tourist ticket. Finally the plane taxied out to the takeoff spot where they revved up each engine and the next thing we were speeding down the runway and off into "the wild blue yonder."

Paul Shaver and Paul Cannon

This was my first time to ride a big airplane. There was such a mixture of emotions in my heart. I was glad I was going as it was the answer to my heart yet I felt like crying because I was leaving all my friends behind and we were going into a world of the unknown.

The Rockies were beautiful with snow all over them. We had about 30 minutes in Denver and got a quick bite to eat but we had to choke it down fast. It was night when we arrived in Chicago. Here we changed planes to American Airlines. They also let us through without paying overweight for the recorder because United had done so. When the plane took off, a light fell off the plane so we circled back and landed. This was the beginning of many problems that would tear at our soul throughout the whole trip. We arrived in New York City an hour late and took a bus downtown where we got a hotel one block from Times Square. We all fell into bed weary to the bone.

## On Our Way

The next morning, after breakfast we walked about New York City and took a few pictures. After checking in at the air terminal downtown we caught the bus to Idlewilde (now Kennedy) airport. There we boarded the Pan American Clipper, a DC-6 B plane, at 1:45 in the afternoon and flew to Boston. From there we flew to Gander, Newfoundland where we mailed a few cards back home. After a short stopover for fuel in Reykjavik, Iceland, we flew onto London, arriving about 8:30 the next morning. What a beautiful sight it was to watch the sun rising above the clouds. Because of a low ceiling and other aircraft, our plane had to circle the London airport at a low altitude for quite a while. It was neat seeing the quaint houses and the countryside.

Finally landing, what a job it was to clear customs and immigration. We took the bus downtown and got a bite to eat. Food at the time was difficult for the British to get but we were able to get some eggs and coffee with toast. Since we had a little time, we hired a car to take us about town. The weather was bad but we still took some pictures. That evening about 10:00 we flew to Paris on British European Airways. The plane was a two-engine "jobby" with the wing on top.

Looking back now, it is amusing as they not only weighed our luggage but they weighed each of us as well. Fortunately, none of us were too heavy. Again, we got the recorder through because the other airlines hadn't charged any extra. We had to make a stop at Brussels, Belgium then on to Paris. They didn't give us any trouble going through customs or Immigration at Paris either.

Taking a bus downtown we saw the Arc de Triomphe on the way though it was way past midnight. We got a fairly nice hotel and a bite to eat though the prices were considerably high. It had been a long day so again we hit the beds exhausted. We were to get up early but being so tired we slept through. A car was to pick us up at 1:00 p.m. but we were still asleep. We had lunch then walked about some and rode the Metro seeing what places we could. We saw the Seine River, the Opera house, the Palaces, the Eiffel Tower and many other sites.

We had supper at the hotel but it was terribly expensive. It hurt to spend mission money that way. We had nothing to do with buying the tickets because they were given to us and were the cheapest way to go. On side trips we always spent our own money, never using mission funds. To us, that was a sacred trust. Later that evening, all four of us walked downtown and had a cup of tea on the sidewalk. Then Max and I went back to the hotel while Erskine and Paul went to a show.

### Murphy's Law Kicks In

Arising early the next morning, November 15th we got a taxi to take us to the Notre Dame Cathedral where we walked around looking it over and then on to the downtown terminal. Checking in at Pan American Airlines we were told that it was too foggy for the plane to land so we couldn't leave. Quickly we transferred to Air France which was to leave at 12:30 that afternoon for Rome. At 2:30 we left the downtown terminal for the airport. That was a harrowing experience as they drove so crazy in France. We waited at the airport until 6:30 that evening after checking through customs and immigrations.

Finally we boarded an Air France, Lockheed Constellation for Rome. We thought surely that we were on our way but the fog was really rolling in. So we taxied out to the runway where they revved up the engines and pulled out on the runway and came back to the terminal. How disappointing! I was so disgusted that I forgot to check back through immigration.

### Only Alternative Was to Take the Train

We went back to the terminal downtown where we transferred to the train. To us the train station was terrible as we had such a long wait. However, they did let us wait in the passenger car. By this time we felt about half starved so I went to a food stand using what little French I had remembered from High School to get us a ham sandwich and a cup of coffee.

In those days, no one showed you which train was which so we found a porter and he showed us where to go. Erskine wanted to tip him too much as he didn't realize the greater value of the American dollar. Paris appeared to be such a wicked city to us. Eat, drink and be merry seemed to be all they cared about where we visited. I was thoroughly disappointed in some things in Paris.

We rode the night train through France, Switzerland and Northern Italy. Max and Erskine had a compartment to themselves as well as Paul and me, so we stretched out on the seats and got a little rest. As the day broke, we were in the Alps of Southern France crossing into Switzerland.

At the border of each country the customs and immigration officials came on the train and looked at our luggage and stamped our passports.

Going through the Swiss Alps and by Lake Geneva we saw some of the prettiest sites we had ever seen. The Alps looked a lot like the Rockies except for the terraces all up the side of the mountains. It was such a beautiful ride.

## Trouble again

When the train entered Italy we had trouble keeping our recorder because they didn't know what it was. They thought it might contain something banned or illegal so they wanted to take it apart to find out. Fortunately Max persuaded them to seal the box so we could take it through Italy. While he was arguing with the officials we held up the train by not getting fully in but standing on the steps until we could bring it with us.

We had to transfer trains in Milan and it happened to be the old coal burner type. Northern Italy was absolutely gorgeous as the railroad snaked down the mountain sides. At times we could see the train engine as well as the caboose since we were in the middle of the train. By the time we reached Rome we were black with smoke.

It was about 8:00 that evening when we finally arrived in the city of the Caesars. The train depot at Rome was really beautiful and magnificent. They told us it was built by Mussolini. We got a nice hotel downtown and a bite to eat and again fell into our beds exhausted. We had been on our journey now for six days. It was hard to get used to all the different kinds of money and languages.

The next morning we arose early and had a wonderful breakfast of ham and eggs. We met an American that got caught in Italy before World War II and lost his U. S. citizenship. He took us around the city so we could visit the Vatican and go into Saint Peter's Basilica as well as visit many of the old Roman ruins. He even drove us down the old Appian Way to the three taverns where Paul was brought into Rome. Then he took us through the catacombs which made the greatest impact on us. This made us more determined than ever to be worthy messengers of the gospel they died for. The Coliseum just reinforced that feeling as we could envision the thousands of martyrs that gave their lives for Christ there. How could we do any less? Rome had so many interesting sites.

Time ran out so we had to rush to the airport after getting dinner, which wasn't very good. The Roman airport was very sloppy in comparison to the Railroad Station. We left Rome on a British European Airways, two engine plane about 3:30 that evening.

## Paul on the Island of Melita

The Mediterranean was absolutely gorgeous as we flew to the Island of Malta which is the old Island of Melita that Paul was shipwrecked on. We landed at the Malta airport about 7:00 that evening.

The British European airlines put us up in the finest hotel and paid for all our expenses. We went downtown and the main street was just packed with people. They seemed to walk up and down the streets for two or three hours then go home. No car could pass on the streets as there were so many pedestrians. We had a wonderful supper of fish, steak and all the trimmings courtesy of the airline at the hotel.

### Africa at Last!

Any Missionary will tell you that when you decide to go to the mission field that all hell breaks out against you. Everything that can go wrong will go wrong. Such was our case as we journeyed onto our destination in West Africa. We didn't know it on this sleepy little island of Malta but we would soon find out. This was the day, November 18th that we would actually set foot on African soil. Excitement filled our minds as we sat at breakfast provided by the airline. They had awakened us at 6:00 that morning as we had to leave for the airport at 8:30 and fly to Tripoli, Libya on the same plane we came in on. Why we stayed overnight, I don't know but it was wonderful.

### To the Shores of Tripoli!

Tripoli was a strange and interesting city. It was like you stepped back into the days of Jesus. Americans were dearly loved as it had only been about eight years since our troops had liberated the country from Adolph Hitler's regime. British Overseas Airways took us downtown in a bus and put us in Hotel Uadan, one of the finest and paid for our room and all our meals.

A Jewish fellow on the plane from Rome wanted us to contact his friend in the city, which we did. He was a Firestone representative and he gave us a grand tour of the city. He showed us many interesting sites. One part of the city was ultramodern while the other part was tremendously poor. The market was something else. They sold camel meat but flies were all over it. It was wonderful to walk through all the Bazaars & shops. It was quite an experience and didn't cost us anything.

### Now You Do, Now You Don't!

We were scheduled to leave at 9:00 that evening because they didn't want to cross the Sahara Desert during the heat of the day. The plane was late, so they had us stay at the hotel until it arrived. The night in Tripoli was out of this world with a large, beautiful moon shining on the city. We walked out on the back porch of the hotel which was right on the Mediterranean coast. Max and I walked downtown enjoying the beauty of the city while Erskine and Paul went to an Italian show. Finally at 45 minutes past midnight, they took us to the airport where we waited till 2:30 in the morning when the plane arrived. An hour later they took us back to the hotel because an engine had failed on the plane.

They couldn't repair it so they had to fly a new engine from London then install it on the plane.

## Crossing the Sahara Desert!

We finally left Tripoli at 10:30 in the morning on November 19 flying right across the middle of the Sahara Desert. What a sight that was! It was so enjoyable to see. We flew at 19,000 feet but you could see clearly the mountains and plains of the Sahara desert. The desert was not only sandy and rippled but it was brown, red and black. It even looked like the soil drifts. I never realized it was so mountainous. They pointed out Timbuktu, the famous French Outpost, as we passed over it along with other villages.

It was night when we arrived at Kano, Nigeria, our first stop. They took us to a hotel where they served us supper, courtesy of the airline. We waited a few hours as they had to contact Lagos to have the lights turned on but soon we found out the engine still had problems. They gave us rooms at the hotel while they repaired the engine on the plane. The next day, the airline rented a bus and took us on a tour of the city. There were huge piles of ground nuts (peanuts) in several places. The dye pools were interesting. Kano was an entirely different world than anything we'd seen so far. Looking back, all I can say is thank the Lord we didn't fly on into Lagos that night. Indeed He superintends our lives.

## Arriving in Lagos

Leaving Kano for Lagos, Nigeria we arrived about 10:30 in the morning on November 20, a full day late. It was a funny feeling when we stepped off the plane. The temperature was very hot and steamy with a lot of humidity and we were all dressed in all wool suits. Customs and immigration were not much of a problem but they would only give us a seven-day tourist visa which would really complicate things and give us many hours of anxiety. Since no one was at the airport to pick us up, we took the West African Airways bus downtown to the terminal. Again we tried to find if anyone was there to pick us up but we couldn't locate anyone. Sidney Elton, the Apostolic Church of Wales Missionary was supposed to pick us up but had given up hope and gone on back up to Ibadan. To this day, I have never understood his reasoning. Why couldn't he find out from the airline when the plane would be in?

Our first meeting was to be in Ibadan, a city about one hundred twenty-five miles North of Lagos. Chief Ackinyelle of the Yoruba tribe had invited us. He was one of the thirteen Chiefs in the House of Chiefs that governed Nigeria under the British Government in those days. He had been converted to the Lord some years before and worked closely with Sidney Elton, the Missionary. Dr. Wyatt had started the meetings a few days before and we were supposed to have been there at the start.

## A Frustrating Experience!

We tried calling Ibadan to see if anyone knew of Sidney Elton or the Americans but we couldn't reach any one of our party. What are we to do? Every fiber of our being seemed to panic. We had been so enraptured about the trip up to this point, envisioning the Lord doing such marvelous things. Now, we felt terribly let down and discouraged.

With all the delays beyond our control, and no one here to meet us caused negative thoughts to arise in our minds. "Could we have missed God?" "Are we really supposed to be here in Africa?" If so, then why have so many things gone wrong? Out of this we discovered that frustration often changes us and puts something rich into a person's life if we are diligently serving the Lord. Of course we couldn't afford those negative thoughts, so we didn't allow them to dominate our thinking. We then began to see what we could do about the situation. We knew the Lord would help us some way. He didn't bring us this far to leave us.

## Cultural Shock - Big Time!

The sights and sounds of Lagos soon made us forget our disappointments. What a study in contrasts. There were shiny new cars passing a slowly moving cart being pushed and pulled by three or four men. Men wearing flowing, colorful robes would walk by with a friend in cool western dress. Well-dressed men and women would pass people with hardly a stitch of clothes on yet pay no attention to each other. Some were working while others were begging in the street but no one gave a second thought. In some places there were dirty, mysterious looking shops that fronted on the streets, while often a lovely home could be seen setting back from the street, surrounded by a sturdy wall with broken glass, on top of it. There were stately homes with well-kept lawns surrounded by tall, graceful palm trees and bright green shrubs with red, white and pink flowers. Close by them would be mud huts with thatched or rusty tin roofs and shabby walls. They seemed crowded together as if for friendship or protection.

The smells were a blend of burning charcoal, cooking fish or meats with various spices along with the open sewers that remained with you long after you left the city behind. It was amazing to see the way folks lived in such dirt and filth in some parts of the city. It certainly touched our hearts, filling them with compassion for the needy. Of course when we went through we didn't know that some parts were the slum of the city as all cities have their own slums.

## If We Could Just Make it In!

We didn't have any address in Ibadan but we knew if we could just get there that we would find our group. So we hired a young Muslim man with a "kit car" to take us to Ibadan. He wanted an enormous amount of money at first to take us but finally we settled on six pounds in English money. At the time an English pound was worth about $2.62 in our money. We didn't know of any places to eat so we bought some crackers, English biscuits (cookies) and a little candy to eat along the way.

It was shortly after noon when we hired the young man so we loaded our luggage into this very small automobile and climbed in. He drove all over Lagos, through parts where the streets were very narrow, to tell all his family what he was doing and say goodbye. The evening shadows were lengthening fast when we pulled out of town at 6:30.

Since Nigeria was an English Colony, they drove on the left side of the road. The driver almost scared us to death at times as he would drive on the right side of the road and when meeting an oncoming Lorrie or car he would pull back to the left side at the last second. Max sat in the front seat and twice he had to grab the wheel to keep us from hitting another car or truck head on. It didn't seem to bother the young man as he was a happy go lucky type of person.

### Moon Struck at Midnight!

Close to halfway, we began to hear a grinding, clunking sound coming from the rear of the car. Pretty soon the rear axle broke and he pulled off the side of the road onto a flat spot. Here we were stranded; it seemed, in the middle of the jungle close to midnight with no one who could speak our language. I think every car and truck stopped to see what the problem was. They would jabber in their languages and just laugh and laugh. They were having a great time at our expense.

How could we ever forget that night with the jungle all around us and a big full moon rising? I had heard all my life about being "moon struck" now I knew what it meant. It was so enormous in size and bright that it seemed like day. The long shadows of the trees and the vines created an eerie feeling in our minds. You talk about feeling lonely. All of us felt so alone with no one to help. What could we do?

After a while a tractor-trailer stopped to see what was wrong. He had taken a load of cocoa beans to Lagos to be shipped out and was returning to Ibadan. He told us to hop aboard and he would take us on to the city. Max rode in the front and almost roasted while Erskine, Paul and I rode on the trailer covering up in our overcoats to keep warm. The trailer was loaded with burlap bags, so we rode on top of them. It was so damp; our clothes became soaking wet by the time we arrived in Ibadan.

The driver knew the city very well and after asking a couple of people, took us to the British Rest House where Sidney Elton, Dr. Wyatt, Raymond Hoekstra and Vernon Sanders were staying. It was 3:30 in the morning when we arrived. We quickly fell into bed, weary to the bone. But we had a problem. They didn't have enough beds so we all slept on chairs that we put together while Doc slept alone on a small cot.

## A Fly in the Food!

They didn't awaken Paul and me so we didn't get to go to the morning meeting. It was just for the ministers that day and they thought we needed the rest. We had our meals at the rest house which were not too bad but on the other hand not so good either. We were all sitting at a couple of tables in a shed type of building with a corrugated tin roof. It had short walls about three feet high but no windows or screening as it was wide open.

This was our first meal here. They brought our plates with the food on them and it looked good. However, mine had a huge bug flapping around in the gravy. Someone said, "Don't worry about the fly. It won't eat much!" However, I handed it back to the waiter and he just took it to the wall and raked the fly off outside then handed it back to me. All the fellows just roared with laughter. They wouldn't bring me another plate as that was all they had. So I gritted my teeth and began to eat where I thought the big bug hadn't been. It had been so long since we had a decent meal. All of this didn't matter very much as we would soon be in the meetings which we had looked forward to for so long.

# The Meetings Begin!
# Chapter 4

Our first night to be in the meetings was on Saturday, November 21, 1953. It was a time that could never be forgotten. There's no way to describe that meeting so you could have a sense of what it was like to us. There was such a huge crowd, estimated at well over 15,000 people assembled on the Race Track in Ibadan, Nigeria. There was no way for us to determine the size of the crowd. When I was a Boy Scout in my teens, I had been an usher at the football games in the LSU stadium in Baton Rouge and this crowd looked as large as that. I had never seen such a huge mass of people gathered for Christian purposes. It was mind-boggling to see such a mass of humanity with such enormous needs. Their anguish seemed to be reflected on their faces. They were there out of desperation.

The noise and activity of the meeting were in full progress when we arrived at 5:00 in the evening to start. Just one look at the suffering and the broken hearted was more than enough to cause anyone to understand why a cry of anguish was born in our hearts that night. It made me think of the uncounted millions of unreached people throughout the world that were without Christ and without hope. We knew that we had the answer through Jesus to bring salvation, deliverance and healing to this people. Beyond a shadow of a doubt, we knew it could lift a whole civilization into the joyful benefits of the Kingdom of God. That was what this meeting was all about.

## The Word of God Came With Power!

The crowd had been singing and dancing for an hour or more being led by the young local ministers who were having a time of their lives. When we arrived, one of the older ministers stepped up and pulled the coattail of the young minister leading the singing and he sat down. We remarked to each other that it's too bad that we can't do that in America. Then they began the real song service. To us, their language didn't lend itself to beautiful singing. But I'll tell you what! No one could compare with them when it came to clapping their hands. It was absolutely amazing and with such beauty and skill. I couldn't even begin to describe it. The noise level was extremely high with thousands upon thousands singing and clapping their hands. When Dr. Thomas Wyatt stepped up to the microphone that vast throng of people became strangely quiet and every eye was upon him. They gave him their undivided attention. It was like they hung on every word he spoke. Since Nigeria was an English colony, there were many that understood him before the interpreters could translate it.

## Simple Message - Yet So Powerful

Dr. Wyatt's message was very simple and yet outstanding. It brought hope and created faith in their hearts. He never preached above their intelligence level. You could sense he was a master in handling a situation like that and he had such an anointing of the Holy Spirit. He always seemed to know just what he needed to do. While he was preaching, you could feel the level of the people's faith rising. You knew there would be outstanding miracles that evening as the Lord Jesus met these people. We sat there on the stadium benches in awe of what the Lord was doing. We all knew that we had some big shoes to fill in the coming days. Would we be able to do it or not?

Doc (as we called him) closed his message by praying one prayer en masse for all the sick, urging them to believe the Lord for a miracle. Could he pray! It was not an intelligent type of prayer thought out before hand but went right to the needs of the people. You knew instantly that he was in touch with heaven. Suddenly there was a great excitement that swept the whole multitude as the Lord began working in healing and deliverance. The noise and emotion level began rising higher and higher as the people cried out to the Lord for His touch on their lives. It was a cry that you could somehow feel in your very body and it penetrated into your inmost being.

## Nearly a Disaster!

Not wanting to feel completely useless during all of this, we stepped up to the rail where the crowd stood and started to lay our hands on some of the sick people that were crowding to the front. Such compassion flooded our souls for them. It almost broke our heart and our eyes filled with tears. At times we leaned out as far as possible to reach all that we possibly could, just to touch them and they seemed so appreciative. All of a sudden, dozens of hands grabbed onto me and pulled me over the rail and on the tops of their heads. I found myself in a prone position on the tops of people's heads, being pulled further into the crowd. They were passing me around on top of their heads to others. All they wanted to do was to touch me or put my hand on their head. I almost panicked. With all my strength, I got my hands free and grabbed a metal post on the rail and pulled my way back up onto the stands as they clung to my legs. It took all of my strength and Paul Shaver's to accomplish that feat. From then on, I wasn't much on the laying on of hands in a large crowd and we would do exactly as Doc did that evening.

He always pitched the direction of his message to build their faith to act and do something and then he would pray one prayer en masse for the whole group as they were doing whatever he asked them to do. It was so effective in bringing healing and deliverance to those in great need. He never backed up from the most terrible need but believed implicitly that the Lord was going to meet them. And it worked with absolutely astounding miracles happening all around. It seemed that wherever you looked, miracles were taking place.

### It's Testimony Time

The African minister in charge asked for testimonies of those who were healed. Multitudes crowded up to the platform, side by side to testify of what the Lord had done for them. There were those who had been lepers, the lame, the halt and the blind as well as many other illnesses that were healed instantly. In fact, you name it and it was happening. It seemed that the whole crowd was stepping out together to come to the platform to testify of healing at the same time.

Surely, this was the way it should be happening. At first there was the worship of the Lord in singing. This was followed by the preaching of the Word of God with the Holy Spirit sent down from heaven and then came a mighty move of the Spirit of God in the deliverance of the people. It all blended together so beautifully.

This was our first service in Africa and we would never, ever be the same again. My, how our hearts were moved as we prayed and wept with that great multitude of wonderful people that evening.

### Meetings Can Be Great But Life Uncomfortable!

When it was all over, we had supper back at the rest house. Again, we had to makeshift for beds since we only had five single beds and there were six of us. We put two of the beds together so Max, Paul and I tried to sleep together with me in the middle on the hump. Needless to say, I didn't sleep much but such were the discomforts we would face in the coming months.

It was that night at the race track in Ibadan when reaching the masses began to weave itself around the strings of my heart. These meetings seemed to create in all of us a fresh faith in God, and brought us an incredible freedom to preach the gospel through interpreters.

### Difficulties Prepare You

Looking back on all the difficulties we experienced, going through Europe and in Africa getting here, especially at the airport in Lagos with no one meeting us was disheartening. After being stuck in the middle of nowhere at midnight and then to be a part of such a great meeting really changes a person's thinking radically. It made us look at life as well as the ministry entirely differently. You begin to understand a little bit about the disappointments and trials that come as being a part of God's plan to endow you with His power. It seems like the soul never really knows tranquility, until it passes through the anguish of desperation. Being in that hopeless situation, we had almost despaired of even getting to Ibadan. We had even started to wonder about our calling but in that meeting, the darkness of defeat turned into a glorious victory. No doubt with all of these problems the Lord was allowing our faith to be tested along with our love for Him and His work. In actuality, He was just preparing us for the things that were ahead.

It's like in Genesis 1:5 where the Bible says, *"And the evening and the morning were the first day."* Our glorious morning of great victory was preceded by the evening of despair. Looking at it closer we notice in Genesis that evening is called "darkness" and morning is called "light," and yet when the two are put together they are called day which is the name that is given to the light alone. So it took our evening and our morning to make up our day. Light always penetrates the darkness. Such was our time in Africa among such needy people.

## Our First Sunday in Africa

On the twenty second of November, it was a beautiful Sunday morning that had dawned. The decision was made for us to pair off and go to the local churches to minister. Erskine and I went to one church while Max went to another and Vernon Sanders and Paul Shaver went to another. I spoke a few minutes and Erskine followed with the message. Dozens of people were healed in the meeting that morning so we came back to the Rest House rejoicing. The others also came back with a glowing report. We all felt a little like the Seventy disciples must have felt in Luke 10:17-20, *"And the seventy returned again with joy, saying, Lord, even the devils are subject unto us through thy name. And he said unto them, I beheld Satan as lightning fall from heaven. Behold, I give unto you power to tread on serpents and scorpions, and over all the power of the enemy: and nothing shall by any means hurt you. Notwithstanding in this rejoice not, that the spirits are subject unto you; but rather rejoice, because your names are written in heaven."*

Dr. Wyatt and Raymond Hoekstra didn't go to any of the meetings that morning but stayed at the rest home to do the Wings of Healing radio sermon. Doc Wyatt almost always scripted out his radio message but Brother Hoekstra had fooled around so much it didn't get done. So I finally typed the full transcript of the message for Doc when I got back. He always read his sermons on the air. When you're speaking on thousands of radio stations, a little "and uh" costs a lot of money. He was so good at reading his sermon that no one could tell he was doing so.

When we went to the evening meeting at the Racetrack, we made the tape for the broadcast first. Then after a time of singing and rejoicing, Doc preached another great message and yet it was so simple that a small child could understand it. This was his last night in Nigeria. The response to his message was great even though there was so much noise on the platform that many people couldn't hear it clearly. Still with all of that, there were such a large number of people healed and delivered. It seemed to be a duplication of the evening before.

Again that night, Paul, Max and I would have to sleep together on the two beds pushed together. It didn't matter too much as Dr. Wyatt, Raymond Hoekstra, Max and Paul left about 3:30 in the morning for Lagos to go to Ghana. They took Erskine and my passport with them to Ghana to get our visas renewed at the British Consulate in Accra. We didn't know it, but this would give us some very anxious moments.

### A Shaky Start

This left Erskine Holt and me, along with Vernon Sanders, to carry on the meetings. Actually, Vernon Sanders was not one of the team from Wings of Healing but was a friend of Dr. Wyatt that wanted to come along. His wife was the preacher in the family and pastored a large church in Denver, Colorado. Nonetheless, since he was with us, we always included him as part of our team.

The time had come when we'd find out if we could carry the meetings on with success. We began the 23rd of November with Erskine speaking in the morning meeting. He set things out straight from the shoulder. Up to this time they only permitted ministers to come to the morning meeting which was held in one of the large churches. At last they let everybody come.

I was a bit disappointed in the service though. All of us were kind of let down with the others leaving. It took the "wind out of our sails." I said a few words in the night service and Erskine preached but the meetings never came up to the level of the previous ones we had with Dr. Wyatt. This was disappointing to me and caused me to pray much about it. There were great results but didn't it come up to my expectations. Maybe my expectations were too high but I really felt that we were going to be able to carry on the meetings with the same intensity and results.

It always amazed me how those people could sit on the ground in the hot evening sun and listen to the gospel being preached. My heart was broken when we left the service that evening because of such tremendous needs of the people and our inability to minister to those needs. It seemed that everyone was sick especially the children.

### Another Day - Another Adventure

There was quite a crowd in the church on the morning of the 24th. I spoke for a little while on the oneness of the body of Christ. I told them that if we knew the Lord, whether we were African or American, Anglican, Baptist, Methodist or Pentecostal, we were brothers and sisters in Christ and equal with each other. All of us belong to the one church that makes up the body of Christ and there is no distinction in races. This really excited the people and would become a theme for us.

Erskine would then take the rest of the service but it didn't rise to the level we expected. Erskine was a great fellow & wonderful preacher. I loved him dearly and we got along very well together. He had such a keen sense of discernment as well as a terrific prophetic anointing. Still I was afraid that some of the things he did while ministering would do more harm than good. At least they were unnecessary.

## Bad News!

Sidney Elton came back from Lagos in the afternoon with bad news and said that he could only get us a fourteen-day visa as they couldn't renew a transit visa for more than 14 days. However, Max kept our passports and took them to Accra with them in order to get us a longer visa. We had called them in Lagos and asked them not to take our passports out of the country but to mail them back to us in Ilesha. They didn't do this and it would give us many anxious moments in the days to come because this had us in a foreign country without our passports and a visa. It was foolishness on our part to have done it this way but we were all "green horns" at all of this.

Some will say that we should have been better planned. No doubt that is true, but if we hadn't gone when we did and like we did, we would not have seen all the needs met that we saw. Some of those would have slipped into eternity without Jesus. This way, many thousands were saved, filled with the Holy Spirit, delivered and healed that would have been missed if we had delayed. Erskine again took the preaching in the night service and this time there was a good response. We personally needed this break. Many blind, deaf and mute as well as lepers along with many other illnesses were healed.

Vernon Sanders and I slept together while Erskine slept by himself as we only had the two beds. That evening at dinner another big fly was in my dinner, so I gave it back to the waiter but he only raked it off as he did before and gave it back to me. I thought, "Oh well, this is Africa and you have to live with things like this." In fact, you learn to take things in stride and not let it bother you as they become nothing but incidentals.

## Now it Is Only Us and Africans

The next morning, the 25th, Sidney Elton, the Apostolic missionary and his family left for their home in Ilesha leaving the three of us alone. They left us a little car to drive up to Ilesha after we finished the meetings. Erskine again spoke in the morning meeting and did a really good job. He called for those that wanted to be filled with the Holy Spirit to come to the front. Many people responded and we laid hands on them for the Baptism of the Holy Spirit. There was a mighty outpouring and about 50 to 60 people received the gift of the Holy Spirit. The Africans were absolutely thrilled as well as us.

## My First Message in Africa

Vernon Sanders said a few words in the evening service and I preached. This was my first real shot at ministering the word in Africa and it would thrust me into the time of my life. I did my best to do it like Doc Wyatt did. There was a tremendous response to the Word with a great many people being healed and delivered. Most of them were Muslim which was a real change, as up to that time it was mostly the Yoruba people who mainly responded. This was the beginning of large numbers of Muslims turning to Jesus in our meetings. We began to realize the best way to win Muslims to the Lord was not through argument and debate but through loving them and ministering healing to them and their families. By in large, we learned that if you can heal their sick, you won't have any trouble ministering to the Muslims. They were hurting and sick people just like all the rest.

Up to this point we hadn't gotten much mail but I finally got a letter from Mildred. This was the second one I had received from her but I hadn't gotten any from anyone else. Let me say this! It's so important to communicate with missionaries on the field and keep them abreast of things at home. It can turn a difficult time into a joyful time. It was always a refreshing time for us to get mail from home and it encouraged us immensely. It kept us connected, which was so vital.

## Our Last Meeting in Ibadan

November 26 was our last day of meetings in Ibadan. We introduced the laying on of hands and prophecy in the morning meeting. One of the African pastors or one of us would call a person or a couple to come up and kneel on the platform, and then we would collectively lay our hands on them and pray for them. The power of the Holy Spirit would come upon them and us and we would begin to prophesy over them. They would break and weep as the secrets of their hearts were revealed and the Lord expressed His will about their lives and ministry. We prophesied over quite a few people, even a woman which was contrary to the men's belief but they accepted it wholeheartedly.

## A Dandy Illustration

The evening meeting was held outside in the rear of one of the churches with Erskine doing the preaching. We didn't have a public address system which made it tough to reach the large crowd. We managed all right in spite of the obstacles because we learned to project our voices. Erskine prayed for the sick, and then I prayed for folks to receive the Baptism of the Holy Spirit. The Lord was so gracious as so many of them received without our hands even touching them. We found that the African people were so hungry to receive the in-filling of the Holy Spirit and they would receive that experience so easily.

Many of the people that came to our meetings were not Christians but were idol worshipers. In conversing with them prior to each service, I would say to them, "I can't understand why you would bow down to a statue that you have made with your own hands. You made it and you know it is just dead wood with no life in it." Their reply was, "We know that there is no life in the idol but we lay our hands upon it and pray to our God to come and inhabit it and we believe that he does." This provided me with a message that I often used when calling for people to receive the Gift of the Holy Spirit and it brought in thousands.

I would say to the great crowds of people, "You make an idol, and then you place your hands upon it and pray for your god to come and dwell in it. You believe that he does but you have no proof of it. Let me show you something that is even greater. We, in prayer, ask Jesus to forgive us of our sins and He does the moment we believe and we have the witness within us. Then we ask Him to come and fill us with the Holy Spirit. Then the God, Who made the heavens and the earth, comes and dwells in our hearts by His Spirit. This is more personal than in an idol. You will know beyond a shadow of a doubt that you have received not only by the great joy and presence of the Lord you will feel. You will also begin to speak in other tongues as the Holy Spirit gives you the utterance." Because it was given in a spirit of humility and love, it seemed to take all the barriers away and they would open up their hearts to the Lord. It was always thrilling to see when they opened their hearts to the Lord. Such joy came to them just as the old song says "It is joy unspeakable and full of glory."

## Problems Still Continue!

The morning of November 27, we were to leave Ibadan and go to Ilesha which was farther North in the Interior of Nigeria. Sidney Elton sent Joe and Roger, two of the Yoruba brethren, from one of the churches in Ilesha to help us get there. They came for us but Joe had to go on to Lagos and mail the portable tape recorder that Dr. Wyatt and the others had forgotten in Sidney Elton's car. Roger came to show us the way up but he couldn't drive. Fortunately I had gotten an International Driver's License before leaving Portland.

We didn't know exactly where Sidney Elton had left the car to be repaired so we looked and looked and finally found it. It was in a shop but it was all torn down. The man said he would have it ready at 4:00 that evening. We waited around all day, spending the time just looking around, trying to amuse ourselves. Vernon Sanders stayed at the shop and persuaded them to finish the car. Finally we left about 8:30 that night and headed for Ilesha. It was dark as pitch and we had to drive on the left side of the road, British style.

I had never driven a right handed steering car before. It was so different from what we were used to. We got about ten miles out of Ibadan and had a flat tire and we didn't have a light of any kind. Somehow, we put the spare tire on in the darkness as I had great feeling in my fingers. When we let the jack down, it was flat and we didn't have a pump. Roger stopped every Lorrie that came by and finally one had a pump but we had to repair it first. Finally, we got the spare tire inflated and were on our way. I drove all the way to Ilesha which was 85 miles of narrow crooked road. It was sure strange driving on the left side of the road. When we got to Ilesha, Sidney gave us our mail. That was a good antidote for all of our problems that day. I had a letter from Lorraine Burnett, the Secretary of Bethel Temple in Baton Rouge, Louisiana, my home church, with a check for fifty dollars. Though we were fully funded by the Wings of Healing, it was great that my home church remembered us as well. This gave us some personal spending money.

There still wasn't any word about our passports and time was running out on our transit visa. The next morning we sent Max a wire trying to get information about our passports. We went to the Post Office but there wasn't any mail or word about them and our airline tickets.

## My First Missionary Compound

Sidney Elton had built quite a missionary compound at the outskirts of Ilesha. It was very modest housing but nice, with a decent room for the three of us. Years earlier, he had planted orange, grapefruit and other fruit and nut trees as well as banana trees. This was really in the bush as they call it. There were no electric lights except at the Elton's compound because they had a portable electric power plant.

Sister Elton and her cook fried some tomatoes with bacon and served them to us along with some oatmeal with powdered milk for breakfast along with oranges, grapefruit, bananas and pawpaw (papaya in the Latin world) grown right in the Elton's yard. There was a huge Juju tree in their yard; in fact this was a Juju grave at one time.

It was sure enjoyable to sit on their front porch and watch the various lizards do what they do. There were several different kinds and they became very friendly with us, especially the big red and purple headed ones. They would come and take food right out of our hands and eat it. Inside, it was interesting to watch the transparent lizards crawl across the ceiling & walls. When they would catch a fly, you could see the fly inside of them.

## The Meetings Continue

We didn't have any meeting in the morning in Ilesha but in the evening we did. The African ministers pretty well ran the meetings here including the song service. Erskine preached and there were quite a few people with various diseases healed and delivered such as blind, deaf and dumb, lepers and you name it. Major miracles seemed to be the everyday thing in all the meetings. We were disappointed at the turn out as the crowd was only about 1500 people. They sat directly on the ground whereas they stood in the other meetings up to this point.

Sunday morning, November 29 was another beautiful day. Erskine, Sidney, and I went to one church while Vernon, Sister Elton and Ruth, their daughter, went to another one. I spoke a little bit and it ministered to the folks and they seemed to enjoy it, then Erskine preached. It was a good meeting with many being met of the Lord in healing and salvation.

When we returned home, we had a lovely dinner of fresh orange juice and dyker, which was a small African bush Antelope, with several canned vegetables. It was so interesting to watch how the English ate their food, putting it on the back of their fork. The Elton's were such a wonderful family and so easy to get along with. We had a lot of fun with them. They were great sports when we kidded with them about their English ways. They had come to Ilesha, Nigeria back in the latter 1930's and began the work. This put them here between 15 and 18 years as missionaries. They seldom went home to England as they considered this home.

Though it was Sunday, we did get some mail. Finally we had a letter from Max and Paul from Ghana saying they had to take our passports to Accra and that they mailed them from there but they didn't say where they mailed them to. So we were still in the dark about our passports.

### We Insisted on Reality in Healing

Again Erskine preached in the evening service with a large crowd in attendance. Many afflicted people were healed, most of them had been blind and now they could see clearly. We never would hold up our fingers before a blind person to get them to tell how many fingers we held up. Doc Wyatt was always against that kind of a thing, saying it was trickery. When the blind were healed, they saw clearly and didn't need anyone to guide or test them. The same was true with the deaf. None of this stuff of snapping your finger behind their ear or clapping the hands and asking them if they could hear. When their ears were healed without anyone touching them, they grabbed their ears and yelled in Pigeon English, "I can hear, I can hear!" It would always electrify the crowd and they would stand and give praise to the Lord. It was always our custom to insist on the real thing, with no gimmicks and no faking.

That night the Harmattan wind started blowing and we felt like we were freezing all night, especially Erskine as he slept on the cot. We didn't have much of anything to cover ourselves with so we slept in our clothes and put our overcoats on top to try and keep warm. Still, it was awfully cold. They told us that the Harmattan is a strong, cold North wind that blows off the Sahara Desert in the winter time and brings fine particles of sand down with it.

## Babalola the Prophet

That Sunday afternoon, Babalola, the prophet, as he was called, came to see us. This was my first time to meet him. He had two letters for us that he had gotten in Ibadan. One was for Doc and one for me but he said he had lost them. He was quite the guy and very friendly as most of the Yoruba people were! He was a big man, about 6 feet 5 inches in height, weighing about 225 pounds I would guess. Usually when he was with us, we would always have him close in prayer. He didn't need a microphone because when he opened his mouth to pray everyone could hear him regardless of the size of the crowd. His mouth was very large and when he opened it wide in praying, it looked like I could put my fist inside and not touch his teeth. No doubt the Lord made him that way as he had ministered to crowds numbering into the tens of thousands without a loudspeaker. He was a special man to me. I can still hear him closing in prayer. It sounded like this: Lo de cro Jesu! The crowd would shout a loud "Amen!" Then he would repeat it, "Lo de cro Jesu!" The crowd again would shout a hearty "Amen!" Then he would finish it with: Lo de cro Jesu Christi, Olu Wa-a-a Wa-a-a-a-ah! He dragged out the last sounds and the people would give a loud "Amen." What a man!

## The Voice of God Came to Him

Just after Sidney Elton arrived in Nigeria, Babalola was employed by the British government to operate a tractor in building roads. One day while hard at work, he heard an audible voice say to him, "Get off this tractor and go preach my word." Babalola was an unbeliever at the time without any knowledge of Jesus or God so he didn't know what to think of the voice. Therefore, he just kept on working. A while later, he heard this voice again saying, "Get off this tractor and go preach my word." He just ignored it and kept on working. The next day while operating the tractor, the voice spoke again. This time the voice said, "Get off this tractor and go preach my word or I will stop it and it will never run again." He didn't and pretty soon the tractor just quit running. He tried and tried to start it but it wouldn't start. They took it to the shop and the mechanics tried to start it but to no avail. So they tore it apart and put it back together but nothing they did would work. They were never able to get the tractor started.

## The Voice Said Go

The voice said he was to go forth throughout the land and raise his voice like a trumpet and declare God's word to the people. He would heal the sick with the water of life as the bell of freedom sounded. He was then told to go into the city and he would meet a certain man and it would be told to him what he must do to be saved and to fulfill the ministry he was called to do. That man was Sidney Elton who explained the way of salvation to him. He accepted Christ as his Savior and was filled with the Holy Spirit, speaking in tongues as the Holy Spirit gave him utterance. Sidney took him under his wing and taught him the fundamental truths of God's word. Soon Babalola began preaching the Word and signs and wonders began to follow him. Great crowds of people would gather to him all over Nigeria for several years. This was during the latter Thirties and early Forties.

Then there began to be a lot of social unrest among the people so the British Government wouldn't allow any large crowds of people to assemble. Babalola wouldn't stop and kept up his preaching with the large meetings, so they arrested him and threw him into prison. They mistook his calling the people to freedom as being political instead of spiritual. After being in solitary confinement for several years, it broke his spirit and he never arose to the great ministry that he had before. When we met him, he was only a shadow of the man he had been, though he still carried a lot of influence with the Yoruba people in particular. He added a lot to our meetings in Yoruba Land by just being in them and he rejoiced to see the great meetings with such tremendous results. However when we went into other tribes and cultures they didn't know anything of him but we still honored him for his past work.

### Extreme Cold!

We awakened early the next morning, November 30, feeling about frozen. It got terribly cold during the night and it carried on even into the morning but it warmed up about 10:00 and became really hot. Since many of the people could speak English, I led worship in the morning meeting. We really wanted the people to enter into the high praises of the Lord because it is out of the Lord's presence that power flows to meet the needy. We knew that we must bring them into a participatory thing rather than being spectators. For the first time they began to sing in the Spirit as the Lord met with His people and it was wonderful.

Erskine preached but he still preached a few things that didn't seem quite right to me. At least, they were not the way Doc Wyatt had taught us to do. For several years, I had seen it work so well in Doc's ministry at home and abroad and wanted to do it exactly as he did. I found that a lot of peripheral stuff in Christianity didn't help at all, so eliminate it. Just stick to the point of building their faith and God will honor that.

### Problems Still Plague Us!

When we got back to the missionary compound, we had a wire from Max saying they had mailed our passports and to see the letter but there was no letter. Again they didn't say where they had sent them, whether to Ilesha or Ibadan or Lagos. We would have to leave the country in two days, which was Wednesday, but we would have to leave Ilesha the next day as it takes a full day to make the trip to Lagos. We were perplexed to say the least but we would continue doing our best regardless of the situation and trust they would make it on time.

## People Came from a Long Distance

Erskine preached again in the evening service and there was quite a good response. Nine people had heard about the meetings and came two hundred fifty miles to be in them. What a needy bunch they were! Five of them were blind, two were deaf, one was a leper and one was a cripple. How they ever made it is a big puzzle but all of them were healed. That made it a highly profitable trip for them. Many more were also healed besides those. Among those healed were many Muslims and because of it, they were converted. Every day, wires and letters came in from chiefs and ministers for us to come and hold meetings in their towns and cities, even from the Muslim North. It seemed that Nigeria was wide open for the gospel. Babalola wanted us to go to Eastern Nigeria across from Calabar for a meeting and he said it would be a tremendous meeting. Oh how I wanted to go to all of these places.

Calabar was a port where many missionaries entered Nigeria by ship. On the island in the harbor is a missionary graveyard where many missionaries were buried. On some of the tombstones were engraved the time they entered Nigeria and the date of their death. Some of them didn't live any longer than two weeks in this harsh land of malaria and typhoid. They paid the supreme sacrifice to bring the gospel to this land. May the Lord honor their sacrifice!

We were so anxious to hear from home but still there wasn't any mail from the states. Having to get out of the country for the lack of a longer visa, the prospects didn't look very good for us getting back into Nigeria regardless of the calls coming in. How would we get out of this predicament?

The first of December was another very cold night in Ilesha, Nigeria. In fact, we were so cold that we felt like we almost froze because of the Harmattan season! It's hot in the daytime and very cold at night. It dries your skin and causes it to crack open. Sleeping on an army cot, you get the cold from below as well as from above. We just didn't have sufficient bed coverings so we slept in our clothes and put all we could find on top and on the bottom.

## Last Meetings in Nigeria for a While!

This would be our last meeting in Nigeria for a couple of months. I led worship in the morning meeting. It was so thrilling to see the people really enter into worship and praise again. We felt worship was such a vital part of the meetings. Without it there wasn't any power of the Holy Spirit to work.

We didn't do as some of the Evangelist did in America, come in after the singing and worship was finished. We believed that the speakers needed to flow in worship just as much as the people. It was in worship that the Spirit of the Lord would quicken and empower us to do the preaching with great power.

Erskine spoke a few words then we laid hands on and prophesied over many leaders, even some missionaries. The amazing thing was how the Lord met all of them. Such a breaking and weeping always came as the word of prophecy came forth over them. The Lord let them know He knew the secrets of their hearts as a proof that it was Him speaking. Yet it was never anything that was embarrassing to them. In fact, on numerous occasions, they had certain events in their minds that had happened to them which they asked to be revealed if this was God. Invariably when they did this, such weeping would occur as the Lord expressed His love and direction for their lives.

We started at 9:00 in the morning and didn't stop until 1:30 that afternoon: a four and half hour stretch. We sure were tired and weary afterwards. I've often remarked years later that the prophetic just drains a person whereas in preaching, you restore your soul. As truth is preached, it has a way of setting a person free including the one doing the preaching.

### A Poor Translator!

Our interpreter in the morning meeting left a lot to be desired. We found out quickly that an Interpreter can either make or break you. It's imperative that you have a good interpreter that can get into the same flow of the Holy Spirit as you. In the evening meeting Erskine came down with a tremendous headache so I spoke. My heart was always so thrilled to see the Lord working so mightily by His Spirit. What a joy it was to be a little instrument in the hands of our wonderful Lord to meet such tremendous needs. There were so many, many being delivered from all kinds of maladies. If I told all of them, it would make this book so large. The crowd was huge that turned out for our final meeting. This made all the discouraging things that we experienced worthwhile. We left with a deep satisfaction in our hearts that we had done the will of our Heavenly Father and many suffering people had their needs met and their lives forever changed.

### The Wait for Our Passports Is Over!

When we arrived back at the compound, our passports and plane tickets had finally arrived from Max in Ghana. Hallelujah! What pressure this took off of us! We had tried to get the ministers here in Ilesha to build a canopy for the meetings but they never did. It seemed that the people in Nigeria would rather gather in the wide-open sun than under a canopy. The sun and the heat didn't seem to bother them as a rule.

It had been a long day of ministering and we were very tired. So right after supper we went straight to bed since we had to rise very early. Babalola's driver was to take us to Lagos to catch the plane. He was supposed to be at the Elton's at midnight but he wasn't. Sidney Elton had to go and try to find him. He went to his home where he found him fast asleep. There is no telling when he would have come for us.

### Gold Coast, Here We Come!

Sidney Elton, Erskine Holt and I along with a driver left Ilesha at 1:00 in the morning on December 2nd after very little sleep. It was a very tiresome drive from Ilesha to Lagos. Part of the problem was our driver would speed up and then let off on the gas keeping you constantly in motion. He really drove fast over that narrow little road just as most Nigerians seemed to do. We arrived in Lagos at 6:30 in the morning, traversing the 186 miles of narrow, winding road in five and one half hours. It seemed to us like it was two nights long.

We stopped at the Christ Apostolic pastor's home in Lagos and had a few minutes of prayer with him then went to the immigration office. We were the first ones to arrive at the office and we were able to get an extension on our tourist visa. Whew! Did we sweat that one out because we were already two days late. Major Chatterton, the English Immigration officer in charge, was very friendly to us and gave us a one-month visitor's visa for Gold Coast. For some reason, he was against the Wales Apostolic Church and made Sidney Elton pay his own bond as they had canceled the Apostolics. Unknown to us there was a lot of religious infighting going on behind the scenes. They would fully manifest themselves later and present some real problems down the line.

# The Ghana Meetings Begin
# Chapter 5

Erskine Holt and I checked in at West African Airways Corporation in Lagos and had our return tickets changed. They gave us all tourist class back to Portland. This paid the extra charge for our trip to Accra and we had twelve pounds left over ($36). After this, we finally could get some breakfast. Paul Shaver would have said, "My stomach feels like my throat is cut."

## A Flight to Remember!

We boarded a small, but old two engine plane at 3:30 in the afternoon. It looked like something another airline had discarded or they had put it together from the scrap pile. We taxied out to the runway where the pilot revved up the engines and then came back in. In a few minutes we took off. We had no idea what that was all about but we held onto the Lord in prayer all the way. Flying this low gave us a wonderful opportunity to see the countryside with its vast jungles and villages. I could hardly hold back the tears as I looked out at the mud huts and thatched roofs of the various villages along the route. There was such a love for this people that came into my heart. I knew that many of these had never heard the gospel and someone must take it to them.

## Finally in Accra!

We arrived in Accra, Gold Coast at 5:00 that evening. Their time was one half hour different from Nigeria. We couldn't help but thank the Lord for a safe arrival. However, it took us a long time to go through customs and immigration. They wouldn't let me bring some ebony things I had purchased in Nigeria until I told them I wanted to mail them home.

We were able to talk to Max and Paul along with James McKeown, the Missionary, for only about 10 minutes. This was our first meeting of this wonderful man who seemed a bit cold but soon became a very dear and close friend. What an introduction! They simply gave Erskine and me our itinerary and left for a meeting in Odumasi that night. We would have the huge meeting in Accra since it had continued from when Doctor Wyatt was there. However, we were extremely tired since we had no sleep hardly the night before. But they say a preacher must be ready to preach, pray or die at a moment's notice so we did.

Erskine preached and I just spoke a few words of greeting. What a meeting it was! Many people were healed and delivered in spite of us being so weary. This absolutely amazed me. We discovered that the power and presence of the Lord never were dependent on how we felt.

We stayed at Jim McKeown's home though he was gone with the other team but his wife was there and she along with her maid took good care of us. She was a quiet and unassuming person with a deep love for the African people and they responded accordingly.

## No Morning Meetings for a While

There was no morning meeting the next day, December 3, as they had been going on for more than two weeks. Doku Ocansey, one of Bro. McKeown's leaders, took us to the immigration office where I applied for a visa back into Nigeria. Erskine tried to get a reservation to go home for the sixteenth of December but it was filled so they put him on the waiting list. We did get Max a reservation for December 30.

At last we were able to find a dry cleaner to put our two suits in. We had worn all wool suits on the flight as that was the custom in those days in traveling. Besides it had been cold in Portland and Europe so the wool suits were really good for that. But in the tropics, they were too much!

### Newspaper Article in Accra, Gold Coast

Here is a copy of an article that was the front page headline in the local newspaper, The Spectator Daily, Accra, Gold Coast while we were in the meetings there. It speaks for itself.

### The Lord Works in Spite of Things!

---

**WINGS OF HEALING TEAM**

**BREAKS ALL BARRIERS!**

**THE SPECTATOR DAILY**

**ACCRA, GOLD COAST, WEST AFRICA**

**Wonderful Cures By Healers**

by Our Own Reporter

IT IS not for mere curiosity that thousands of people flock James Town Square, Accra, every evening these days. There is something to bear witness to.

The Wings of Healing team has made the place famous by their wonderful cures, not for their name or glorification but to glory of the Lord Jesus by whom they accomplish the healings.

Personal testimonies borne publicly on the platform give true account of what is happening. You only have to believe to be healed.

Thousands more will be at James Town Square this evening. Many come from long distances, miles around, and could hardly leave the place at closing hour. The wonderful events of the evening in the name of Jesus glue them to the spot.

There, truly, the sick are cured. I met a man there who for many years could not walk. His whole waist had been like one piece of iron bar. He could not stretch himself. In fact, he was carried there.

But by the godly spiritual power of the healers this man is gambolling about today — singing praises to Jehovah. And this is only one example of the wonderful healing in progress in Accra today.

Doubtless the writer will be present this evening for his own testimony.

---

We gathered with the huge crowd in the evening service and Erskine preached. It was a very good meeting with the Lord's presence mightily in our midst. However, I had a problem with some things Erskine did and couldn't quite go along with his idea of mass impartation of the gifts of the Holy Spirit. In spite of that, many people received wonderful blessings and healings from the Lord.

It always amazed me that our doctrine may not be absolutely correct yet when you minister in the love of Christ and the compassion of the Holy Spirit, the Lord works in wonderful ways. After all of that, we laid our hands on many of the sick and prayed for them. There were so many more people healed from all kinds of major infirmities.

Again there was no morning meeting on December the fourth. So with a little time off, we went to a wood carver's place and had some small things made for our family and friends. We would have to pick them up later after he made them. We had to be very careful about which wood we selected as the government wouldn't allow several kinds of the lumber to be taken out of the country. It was sure hot during the day and just a little bit cooler at night.

It fell my lot to preach in the evening service where we had a good worship service and a great move of the Holy Spirit. After preaching a simple message and praying en masse for the whole crowd, I just stepped back from the mike and waited as the Holy Spirit began to heal. Suddenly the Lord's presence swept over the crowd and so many people were healed of all kinds of diseases that you can imagine. There seemed to be nothing that was too hard for our Lord! My heart was so thrilled to see God working and meeting the enormous needs of so many hurting people and do it on a wholesale basis.

However, with all that going on around us, we still longed to hear from home but there wasn't any mail. I can never forget how lonesome and bored we were at times in spite of all the things going on.

### Finally, a Day Off!

On December 5 there wasn't any meeting at all as the people were just tired out after more than two weeks of continuous meetings twice a day. Many of them had been staying all night under the canopy as they had no other place to stay. They just rolled out little straw mats on the ground and slept on them.

We got word that Max and Paul were up North and across the river in Transvolta with Jim McKeown and were having great meetings. Erskine and I made good use of the time off by going downtown and getting a much needed haircut. While there, we decided to go through the market. To our American minds, it was terrible because we were not used to seeing such things. Accra was nicer in some ways than where we had been in Nigeria with a lot more people speaking English. However, the temperature really began to soar as it was much hotter.

Doku Ocansey came and took us to his home and drove us by the seashore. It was really beautiful. They say the water is warm all the time. His cook fixed us an orange squash to help cool us but he made it too strong and it made me a little sick. They brought us some of Doku Ocansey's African clothes so Erskine and I dressed up in the African attire and they took some pictures of us. Did we ever look different? It seemed to thrill our brethren to see us dressed like them. But they were so gracious anyway.

### Back to the Meetings

There was quite a large crowd under the canopy for the morning service on December 6. I was supposed to speak but Erskine got up and tried to tell them about worshiping God in the Spirit and spoke for a solid hour. It really turned me off as I just couldn't agree with him on some of the things he was saying. He explained to them how to hit a certain tone and even demonstrated it. Then he told them to sing hallelujah over and over.

Rev. & Mrs. Ocansey and Paul

I was so repulsed by him trying to teach the mechanics of worship that I would have gotten up and ran if it wouldn't have hurt things. In all the years of revival, I had never seen nor heard of anyone doing such a thing. We had always left that up to the Holy Spirit to orchestrate. It just didn't seem right to make rules for singing in the Spirit. My reasoning was that we needed the spontaneity of the Holy Spirit, not the mechanics of worship. I have found, all that is needed for them to enter with us into worship is to see and hear us actually doing it. This would inspire them greatly.

That is why we were so opposed to ministers running in after the worship service is over. You have to actually be a part of the flow of the Holy Spirit among the people. They will follow if you will lead. This was the only time that Erskine did this and I'm sure it taught him a great lesson. I might say that we may have disagreed on things but we were never disagreeable with each other. He was a great guy to work with and I had great respect for him.

## Baptized in the Ocean

In the afternoon the pastors had a baptismal service in the Atlantic Ocean with more than 100 being baptized. These were the ones that were a part of Brother McKeown's group and were the ones converted after the last baptismal service which they had a few days earlier. It was hilarious to watch. Johnnie Mallet was baptizing them with the help of other pastors. They would put a person down into the water just when a big wave would come and dunk them all. Other times, they would start to baptize one at the peak of the wave and by the time they got them low enough in the water, it was gone and they were lying on the sand bottom. It was such a wonderful time for the people as they were so filled with an abundance of joy.

## Another Group Filled with the Holy Spirit

We had to hurry to get back for the evening service. It was another great time in the Lord. I preached and at the end of the message, asked for those who wanted to be filled with the Holy Spirit to come forward. About 200 came forward and we gave them instructions on how to receive the Holy Spirit. We always included the matter of asking the Lord to forgive their sins and led them in a prayer of repentance. What a thrill to see all those faces with tears running down their cheeks as they earnestly sought the Lord. During that wonderful time we would move between them and lay our hands gently on them for the Baptism of the Holy Spirit. Suddenly they would be overwhelmed with such joy and they would begin speaking in other tongues as the Holy Spirit articulated the words. Almost everyone received the Baptism of the Holy Spirit. What a happy crowd!

When things quieted down, we prayed for the sick and such a wonderful move of the Holy Spirit came among them. It never ceased to amaze me at all the tremendous miracles happening all around us. At times I thought the Lord was doing it in spite of us and not because of us. We never felt worthy of any of this. It was all by His marvelous grace.

## A Letter and a Guinea Pig

I was so thrilled that I finally got a letter on December 7. It was from my sweetheart, Mildred but none from anyone else. There was no morning service today and this sure made it lonesome. With just one meeting a day, we had too much time to think about ourselves and home. It's like the old saying, "An idle mind is the devil's workshop." I much preferred being busy all the time as that was what we came over for. The weather was terribly hot but it was fairly cool at night. We had been telling our cook how good the African duiker was that we had in Nigeria and wished that she would get some and cook it for us. So she announced that this was the day and she had prepared African duiker for dinner. Erskine and I were absolutely thrilled at that. We sat down to eat and took some of the meat but it looked kind of strange. It had a funny looking skin with a few short hairs protruding out of it. A duiker was a small bush antelope and was skinned just as beef is done. So we knew this could not be duiker, consequently we began to question her. This was a big mistake! She kept insisting that it was duiker and we told her it wasn't anything like the duiker we had in Nigeria. Then she told us it was like the little animals that Doku Ocansey raised in a pen at his house. Oh, Oh! We then realized we shouldn't have asked all the questions and do as the Scriptures said, *"Eat what things are set before you, asking no question for conscience sake."* What we had for dinner was a guinea pig. Yuck! It was all we could do to keep from heaving it up. Erskine began to look pale around the gills and I thought surely he was going to lose it, but we both kept it down even though it was very hard to do. From that day forth, we would never again ask for duiker.

Erskine preached in the evening service with the crowd holding up nicely. Many, many more people were saved and delivered from all kinds of things at one time. It felt good to "get back in the saddle again" as it was such a joyous thing to be involved in such tremendous meetings.

## A Crowd Excites the Preacher!

There wasn't any morning meeting on December 8. Erskine went downtown to check on his reservations to return home but he couldn't get any for the 16th so he got one for the 30th of December with Max. In the evening service we had the largest crowd of the meetings. There is something about a huge crowd that just turns a preacher on. What a delight it was to speak in this meeting. The Lord's presence was there in such a mighty way and He confirmed His word with signs and wonders following. So many people of all walks of life were healed from all sorts of sickness and diseases. It is always thrilling to see the Lord instantly heal anyone but it was especially wonderful to see Him heal the children.

In all of our evening meetings, we always gave an invitation to come and accept the Lord after the healing time was over. We felt this was the most important time of all so we didn't hurry it. There were always hundreds and many times thousands that came forward to receive Christ. Usually the one that didn't preach would give instructions to them on *"How to receive the Lord into their hearts."* Then we would lead them in a sinner's prayer of repentance and pray for and with them. The glory of the Lord would come mightily upon them as they wept their way into the Kingdom of God. This was our last service in the canopy in Accra and brought to a close more than three weeks of amazing meetings in which thousands upon thousands were saved, healed and delivered. They began with Dr. Wyatt and we carried them on. The thrilling thing was that the crowds and miracles were just as great with us, proving to all involved that Dr. Wyatt's vision would work. It was transferrable!

> **Another Newspaper Report**
>
> ### Wings of Healing
>
> GENTLEMEN What a great team you are. There has been nothing like it. Pass through Britain; you should, and tell them over there the good message. Don't give them only B19's and B36's plus H Bombs. Here is something really excellent for mankind, better than Economic Aid, you will agree. Which reminds me that it is only in the United States the Healing Art Gospel is well founded and recognized. You represent the very good side of America indeed. When the lame walk and the blind see by your belief in Christ, a belief which is so infectious as to make others believe, I am sure that Christianity will, sooner or later, win the whole town. May those who have different views not criticize but work with them and try to help all in need. Human frailty cannot do these wonders in the name of the Lord. Amen – JR

### On to Suhum

The morning of December 9, we had breakfast then packed our things to leave. We hired a Lorrie to take us to our next meeting in Suhum, which was a little ways North of Accra. It wasn't very far but it seemed like a long way because of the condition of the road and riding in the back of a small pickup truck. It was only about 46 miles but we had a flat tire before we got there.

Upon our arrival, they put us in the government rest house which was very nice except there was no running water. Since there was no hot water heater or stove, we had to take a bath as well as shave in cold water. When we took a shower, someone had to hold a pitcher of water over a wall and pour the cold water over us. I was running very low on razor blades though I had bought some in Accra but they wouldn't fit.

We hired a Christian brother to go with us and he did our cooking on a small charcoal burner. He was a very good cook regardless of the

On the Road to Suhum

primitive conditions. A Christian sister also went along to do our washing and cleaning. They took really good care of us. We were always treated royally. What a delight to talk with those who could speak English. With many of those who couldn't, we learned some of their words and it would thrill them to no end when we would try to speak in their language. We always did our best to speak to the "little" people, the ordinary folks, when we came to the meetings and when we left. They loved it when we said goodnight or good evening in their language. We just wanted to show them that we were ordinary people exactly like themselves.

### Bamboo Canopy

They had erected a canopy of bamboo poles with palm branches on top, right in the middle of town. However, there was no electricity so we didn't have any lighting or PA system. For that reason we had to have the service early in the evening. Erskine preached the first service but we thought the crowd was small for some unknown reason. There were only about a thousand people that came out and it seemed very small as we were used to so much larger crowds. They were not very responsive either in their singing or to the message preached. This didn't seem to matter because there were a great number of people healed anyway. Quite a few lepers were healed completely as well as many deaf and the blind. Leprosy seemed to turn an African's skin white in the infected part. When they were healed, the white area instantly became black or brown just like the rest of their skin. It was a sight that I will never forget as long as I live. This wasn't a rare thing in the meetings as it happened hundreds of times and in almost every meeting. It just seemed that the Lord had extra compassion on the lepers. They were so hopeless and it would break our hearts when we saw them.

When the blind were healed, they just shouted loudly, "I can see, I can see!" Likewise with the deaf, they would grab their ears and shout, "I can hear! I can hear!" They were so excited that they would jump up and down in place and it would turn that crowd into a mighty crescendo of praise to the Lord. Let me tell you, if we had that happen to us, we would jump up and down with excitement too. My! How that electrified the crowd! They would instantly lift their hands and begin worshiping the Lord. Indeed, the Lord was getting all the glory and praise.

## Dark as Pitch

After the meetings we loved to sit outside and look at the starlit heavens. It was so dark at times, and you could hardly see your hand in front of your face. We found quite a few of the constellations over a period of time. Really, one has to use their imagination quite a lot to connect the stars in order to see some of the constellations.

This reminded me so much of when I was a boy and living in the country in Southern Louisiana. We would sit on the porch and look at

Paul behind Government Rest House

the heavens by the hour as we had no television or radio. This helped to pass the time as we usually got bored stiff with nothing to do. Every evening about an hour or so after dark, a little animal called the Bowiea would begin his cry. It sounded like a baby crying and made chills run up our back. It always made us have such a lonesome feeling for home.

## Problems, Yet God Works

Erskine preached in the morning meeting of December 10 and did a great job. He directed it toward healing and there was a very good response. A great many of the people were healed instantaneously of all kinds of sicknesses, afflictions and infirmities. However, it seemed to us that the people here didn't seem to move as freely as they did in the other places. I don't know the exact reason but it seemed like they were just not getting what we said. It could have been our interpreter but not entirely. They had an Apostolic of Wales sign out in front of the meeting place and Erskine asked them to take it down and put up a sign that said "Undenominational Meetings." The reason for this was we wanted any and everyone to be able to come to the meetings regardless of their religious affiliation. Instead they put up a sign that said "Latter Rain" which we didn't like either. On some things, you can't win for losing.

## Ever See a Two-Foot Yam?

In the markets and along the road side, we saw these huge things that looked like logs stacked up. We enquired what they were and were told they were yams. Being from Louisiana and growing up on a farm where we raised lots of sweet potatoes which we called yams, I was amazed at their size. They grow on a vine similar to the sweet potato but are nothing like them at all. I had never seen such huge yams before. They were about six to eight inches in diameter and about two feet or more in length. They were white inside, about the color of an Irish potato but very dry and stringy when they were cooked. We tried some of the yams for lunch. They were very good in a way but a little too starchy and stringy for my taste at the time. This was one of their staple foods and they fixed it several different ways. They told us they would cut down the jungle and burn it then mound up hills of soil and plant corn and yams in the same hill. Each year the process would be repeated as the rains would wash the top soil into the streams.

## Tough Time Preaching

The evening crowd was quite a bit larger than the evening before and it was my time to preach. It was a very difficult time. In fact it was the hardest that I have ever had in preaching up to this point. It seemed my words were hitting me right in the face. I just couldn't get the people with me. In spite of all that, the Lord healed quite a good number of the people. Some of them had been blind and others deaf as well as many other diseases and afflictions. We found out again that the results of a meeting had nothing to do with how we felt or how we preached. It was the Lord orchestrating the meetings and not our ability that produced the results. We were so thankful for that!

## The Lord Meets the Children

Erskine wanted to pray for the children in the morning meeting of December 11 though I was supposed to speak. So that was what we did. He was my senior and I let him take the lead. We just had the children come to the front and we moved among them laying our hands upon them and praying. Many of the children were healed instantly and it really excited the crowd.

We then prayed for the adults, using a healing line. Somehow I just didn't care for a healing line and my faith just seemed to take flight, but

Erskine loved it. Quite a few of the adults were healed of various afflictions. We found that once you start a healing line with the laying on of hands then you are obligated to finish it. Often that would take hours upon hours as there is no place to stop till the last person is prayed for. I found that if you didn't build the people's faith through the preaching of truth then you would have to resort to the laying on of hands. On the other hand, if you built their faith through the word, you could have them do most anything like "take a half step forward," when you prayed one fervent prayer for the whole mass of people. Actually, the praying of the one prayer brought greater results by far.

Erskine preached in the evening service with the crowd being much larger than the evening before with most of them sinners. Great numbers of them came to Jesus as a result of so many of them being healed and delivered. There is something about seeing miracles like that to cause people to accept the Lord as their Savior.

### A Taste of Home!

In the morning service December 12, Erskine was to speak but we felt the Spirit moving in the prophetic. So we began laying on of hands and prophesying over some of the people. I am not his judge but it seemed to me that Erskine loved to prophesy an office of Apostle, Prophet, Evangelist, Pastor or Teacher over certain ones. I didn't agree with him on that because to me, it is the ministry that makes the office and not the reverse. In spite of my feelings, the Lord was so gracious and met His people. Some of them just wept and sobbed when the secrets of their hearts were opened.

Max, Paul and Brother McKeown arrived as we were prophesying over the people, then we went to the rest house to discuss further plans. Paul brought two packages from Mildred. They were really nice Christmas presents. She sent me a fruit cake which I shared with the others and all of us thoroughly enjoyed it. It was a taste of home. Max talked to Erskine about staying and going home with him on the 30th of December. So he decided to be a martyr and stay (he couldn't have gotten out anyway). It provided us a good laugh just the same.

### On to Swedru

Jim McKeown, Max and I went to Swedru as I was tired of some of the things Erskine did and it was better that we separate for a little while. I loved him dearly and we got along great. The only thing was that I felt we should do things like Dr. Wyatt did them because they worked so mightily but Erskine was his own man and always did things his own way. Somehow, the vision of Dr. Wyatt gripped my heart and the way he did things was the way I wanted to do them. Actually, they worked so much easier. On the mission field we found that you can get touchy very easy, especially when things don't go the way you think they ought to. We all had our times but we never let them linger or divide us.

Erskine and Paul teamed up together for a while and went to other places. This was a good change for all of us. In Swedru, they put us in a big two-story house that was a business school. Max and I slept in the same room on our canvas cots. I say slept but that is a misnomer as there was so much noise going on we couldn't sleep. Quite a few other ministers stayed there as well and they stayed up until after midnight and were up at daybreak, talking loudly and laughing. The first service was in the evening with Max preaching. He sure preached a wonderful sermon. The place was packed out but our interpreter just couldn't seem to get our message across to the people. He just couldn't get in the same Spirit with us. Consequently, people didn't respond very well. So we didn't pray for any of the sick. You could sense their faith was not built up enough and we would wait till the next day.

## My First Morning Meeting With Max

There was a good crowd out in the morning meeting of December 13 with Max doing the preaching. What a joy it was listening to him declare the word. I learned more by listening to him. Our interpreter was still struggling, consequently the people just didn't respond again. We found out part of the problem was that a dissident element was causing us a lot of trouble with the people. We also discovered that James McKeown was a very peculiar fellow and hard to understand but we really liked him.

Max preached again in the evening service. In fact, he preached two sermons. The people still wouldn't respond. So he told them to do something if they had to shove a preacher aside and breakdown a fence and he demonstrated it by pushing a preacher aside and breaking down the railing on the platform. Suddenly a wave of the Holy Spirit swept over the crowd and the Lord began healing people all over the place. Quite a good many were healed. One leper whose face was one big sore and was so crippled that he couldn't walk, instantly leaped to his feet, jumping all over the place and rubbing his face. We could see his face literally drying up before our very eyes and he was perfectly healed before we left that evening. It was amazing to watch him being restored.

The afternoons were terribly hot so Max and I got in the shade and talked over a lot of things concerning the work in Ghana. This insight would help us immensely in the coming months.

## Not All Meetings Great!

I preached in the morning meeting of December 14 along the lines of revival, dealing with the matter of it being a heart work. Revival starts in the heart of people. We didn't pray for the sick as that didn't seem to be the direction the Lord led us.

Max was supposed to go to Asamankese but Brother McKeown thought that he should go to Sekondi so he waited till Paul came. It was too late in the day for me to join Erskine in Asamankese so all of us stayed in Swedru.

I preached in the evening service but the crowd wasn't very large for some reason. That was a disappointment. It may have been because it was a Monday night. Perhaps it would have been better to close on Sunday evening rather than Monday. In spite of all the difficulties and disappointments, quite a number of the people were healed, but the meetings still hadn't broken open to our expectations.

Paul brought me two letters from Mildred, one from my Bible School room mate, Howard Ramer and one from Vernon Sanders in Nigeria. My, how our spirits were lifted by mail from home! Vernon said that Sidney Elton was expecting us to be on the plane back to Nigeria on the 21st but that sure was not my desire.

### In Asamankese

It was decided that I would go back with Erskine so Brother McKeown took me over to Asamankese in time for the morning meeting, December 15. Max and Paul continued on in Swedru for another night. Erskine did the preaching and afterwards we prayed for the children. So many of them were healed and delivered from all kinds of physical illnesses. In the afternoon, we met with Peter Newman Anim, the head man of the Gold Coast Christ Apostolic Church and his lead men to talk about the outpouring of the Holy Spirit. We set it out very straight forward to them and they seemed very open to it. They came with many questions and fears of things they had heard but we answered them all very well it seemed. Erskine was really gifted in that way.

It was my time to preach in the night service but I had such a terrible headache. In fact it was so bad at the end; I had them all to stand and praise the Lord and had Erskine to take over. There was a great move of the Holy Spirit as the Lord met the people. Many were healed of so many kinds of afflictions. That is always thrilling to see the Lord work in spite of our frailties. After the meeting, we tried to wire Sidney Elton in Nigeria but it was too late as the office was closed. So we mailed him a letter explaining our situation.

### Laying Hands on Peter Newman Anim

We decided to wire Sidney Elton before we went to the morning meeting on December 16 to let him know that we couldn't come back to Nigeria the twenty-first. After the worship, we felt that the Lord wanted to fill people with the Holy Spirit. So Erskine taught on the laying on of hands for receiving the Holy Spirit and we laid hands on them to receive. About 100 people came forward and almost all of them were filled. This thing really worked.

After this, we laid hands on and prophesied over quite a few. Many of them were from the Christ Apostolic Church including Peter Newman Anim. When they brought him up, he kneeled down beside the chair and we stepped up and began to pray for him. At the time I didn't recognize him though we had met the day before but he was dressed entirely different. We found out afterwards that he was the Chief Apostle of the Christ Apostolic Church. His old name was Kwaku Anim Mensah. Of course the African ministers and Erskine knew him.

Our African brethren led off prophesying, followed by Erskine. They all spoke in glowing tones about him being called to be an Apostle and the glorious things he would do. I noticed that he was not moved at all by any of that. I earnestly sought the Lord for His word as I knew in my heart this man was looking for a confirmation of something. Suddenly I had a vision of him as a boy of twelve years of age in explicit detail. As I began describing it, he began to weep as though his heart was broken.

Afterwards, he sobbed his way to the microphone and told the audience in a broken, quivering voice that he had asked the Lord to verify to him if this revival was of Him or not. If it was, have the young American prophecy about this certain event in his life, describing it in detail. He went on to say that no one else knew anything about it, yet everything was right on. What a great guy we found him to be. He would work very closely with us from then on.

Both of us were very weary as the laying on of hands and prophesying really tired us out. The service lasted until about 1:00 in the afternoon which made a very lengthy service. I preached in the evening service and there was a very good response to the Word. Many, many people were healed and delivered of all kinds of diseases, ailments and infirmities including the blind, deaf and the cripples. Oh, how the Lord works in such marvelous ways, His wonders to perform.

This was our last service in Asamankese. How we fell in love with the people and we would stand around and talk with them after the meeting and try to learn some of their language. This thrilled them to no end. They were such a lovely and jovial people. From that day, the Christ Apostolics were with us in all our meetings.

### In Kumasi

The next morning, December 17, we took a Lorrie from Asamankese to Kumasi. This was a distance of 196 miles with about half of it being on hot, dusty dirt roads. It was very tiresome as the Lorrie was just a small pickup truck with a top on it but it was so crowded. Would you believe it? We had a flat tire on the way. It made me wonder if we could ever go anywhere without any trouble. It was about 5:00 in the afternoon when we arrived in Kumasi. They put us in a nice two-story house. How wonderful it was to have a bathtub and a flushing toilet. Usually they had just a box with a large can in it for the toilet. I was so dirty from the dusty road that I had to take two baths in order to get clean. There wasn't any service in the evening which was a good thing as we were really tuckered out. There was one bed in our room and another thing they called a bed. Really it was nothing more than a couple boards for springs with a kapok-filled mattress on top. It dipped in the middle where the boards had big cracks between them. Erskine being my senior, had the soft mattress and I tried to make out on the other thing but it was torturous to say the least.

## Opposition Comes!

On December 18, we didn't have a morning meeting as we felt it was best to start with the meeting in the evening. It was so nice to have the morning off for a change. Erskine and I walked downtown to get some exercise and just to look around. The sight of the open air markets was not a pleasant experience. The flies seemed to be everywhere, on the meat, the breads as well as the cooked food. The sight along with the smell almost made me sick to my stomach. There seemed to be such unsanitary conditions in that market in those days. The meetings were held in the Prince of Wales Park, right out in the open. Unknown to us, one of the Pentecostal groups from England was doing all they could to hinder the meetings and prevent people from coming. That's sad because they could have had as much a part as any other group because we didn't exclude anyone. It was the smallest crowd that we had thus far, yet the presence of the Lord was so powerful. Erskine preached and about two-thirds of the sick were healed. It was a cross-section of diseases that was healed with the blind, the deaf, elephantiasis, yaws, leprosy as well as many cripples.

## The Lord Meets the Children Again

Erskine really preached a good message in the morning meeting on December 19. Then we prayed for the children and a good number of them were healed. Your heart has to go out to the children. The meeting was held in the church and it wasn't quite full as they didn't do any advertising or promoting. It seemed like they just wanted the meetings to be in their Church and exclude all the others. This was the second place that we had run into that type of thing. It was my time to preach in the evening service and the anointing of the Holy Spirit came upon the crowd in such a mighty way as we gathered in the Prince of Wales Park that evening. As I prayed for the whole crowd at once, over half the people were miraculously healed. There was such a wave of healing that just swept over the crowd. Many more were healed than in the evening before, however there wasn't the great number of sick people attending that we usually saw, though the turnout was quite good. There came a huge tropical storm about 10:30 that night and it was a doozie! I never saw it rain harder in my life. The wind roared and the bottom fell out.

## A Time of Dedication

The church was packed for the morning meeting on December 20. Many people were standing on the outside as there wasn't enough room inside. Erskine gave a short exhortation on the lines of praise and then I preached. The Lord sure was there with such a powerful anointing. What a joy it is to preach under such a powerful influence of the Holy Spirit. The message was on consecrating our lives to the Lord. At the end of the message, I had those to stand that wanted to dedicate their lives to the Lord. It looked like everyone stood so we prayed for them en masse as they really were crying out to the Lord. Oh, how the glory of the Lord came upon them. That is such a touching scene when it happens.

After this tremendous move, Erskine gets up and tries to persuade each one of them to witness to ten people by tomorrow night. He used to do this a lot in the States as well. There were only a few who said they would, so Erskine just walked out. A little later I left as they were taking the offering and things had pretty well run their course. I didn't want him to walk out like that but he insisted he was and he did it.

In the evening meeting he preached on *"I know my Redeemer lives"* but it didn't seem to have much punch. Nevertheless, a good number of people were healed. The crowds, though very large and numbering into the thousands, were still not running as great as they had been in other places. No doubt our problem was this other Pentecostal group was really fighting us and doing all they could to prevent people from coming. When will Christians ever learn?

## Words of Wisdom

It looked to me like Erskine must have had a "burr under his saddle" from the day before. He preached for an hour and forty-five minutes on personal witnessing in the morning meeting of December 2. I couldn't help but think of what Dr. Wyatt used to tell us young preachers, "If you must preach, for God's sake, spare the people." The people just seemed to be worn out. In fact both of us were extremely weary as well. Perhaps the heat and poor beds were getting to us. It seems that a person sleeps but it doesn't seem to do them as much good. It was so hot and humid, especially under the mosquito net, so you roll and toss all night.

Max and Paul were to meet us here before the service began in the evening but they didn't come till afterwards so I had to preach. The crowd wasn't very large and there were not very many sick people remaining. There were a few people who were healed but there was a huge number who came forward for salvation. This made it all worthwhile. When you are used to having huge crowds and one is smaller, though still large by any standard, you tend to wonder why and are a bit disappointed. We have to realize that every soul is important and the size of the meeting is not to be the criterion of whether the Lord blessed or not.

It was so good to see Max and Paul again after the service. They stayed in the Wilbin Hotel, so we went over and visited with them. They had gotten our mail and brought it with them. There were two letters from Mildred. It seems that she was the only one that wrote as no one else had written for quite a while. Even my family and the church in Baton Rouge hadn't written either.

## December 22

The Church wasn't quite filled for the morning service but it was a good turnout by any standards. I exhorted a little while and Paul was to speak but we felt we should lay hands and prophecy over some, so we did. In fact, we prayed over quite a few women this time and it was quite acceptable. What a powerful time in the Lord!

After the meeting, we went to the hotel with Max and Paul and had a wonderful dinner. It was one of the best meals we've had on the whole trip. In the afternoon we were able to borrow a car, so we drove out into the country and took some pictures of the jungle, cocoa trees, cola nut trees and also rubber trees. We broke some of the big cocoa pods open and tasted them. There was a sweet gooey substance around the beans that tasted quite good. The cola nuts were extremely bitter however.

Max preached in the evening meeting on putting your foot on the devil. It was excellent and really blessed the people. There were not very many people healed as there wasn't many sick remaining. This would be the last evening meeting in Kumasi as we must move onto another town and place.

## Questions and Answers Very Profitable

We had our last morning meeting in Kumasi on December 23, in which we prayed over and laid our hands upon quite a few more men and women. The meeting was then opened to questions and answers. All the questions asked were about unity and women. We stressed working together with all groups in love. The Lord wanted to make His people one in diversity and not conformity. While we would never be one big church in a city yet we were all a part of the great Body of Jesus Christ and should not be fighting one another. With women, we wanted them to begin using them in the ministry because *"in Christ"* there is neither male nor female. The way we handled the questions was for Max to answer them for a while then Erskine would answer some and I would follow at the end. Paul didn't feel like doing anything. It seemed to be a very profitable time for the people.

Erskine and Paul left for their appointed place. Max and I left in the afternoon for Wiamoase in the back of a Lorrie. It was only about 31 miles, but off the paved road down an old dirt road, way up in the hills in what seemed like the heart of the jungle. Chapter one tells about the meetings in Wiamoase from December twenty-third to the twenty-eighth.

# Two Youngsters Left Alone
# Chapter 6

### It's Not an Easy Road

It was the twenty-ninth of December in 1953. Paul Shaver and I were now all alone since Max Wyatt and Erskine Holt had left for Accra and then flew on home to Portland. We arose early, had breakfast and packed as we were told we would leave at 10:00 a.m. However, it was 1:00 in the afternoon before they came for us. All of us rode in the back of a Lorrie from Kumasi to Sunyani, which was a trip of about eighty miles. Today, that isn't very far but in those days it was a long way. It was a tough trip as it was very crowded in the back of the Lorrie with so many people tightly squeezed in. We finally arrived at 5:00p.m. at the place where we were to stay. Consequently we had to get settled and cleaned up very quickly as the evening service was to begin at 6:30.

### Can We Really Do It? Let's See!

When we arrived for the first service there was a huge crowd awaiting us and they were already singing and praising the Lord. What a delight it was to walk into a meeting where the people were really enjoying themselves, just singing and dancing and praising the Lord. To us, the big question now was this: could Paul and I carry on the meetings the same as had been done when Dr. Wyatt, Max and Erskine were here? We would find out quickly as this was the time when "the rubber meets the road." As far as we were concerned it was now or never. Actually, to us it was a "do or die" situation. However, there was not a doubt whatsoever in our hearts that the Lord would work the same way, as He is not limited by any certain people. We found that Omnipotence needs no helpers! If it was God with Doc and the others then it didn't matter who the vessels were. All anyone needed was faith in God that He would do it and we really felt up to the task. As F. B. Meyer once said, "We never test the resources of God until we attempt the impossible."

### Our First Meeting Alone

As our custom was, one of us exhorted a few minutes then the other one did the preaching. So I led off with a short exhortation in order to build faith and excitement. This was always a vital part of the meeting and a kind of "breaking the ice" type of thing. It got the people in a responsive mood which made them easier to preach to and build their faith through the Word. Paul then kicked off the meeting by preaching the first message. He really did well and there was such an excitement in the meeting. The Lord's presence was so mighty in our midst.

Right after Paul prayed en masse for the great crowd and they had settled down some, I then invited people to come to the Lord. It was absolutely amazing the tremendous numbers that responded. Thousands of people raised their hands instantly, signifying they wanted to receive Jesus as their Savior. Our problem was, there was no way of bringing them to the front and praying with them since they were all packed so closely to each other and the crowd was so huge. All we could do was explain the way of salvation and lead them in a united prayer of repentance and trust the Lord to do His work. We had no altar workers or counselors to help people as the church hadn't developed to that stage yet. You could see the Lord was really working in their hearts as many of the people, both men and women were weeping before the Lord. Tears were streaming down their cheeks as they wept their way into the Kingdom of God.

After all of this, we asked for testimonies and it looked like all the sick were coming to testify as hundreds lined up. They were all very orderly. There was a great wave of healing that had swept over the crowd when Paul had prayed. Just about every kind of miracle you could think of became a reality. White leprous spots changed to the color of the person's skin at the blink of an eye. Crippled people were standing on their feet dancing and rejoicing. The blind were seeing and shouting, "I can see, I can see! The deaf also were shouting, I can hear, I can hear! Heart problems, lung problems, kidney problems, stomach problems as well as fever was gone in an instant.

With all that going on, the noise level was out of this world. It took more than an hour for most of them to testify even though the African ministers would not allow any of them to be lengthy at all. They were not bashful about stopping a person if they went a little long and it didn't hurt their feelings. This was such a tremendous time in the Lord and with such amazing results.

### The Renowned Steak and Kidney Pie

Our cook had asked us what we would like to eat after the service. We told him that we had steak and kidney pie in Kumasi and really enjoyed it. So he had it prepared when we got back to our room. We both really enjoyed it as it was very delicious.

They had put us in the town mansion but in a very small room. It had only one bed and a small cot. I took the cot and let Paul have the bed as he had carried the weight of the meeting in preaching and praying. By now, we were so used to sleeping on cots anyway. So it was no big deal.

After finally getting to bed, we couldn't sleep very much because it was so noisy. It seems that people talked and laughed all night long but you couldn't blame them with all the excitement of the meetings. Since this was the 30th of December and we were in the midst of the Harmattan season, it was really cold. Sunyani was quite a distance farther North than Accra and that made it that much worse. So we had to sleep in our clothes and use whatever we could find to try and stay warm. I never dreamed that subtropical Africa could be so cold.

## Breakfast Was Something Else!

We arose fairly early and had our breakfast. Here we had a different cook and he wanted to please us very badly. So he prepared some oatmeal which we had with sugar and evaporated milk mixed with filtered water. There was no such thing as fresh milk. We tried to tell him that we didn't want any oatmeal but he was so used to the British custom of oatmeal every morning that he fixed it regardless of what we wanted. He took a firm stand that we must eat oatmeal first as it was so good for us. He then brought us some very smelly fish and did they ever stink! Wow! He cooked the eggs in the same smelly oil and served them with toast. We could hardly stand the smell of the fish or the eggs. We "toughed" the eggs and toast down but we just couldn't stomach the fish. Actually the eggs tasted like the rotten fish smelled. What happened was: they shipped the fish up from the coast with no refrigeration, so by the time they're bought in the market; they are at least two to three days old. You know how quickly fish can begin to smell without refrigeration.

## The King Comes to the Meeting

Since it was so cold, the people assembled pretty late for the morning service. During the singing time, the King of Sunyani came into the meeting. It was a sight to behold! He was sitting in his big gold-plated chair that had two gold-plated poles fitted into brackets so it could be carried. This was transported by eight big, strong, handsome African men with the poles on their shoulders. They were as black as ebony and dressed in short white pants and their bodies were oiled to make them shine. The king had a huge gold crown on his head that looked like it must have weighed ten pounds. He was arrayed in the most beautiful purple robe with pure gold threads interwoven into it. I thought it was the most beautiful cloth I had ever seen in all my life even to this day. What a sight to see as they came bringing in the king! It was magnificent. In fact it was absolutely stunning. No doubt about it, here was royalty!

They put him and his throne directly in front of the pulpit, several rows back. He really participated in the singing and worship. We prayed for him toward the end of the meeting and he just wept his way into the glorious presence of the Lord, receiving Jesus into his own heart.

It was my time to speak, so I spoke along the lines of deliverance and many more people were wonderfully healed. Again, you could see many white leprous blotches on the black or brown skins just vanish before our very eyes, being replaced with the most beautiful brown or black color. This was happening all over the place to dozens of people at the same time. What tremendous joy filled that place when these people fully realized they were healed! There was such dancing and emotion displayed with it being all orchestrated by the people and not by us on the platform. Never once did we try to stir up the people with emotion. It was always with the Word of God to build their faith.

When things kind of settled down, we then instructed them in what it meant to receive Christ as their Savior. This was imperative! You could watch their faces and see when understanding came into their hearts as huge smiles would cover their faces. To quote and old Southern expression of happiness, "They were grinning like a 'possum eating yellow jackets." Indeed, they were exceedingly happy and full of joy.

We found the morning services valuable in teaching the people what accepting the Lord was about and making sure they understood it. When we got back to the room, our cook had prepared steak & kidney pie for lunch again. We reluctantly ate as this was the third time in a row.

## Messages Hard to come by, but God Works!

Paul insisted that I speak in the evening meeting as he said he didn't have anything and neither did I but I went ahead and did it. After all someone had to speak as there were only the two of us. I preached a simple little message to inspire their faith and then I prayed en masse for the whole crowd. Again there was a great move of the Holy Spirit with multitudes of people being healed of all kinds of infirmities. Just like the night before, the blind were seeing, the deaf were hearing and the cripples were dancing. It was so amazing with all the miracles that happened. I was so fascinated to again see these large white blotches of leprosy on people's faces or arms and legs disappear and instantly being replaced with the original black or brown color. You blink your eyes and it was done and you say to yourself, "*I know I didn't see that*" but we did over and over again, hundreds of times.

As was our custom, at the end of the meeting, we invited people to accept Jesus Christ as their Savior. It was a repeat of the night before, with so many people accepting Him as their Savior. Some would ask if these were all the same ones again. No doubt some of them were the same ones that raised their hands the night before, but there were so many more this time. It didn't matter to us if they were the same ones as when they really accepted the Lord, they wouldn't raise their hands anymore. We were not counting numbers anyway. This made a grand and glorious day with so many wonderful people being met by the Lord in salvation, deliverance and healing.

## Harmattan Takes Its Toll!

Preaching twice today, my voice was about gone because of the Harmattan. There was so much of the fine sand and dust in the air that it made breathing difficult. If we were cold, we couldn't help but think of the poor Africans with hardly any clothes. They were probably much colder than we were as we came from a colder climate. After the evening meeting, our cook had prepared steak and kidney pie again but we just couldn't eat it this time. This was the fourth time in a row.

## The Last Day of the Year was Extremely Busy

The last day of 1953 had arrived, the thirty-first day of December. We had been on this trip for over a month and a half now. Again our cook had prepared us some oatmeal, eggs and toast for breakfast which we devoured as we were so hungry because we just couldn't stomach any more steak and kidney pie the night before.

The crowd was huge when I led off with a short exhortation to stir them up. Paul then preached the main message in the morning service. The response among the sick wasn't very much as there didn't seem to be very many sick people left. It reminded me of Mt. 12:15 where *"great multitudes followed Him, and He healed them all."*

Paul instructed them about receiving the Lord and what it meant. He did this in order to give them a Biblical foundation of what they had experienced. We found that it was extremely important to ground their experiences in the Word and we would do this by teaching in the morning services.

## The Village of Odumasi

We didn't have much time to rest after lunch because the Chief of Odumasi, a neighboring village, wanted us to come over to see him and to speak to his people. We had told him that we couldn't come because we didn't have any time. But he kept insisting we come even in the afternoon. So we consented. He promised, "When you come, I will ring the gong for all the people to come together." We were told that when the chief rings the gong, everyone must come immediately. It went back to the time when a warring tribe came against them, and they would assemble to fight.

On the way over Paul and I had a big argument over who was going to preach. I said that I wasn't and Paul said that he wasn't. He usually won out as he seemed to have a stronger will than I did. Maybe it was his German nature which he often bragged about jokingly. Anyway, both of us were so tired and felt preached out. Inspiration seemed to have taken flight and we both struggled to have anything to say.

When we arrived at the village, the king had his men to ring the village gong. To our surprise, more than three thousand people began to gather with the whole village turning out. It seemed that they were coming from all directions as fast as they could. There was no platform or anything to stand on so you could see over the tops of the people surrounding you and this made it difficult to minister to the people in the back. We sang a few African songs and Paul stepped up and exhorted in a few words then I was to preach. No one could imagine the agony I was going through unless you had been there and had done that. I didn't have the slightest idea of what in the world to speak on. My mind seemed totally blank. All I knew was that here was a huge crowd of people who had never heard the gospel before and I must tell it to them.

Suddenly my heart was filled to overflowing with the power and the presence of the Holy Spirit. Acts 13:27- 30 and 38-39 came so forcibly to my mind and I then opened my Bible and began to read those verses. *"For they that dwell at Jerusalem, and their rulers, because they knew Him not, nor yet the voices of the prophets which are read every Sabbath day, they have fulfilled them in condemning Him. And though they found no cause of death in Him, yet desired they Pilate that He should be slain. And when they had fulfilled all that was written of Him, they took Him down from the tree, and laid Him in a sepulcher. But God raised Him from the dead: . . . Be it known unto you therefore, men and brethren, that through this man is preached unto you the forgiveness of sins: And by Him all that believe are justified from all things, from which ye could not be justified by the law of Moses."*

---

**A copy of report that we sent to Wings of Healing**

**Cannon - Shaver Report**

Sunyani, Gold Coast—January 1, 1954

Greetings from Paul Cannon and Paul Shaver.

We closed a wonderful meeting here in this northwestern section of Gold Coast tonight. We won't have much breathing time though, as we have to leave at 8:00 A.M. and travel 130 miles by lorry to begin services in Agogo tomorrow night.

We are oh so happy that we can report that God moved in a mighty way here in this town.

The Paramount Chief of a nearby village was in the meeting and sent word that he wanted us to come to his town and help his people. We arranged to go the next afternoon. Practically the whole village (about 3,000 people) turned out. They were all heathenish with Ju-Ju charms and the like hanging from their arms and necks.

We ministered to them in word and the power of the Holy Ghost and many were healed, including the Chief.

There was a wonderful spirit in the service here tonight. After the preaching we laid hands on people to receive the Holy Ghost and nearly 200 received and many were healed. The Paramount Chief was saved and filled with the Spirit in this Service.

Paul Cannon in Campaign in Sunyani, Gold Coast.

---

When I finished reading vs. 29, *"and they took Him down from the tree, and laid Him in a sepulcher,"* the whole crowd said in unison, "Awe!" Then when I read the next verse, *"But God raised Him from the dead,"* they shouted "Yeah!" Briefly, I spoke on the fall of man and gave a quick historical synopsis of mankind and why Jesus came and had to die. Most of them were totally unconverted and had never heard the gospel before. When I told about when Jesus went into the bowels of the earth and took the keys from the devil and arose from the grave, they really took off cheering. They clapped their hands and shouted "Hooray, Hooray!" Such excitement came to them and they were all with me.

We then prayed en masse for the whole crowd but it looked like only one was healed. The Apostolic ministers with us grew afraid but I knew that God would confirm His word so we prayed again and the first one up was a little boy of two years of age that had been born blind. Then a young girl about 10 was healed of total blindness and she could see perfectly. She kept saying, "I can see, I can see, over and over again. This electrified the crowd as they all knew her. There were a whole lot of people healed of so many different things. When the Master of ocean, earth, and sky calls the shots, things happen.

After this we didn't have any more time as we had to go back to Sunyani for the evening meeting. On our way back, I had the deep sense in my heart that the Lord had come through in what was a big crisis for me. Praise His name! To Him be all the glory!

### Back to Sunyani

Paul preached in the evening meeting in Sunyani and again we had great miracles happening right before the people's eyes. It seemed that the miracles were so much more openly visible here than what we had seen up to this point in other places, even with Dr. Wyatt. The news of what was happening had spread to other neighboring villages so consequently there were many more sick and crippled people that came.

With such astounding miracles happening, there weren't any skeptics to be found. We didn't single anyone out to draw people's attention as these people knew one another very well and knew the health problems they had. We allowed whoever wanted to come up and testify to do so and the crowd would get so excited when they did testify.

After the service we had steak and kidney pie for dinner again. We couldn't believe it. This was our fifth day in a row and it sure got tiresome after that many times. Shortly thereafter, we fell into our cots exhausted but with a great feeling of satisfaction in our souls that we had done the work of the Lord in difficult ways. We had found out that we could carry on the meetings with the same results as when Dr. Wyatt and the others were with us. For this we were so very thankful.

### The Beginning of the New Year 1954

Paul and I began the New Year by continuing to minister in Sunyani, Gold Coast to finish up the meetings there. We had very little sleep during the night as there were some people outside our window making so much noise by knocking on people's doors most of the night. It makes a person wonder if these people ever slept. No doubt they were celebrating the New Year's arrival. However, this went on every night.

## An African Wedding

We went to the canopy early this morning because they were having an African wedding and we wanted to see how they did it as well as be a part. Brother J. A. C. Anaman, our interpreter, officiated at the wedding ceremony and it went very well. The bride was dressed in a plain white dress with the man dressed in Western style clothing. Though it was a very simple affair, it was very nice. An interesting thing to me was that the mother and not the father gave the bride away. After they said "I do" in response to the Minister's question, the mother took the right hand of each of the couple and joined them together as the minister pronounces them man and wife. They kneeled together and brother Anaman laid his hands on them and prayed that the Lord's blessing would be upon their marriage. Then they just got up and walked out shaking hands with the people as they went. That was it! I thought, Shucks! No kissing the bride! (Not me - but the bridegroom.)

## The Laying on of Hands and Prophecy

Paul taught in the morning service on the laying on of hands with prophecy and we laid hands on and prophesied over quite a few people. The Word of Knowledge was so great that the men and women would just break and sob as the word of the Lord hit home and the secrets of their hearts were revealed. This was such a life changing and powerful ministry to these people. They would never be the same again.

After it was all over, I was completely exhausted as the laying on of hands and prophecy was such exhausting work. Again, in preaching, you kind of restore your soul as you preach the Word of the Lord. The Word has the same effect on the preacher as it does the hearer, bringing life. But the laying on of hands and prophecy is so intense in your seeking the Lord for His word and the anointing of the Holy Spirit is so heavy that when it is over, your body feels exhausted.

When we got back to the hotel, our cook had fixed us some chicken for dinner. Oh joy! What a relief it was from Steak and Kidney pie. Whew! Usually, he was such a good cook and the meals were very delicious. However in the evening he fixed some mutton but it was as we often said, too much lamb, ram, sheep meat and mutton taste for us but we ate it and were thankful.

## A Holy Spirit Filling Evening

It fell my lot to preach in the evening meeting. As usual at the end of meetings we would pray for people to be filled with the Holy Spirit as so many had already accepted the Lord as their Savior. When the people came up, we always took a few minutes to instruct them in what to do to receive the Holy Spirit. The next thing we did was to get them to pray along with us in a prayer of repentance. This is where you can see the sincerity coming out as tears would begin to flow down their faces. Along with our African ministers, we then laid our hands on them for the Baptism of the Holy Spirit. It was always amazing to see the Lord filling

The Road To Agogo

them with the Holy Spirit. There were more than 200 that were gloriously filled. Needless to say, there was "joy in the camp that night."

After all of that, we prayed for the sick en masse and many more people were healed and came up to testify of their healing. When the meeting was all over, we tried to make a tape for Portland of the testimonies but there was trouble with the recorder so we didn't get it all. We wanted some of these live testimonies for the Wings of Healing broadcast. During the meeting, the chief of Odumasi was healed of back trouble and bad eyes plus he was filled with the Holy Ghost. You should have heard the crowd rejoice at that. We did get his testimony on tape.

## The Proof is in the Doing

This was our final meeting in Sunyani of which we have many fond memories. What a wonderful and delightful people they were! These meetings proved that a couple of young men when left alone could carry on the vision that the Holy Spirit had instilled within our hearts through Dr. Wyatt. Doubtless, we would have our ups and downs but the downs would not be our fault but rather the lack of preparation and expectations by the places we were visiting. We would have some bitter opposition from a few religious groups at times but we didn't let that bother us nor did we attack them.

We found that in the unreached towns and villages where there was no Christian witness, we didn't need any preparation to speak of. Just the invitation from the king or chief was sufficient and he would ring the village gong. However, where there were several different churches involved, the results depended to a great extent on the unity of the body of Christ in that particular area. It didn't seem to affect the healings and miracles as they were always there. It did affect the size of the crowd and that in turn affected the number of people saved, filled with the Holy Spirit and healed.

## On the Road to Agogo

We began the second day of January by getting up very early and packing our belongings. Again there wasn't much sleep to be had as it was still so noisy all night long. Brother J. A. C. Anaman had a Lorrie come at 9:00 a.m. and took us back to Kumasi. It was a three-hour drive back and we arrived about 12:00 noon. We hurriedly got our mail and had a cup of coffee and Ovaltine as we had to go on to Agogo by Lorrie for a meeting that evening.

On the way, there was an eighteen mile stretch of dirt road that was rough and terribly dusty especially riding in the back of a Lorrie. The whole trip was about 130 miles, total. They put us up at the English Rest Home that was on top of a hill that overlooked the city. What a sight it was to see all the lush jungle lying all around.

## The Largest Crowd Yet

It was my lot again to preach in the evening service as Paul said he was just too weary. I was dead tired too but someone had to do it. Physically, we were not up to it as the only thing we had to eat all day long was bread, butter and coffee and Ovaltine.

We hurriedly dressed and went to the evening meeting. There was an enormous crowd gathered and they were in full swing, singing and worshiping the Lord. In fact it was the largest crowd that we've had up to this time in the Gold Coast including Dr. Wyatt's meetings in Accra.

When we arrived, an older Minster got up and led the official song service. Up to this time they let the younger ministers "try their wings" leading and preaching. There was no canopy erected here and no seats so they just stood for hours in the open field where they had erected a small platform. There were quite a few really great miracles that happened in the evening, such as the blind seeing, leprosy disappeared and cripples walking without any sign of ever being crippled.

However there wasn't as many as we expected since there was such a powerful Presence of the Lord in the meeting and such a huge crowd. It seemed that we just couldn't keep the crowd quiet enough so all of them could hear. Then too, we had a different interpreter which makes a lot of difference. Brother Anaman didn't go with us to Agogo but a brother F. D. Walker did, so he interpreted for us. An interpreter can make or break you when it comes to preaching. By the end of the meeting, I had such a tremendous headache I could hardly stand and felt completely exhausted. The weather was really cool as the Harmattan wind was still blowing very strongly.

January 3 was a Sunday morning so we went to the meeting at the set time but the people were late in coming for some reason. Usually on a cold morning they don't like to get out of their mud huts till it gets warm.

Since there was a little time we went to see the chief in his palace which was nothing more than a large mud hut. We had a good time with him and he was very open.

Paul did a great job of preaching in the morning meeting in which there was a great crowd out, and most of them were, as yet, unreached with the gospel. In those days the term heathen was the term we used and it didn't mean some derogatory thing that they were inferior but simply that they were not believers in Christ as they had not heard of Him. This was the term that was used by most everyone in those days, including the Africans. To us it was a term of endearment as Jesus came to save especially the heathen. There was a really good response to Christ but still not quite what we wanted or were used to seeing up to this point.

### A Gift from the King

In the afternoon, some special messengers were sent by the chief and they brought us a gift. They had two live chickens, three big yams that were about eight inches in diameter by two feet long plus some other things. This was to show his appreciation for our coming to see him the day before. As is the custom, when they "dash" you something (their term for giving) we gave them a couple of schillings as a token of our thanks. You must be very careful that you show your appreciation by giving enough but not too much that would look like you are paying for them as it could offend them. We were fortunate that our cook informed us of the protocol because the last thing we wanted to do was to offend one of them. After all, we came to win them to Jesus Christ.

### 500 Filled With the Holy Spirit

Paul preached in the evening service to a much greater crowd of people than last night. Practically everybody in the village came out for the meeting and then some. Before the sermon, we asked for all those who wanted to be filled with the Holy Spirit to come to the front. Since Paul was preaching, I gave them the instructions on how to receive the Holy Spirit. Then we had a time where we led them in a prayer of repentance and began worshiping the Lord. As the mighty presence of the Lord came down, we then laid our hands on them for the Baptism of the Holy Spirit. About 300 of them were filled and spoke in tongues as the Spirit gave them utterance. After this, we had another group to come up and more than 200 more received the in-filling of the Holy Spirit. This was the greatest number of people filled with the Holy Spirit in any service with just Paul and me ministering. Many of those filled were young people and they received a glorious experience.

When that part of the meeting was over, Paul spoke a few minutes about healing and prayed for them en masse. There were a lot of sick people that were healed but for some reason we just couldn't seem to get the "overflow" we were expecting.

### The Meetings in Dunkwa

We arose fairly early on Monday, the fourth of January and had our proverbial oatmeal for breakfast. We packed our bags and loaded them into the back of a Lorrie which took us back to Kumasi. We arrived at noon so we got a bite to eat at the Kingsway Hotel (such as it was) and both of us got a badly needed haircut. At 3:00 in the afternoon we caught the train for Dunkwa which was 60 miles away. It was 6:00 when we arrived, so we had a quick bite to eat and went to the service.

There was absolutely no preparation here for our coming, so the meeting was held in the church building but it was way too small to hold all the people that had come. Paul spoke a little and I followed with the main message but I was so sick I could hardly stand. I had to hold on to the pulpit to keep from falling as I felt so weak. My head hurt so badly that I could hardly think and my stomach was also upset. I felt so tired and sick that I just couldn't deal with the sick for deliverance. In spite of it, the Lord undertook for us by healing all the sick that came except two people. It is amazing how the Lord works regardless of our infirmities. Brother J. A. C. Anaman interpreted but he didn't do so good either as he was struggling along with me.

We finally had some mail here which was a big thing as we were so homesick too. After the meeting a brother gave me a beautiful black pair of African slippers with leather soles which today are called "flip-flops." They cost him 30 cents and were greatly appreciated. That helped so much in getting out of bed and slipping them on instead of shoes. Besides you could see if a scorpion was on them before slipping into them. In most of the places we would have to turn our shoes upside down when we went to bed to keep the scorpions from getting into them.

### The Arrival of Paintsil

The fifth of January, we began our day with oatmeal and eggs for breakfast and went to the morning service. It was an hour late starting as the people were so slow in gathering because of the cold. Paul preached and a couple of sick people were healed when we prayed for them. It was a rough night sleeping because the beds were horrible. They sank in the middle and it was like we were sitting up all night.

Paul preached again in the evening service and a few more people were healed. J. Egyir Paintsil came up and interpreted for him and what a difference he made. Paintsil got so excited and thrilled with the message that he really excited the people. He was very good at interpreting and a great joy to be around. We were supposed to go to Tarkwa the next day but he didn't get word in time to line up a meeting there so we had to remain in Dunkwa a few more days. You learn to take all these things in stride as communications were extremely difficult in those days.

## A Very Discouraging Time

The next day, the sixth of January a baby in town had died during the night so the people didn't come out much for the morning meeting. There were only about 60 people that showed up at the starting time. I spoke along the lines of consecration and felt I did such a miserable job of it. It was so disappointing in this place. Paul was sick with a cold and my voice was just about gone.

Since Paul had preached both times the day before, I spoke in the evening service as well. There weren't very many people that came because of the threatening weather. A tropical storm came up during the service while I was preaching and the wind blew really hard with the lightning striking all around us. The wind caught my notes and blew them away and the lights went out but I continued preaching anyway and Paintsil continued interpreting. Before the storm, it was stifling hot but it got cold afterwards. A few people came up to receive the Holy Spirit so we instructed them and laid hands on them for the Baptism of the Holy Spirit. There were 16 filled and received this glorious experience in the Lord. This made it worth all our problems.

## Did you ever Get 'Oatmealed' Out?

On January 7, we had our oatmeal, eggs and fried potatoes for breakfast. The eggs and potatoes were great but we were just about "oatmealed" out. We asked ourselves, how in the world can the British eat oatmeal every morning? One of our problems was they didn't cook it to our liking as it was always without any salt. The morning service was to start at 11:00 but it was an hour late and still there were only a handful of people out. Paul spoke for a few minutes and it was quite good. I followed with the main message.

In the afternoon, as I was writing my journal, I could look out the window across the little valley and see almost the whole town. Vultures were flying all around and would light on the roofs of the houses, on the ground and just about anyplace. I never saw so many vultures in my life though growing up in Southern Louisiana, but we had our share of them.

In the afternoon, we walked down to the marketplace for something to do and to get a little exercise. We loved to take a stroll through the market places and meet the people. They were always so friendly and would greet us merrily. This provided a time for the people to get to see us up close and say a few words to us. This meant an awful lot to them to see that we were not untouchables. While there, I bought a piece of goat leather and reworked my Bible case which was getting badly worn.

When we got back to our place, our cook had prepared some corn beef (canned) and rice for dinner. I spoke in the evening service and we laid hands on quite a few and prophesied over them. It was a powerful time but this was the hardest place of all thus far.

## Onto Wassaw Simpa

On January the eighth, we again had our oatmeal and then a couple of eggs and fried potatoes for breakfast. Then we packed and caught the train for Tarkwa at 10:30 a.m. We took a bowl of chicken, cooked African style and bread along with us as there were no places to eat en route. However, there were no utensils, so we ate it African style – with our hands. As an aunt of mine used to say, "Fingers were made before knives and forks."

Paintsil and some other brethren of the Gold Coast Apostolic Churches met us in Tarkwa and took us by car to Wassaw Simpa. They put us up at the Chief's home but that wasn't very good. We slept on our cots that we carried with us, which was all right. However the water to bathe in was so brown before you bathe that you couldn't tell how dirty you really were after bathing. At least you changed "smells." Our cook had prepared some fish and chicken for supper that was outstanding. He sure was a good cook and was provided by the Chief personally.

## A Paralyzed Man Instantly Healed

When we arrived at the service there were between two and three thousand people already assembled and worshiping. When it came time to speak, I led off with a short word of exhortation to break the ice and Paul took the main message. There were only a few people healed in that meeting but they were very outstanding miracles. They had carried a man into the meeting who had fallen from a great height and had broken his spine. He was completely paralyzed from the neck down and almost died on the way. It's a miracle that he lived to be brought into the meeting. It's interesting that his name in English meant "God is alive." After we prayed en masse for the whole crowd, he instantly leaped to his feet, praising God and kept jumping around so excitedly praising the Lord. It reminded us of the cripple that was healed at the gate called beautiful in the book of Acts with Peter and John.

The crowd liked to have gone wild with excitement! They were shouting and dancing and praising the Lord from the top of their voices. Yet they never posed a problem of control. It did take quite a while to get them all settled down so we could have some other testimonies. It seemed like the Lord would just sweep over the congregation after some of the testimonies with another wave of healing. So many unbelievable things were happening all around us as miracle after miracle kept on occurring. This was without us doing anything, just sitting on the platform. The Lord was just reaching out and touching His people. What a jubilant crowd! It made all of our sacrifices we had gone through thus far worthwhile.

### Such Good Food

We had asked our cook just to fix us pancakes for breakfast and nothing more on the ninth of January. He had agreed the night before. However, when we arrived for breakfast the next morning, lo, and behold, he brought us the infernal oatmeal, then he brought us two eggs and sausage for each of us. When we had finished eating those things, he brought us two banana pancakes. By that time we were stuffed and thought sure we were through and then he brought us a large marmalade pancake. That was just too much yet it was so delicious! It really didn't matter if we couldn't eat it all because what we didn't eat they did, even the stuff we left on our plates. Nothing was thrown away; not even the scraps.

### A Rejoicing Chief!

In the morning service, Paul led off with a short word of exhortation and I followed with the main message. However, I really had a tough time with my voice. My throat was so sore as I had caught a head cold during the night. Paintsil's voice was just about gone as well. Paul's had been bad, but his was improving a bit for which we were very thankful.

The chief was in every service and having himself such a good time. What a joy it was to see him rejoicing and praising the Lord along with the people. There were a few people healed in the morning meeting but not great numbers. As usual in the morning meetings we taught on the basics of salvation and living a Christian life. So any healing or miracle was beside the point.

### No Lepers Allowed in Town

They are different here than in other cities as they wouldn't allow any lepers to come into the city. In most cities thus far, there were always hundreds of lepers around and they looked so hopeless. If anything touched my heart, it was always the lepers. My father had helped build the Leprosy Hospital in Carville, Louisiana when I was a small boy. He would tell us of the pitiful plight of the lepers there and perhaps that left an impression on my young mind. Another thing to me was the fact that Jesus took time to heal the lepers.

### Outstanding Miracles

There was a huge crowd out for the evening service with Paul leading off and me doing the preaching. So many people were healed with some of them being such outstanding miracles. It took a long time to allow some of them to testify but that didn't seem to matter to the people. This was the greatest thing that was going on in these parts and they enjoyed every moment of it. Our African brethren handled the testimonies entirely as we sat and rested and listened with amazement. Our hearts were filled with praise to the Lord for meeting these needy people. Sometimes right before your eyes, miracles happened and because they were so great, you would say to yourself, "I didn't see that. I know that I didn't see that." But we did and glorified the Lord along with the wonderful people.

## Polygamy a Problem

It was January tenth and once again we had our proverbial oatmeal and eggs for breakfast. Somehow we still can't get them to understand that we didn't want any more oatmeal. Paul preached in the morning meeting or maybe I should say we gave them a doubleheader. I taught for a while and he preached. I really felt that I needed to cut across some of the old customs of plural marriages as there was quite a lot of polygamy here. They seemed to accept the things we taught because of seeing all the great miracles. In that way, I guess we earned our right to be heard.

After the meeting we tried to make a tape for the radio broadcast as the Wings of Healing was pressing us to get some testimonies and singing, but the recorder went on the blink. Electric recorders were not good over here because most of the places didn't have electricity.

## A Thousand Accept Jesus in Tarkwa

We had to leave at 4:00 in the afternoon to go to Tarkwa for the service in the evening. It was a trip of only 18 miles one way but the chief of Wassaw Simpa had his driver take us in his Studebaker car. There were nine of us in the car. The service started at 5:00 with a tremendous crowd present. They didn't have a canopy so the meeting was out in the open, right downtown. Tarkwa was a gold mining town and a rough one at that. When we began, there was a group of people from a Catholic church, marching up and down the street right in front of us. They were chanting their rituals and all, but it just brought more people out to hear us. No way were we going to fight them so we just went on doing what we always did, preaching the gospel of Jesus Christ.

I began the ministry part of the service by laying a foundation of the Word and Paul preached although he had trouble saying his words. In spite of it all, it was a great meeting with many, many people being healed. Most of those were outstanding miracles. It was funny, because when the miracles started happening, those that were marching in the street stopped and came and joined us.

At the end of the meeting, I spoke a few words about salvation with Paintsil finishing it up as he knew the language. Close to 1000 people gave their hearts to the Lord in that meeting. We had them come to a spot where we had the people vacate so we could deal more closely with them. There is no thrill like that of seeing a thousand people weeping their way into the Kingdom of God. Oh, I tell you, the Lord is real and will make Himself real to anyone who will earnestly seek Him.

It seemed to be such a long journey back to Wassaw Simpa as we were so weary. Our cook had dinner ready when we arrived so we "chopped" as the African people would say (ate dinner). Tired and weary from the long day we fell into bed exhausted.

It was such a good feeling and with a heartfelt satisfaction that we had been the instruments the Lord had used to minister to and heal a lot of people with so many coming to Him. Again, that made our efforts worthwhile. When you consider, "If one soul is worth more than the whole world," what would be the value of all of these! Indeed the angels in heaven were rejoicing as well as us.

## Last Day in Wassaw Simpa

It was January 11th and it seemed I coughed all night. My throat was so terribly sore along with a bad head cold. The enemy seems to magnify things when you don't feel well. Things that ordinarily wouldn't bother you really seem to stand out. Like when we shaved, we had to use a little cream pitcher to hold the water and stand at the window. I used Mildred's picture that I carried with me for a mirror as there was no mirror here and we didn't have one with us.

We were back in Wassaw Simpa where I preached in the morning service on the laying on of hands and we prophesied over some of the people. As always, there was such a breaking and weeping as the word of the Lord went forth over them. Paul preached in the evening with another good meeting with many more getting healed and delivered from all kinds of diseases. This would be our last meeting in Wassaw Simpa as it was time to move on and we were glad because of the physical hardships, though the Chief and his people had been so wonderful to us. What a lovely people with a wonderful chief. We loved them all.

# A Visit to Elmina Castle and On
# Chapter 7

It was January 12th and we didn't sleep much during the night as I was still coughing most of the night. We had to arise early so we could leave at 8:00 for Cape Coast. We were so thankful that the Chief of Wassaw Simpa had his driver take us all the way in his Studebaker car. Riding in the back of a Lorrie was really tough. The Chief was such a wonderful man.

On the way, our driver stopped at Elmina Castle so we could look around and take some pictures. This is one of the most historic towns in Gold Coast as it was the largest slave market in its day. The tears formed in both of our eyes as we walked around this old historic fort where so many young Africans were shipped off to other parts of the world to be sold on the slave market, never to be reunited with their families again. Many of them died en route. It's been estimated that 6.3 million slaves were taken from the Gold Coast alone.

Elmina Castle was built by the Portuguese in 1482 in a region that was rich in gold and ivory. Its original name was El Mina which means "the mine" in Portuguese and had nothing to do with slavery. It was the first permanent structure south of the Sahara built by Europeans. With the discovery of the New World, many plantations were built in the 1500s which suddenly expanded the demand for slaves. Quickly, trade in slaves overshadowed gold as the principal export of the area with West Africa being the principal source of slaves for all the Americas. The dungeons still are terrible reminders of those horrible times.

### How Did They Get so Many Slaves?

We wondered how they got so many people to be sold as slaves. Our African brethren told us that the Coastal Tribes often went inland to war with other tribes and captured the young people and brought them back to the fort where they were sold to the slave traders. However, slave trading was firmly entrenched in many areas of Africa before any contact with Europeans. Prior to the demand in the New World for slaves, they would either kill them but most often used them as their own slaves. In most situations, men as well as women who were captured in local battles became slaves. However, unlike the rest of the world, most of the slaves in African communities were ultimately absorbed into their masters' families as members.

The supply of slaves at first was entirely in African hands as powerful chiefs were known to have been engaged in the slave trade as well as Muslim Traders. Later, individual merchants who commanded large bands of armed men would raid villages and capture people for that purpose. All the horrible things that happened because of the slave trade, made it exceptionally hard for the gospel to penetrate the region. Missionaries tried but most were failures for many years.

This old castle made us realize that slavery was a horrible thing. Though to some, dying in battle would have been a better fate as the living conditions were so horrible, both in the dungeons as well as on the ships that carried them. What a dark spot in the history of the human race. May our gracious Lord forgive us all of such a tragedy!

## In Cape Coast

We arrived in Cape Coast at 1:00 in the afternoon and were hoping that our mail would catch up with us but it didn't this time. We stayed in a really nice home that sat on top of a hill overlooking the Atlantic Ocean. What a lovely view as you could hear and see the waves rolling in. It was cool all the time so this made it good for sleeping. We went to the Post Office and sent Brother McKeown a wire to please send our mail.

## Spirit of Fear

Paul preached in both the morning and the evening service but for some reason both of us felt scared stiff. It just seemed like a spirit of fear was trying to overwhelm us but we went on doing what we always did in spite of it all. We learned that you cannot give in to your emotions as they have nothing to do with the meetings, or shouldn't. You don't have a good meeting because you feel good. It's the Lord that works by His marvelous grace and has nothing to do with how you feel.

In spite of that feeling, it was a good service with some outstanding miracles happening. A woman was carried in by eight men as she was completely helpless but she was instantly healed and danced all around the platform completely healed. This brought a tremendous excitement to the huge crowd as she was known by so many to have been paralyzed. Again, all of this happened when we prayed en masse for the people as we didn't lay hands on people hardly ever in a large meeting. This lesson was learned early on in the meetings as you will be mobbed instantly by people just wanting to touch you.

In walking through the crowd afterwards, people would crowd around you and wipe your perspiration with their hand and then wipe it on their forehead. I guess they thought our sweat would bring healing and the Lord did heal some but it was their faith and not our sweat.

During the service the electricity went off which hindered things a little but they got some gas lanterns and lit them pretty quickly. This of course left us without a public address system. Consequently, we had to learn to project our voices so the people at the rear could hear us. We found that we could do it pretty well without straining our voices. Really, it's quite a technique.

This was the town where Dr. Wyatt had come the year before and had such a great meeting. We couldn't get the same place to hold our meetings as the Methodist wouldn't permit us to have it this time but it didn't matter.

## The Agony of the Preaching

January 13. We had such a good night's rest with the ocean breeze blowing into our room. You can't imagine how wonderful that was! The roaring of the waves acted as a solace as they sloshed against the shore. It made for a peaceful time. We still had our own problems. With preaching so often, it was terribly hard to get something to preach. It prompted an inward struggle that you constantly labored under. With great anguish of soul, we would cry out to the Lord incessantly for something from Him. I finally settled on something to minister in the morning service, but I didn't think it was very good. Somehow the Lord worked anyway because He is so gracious!

## Great Needs - Great Healings

There were such a great number of people healed of so many different ailments in the meeting. A Methodist schoolteacher had taken off of her job to go to the hospital as she was so sick but instead, came by the meeting and was healed. We saw another horrible site - a woman with her left eyeball sticking out about one and a half inches instantly healed. It just vanished and went back into her head, after which she looked normal and could see perfectly. There were such needs that it just broke our hearts and we couldn't help but be moved to tears.

It seems that people always revel in seeing the miracles but somehow with us there were always the constant needs that were so visible, at least to us. So although there were hundreds of outright miracles every night, it was the ones who were still in need that burdened our hearts the most. It's like the Lord said about the shepherd leaving the ninety and nine and going after the one that was lost. We rejoiced for the moment with those who were healed but our hearts still were heavy for so many others that were so helpless and desperate.

To have a little recreation and to relax, we went swimming in the ocean during the afternoon. This was such a lovely beach and it certainly wasn't crowded by any means. So we had a time of our lives for an hour or so each day and it didn't cost us anything. We really enjoyed our time at the beach as it helped us over our loneliness and boredom that would settle in during the afternoon.

## A Moment Seemed Like Eternity

Besides the morning meeting, I also spoke in the evening as well. There was another great move of the Holy Spirit with many more healings. The canopy was packed out and they were standing way back on the outside. There were at least seven or eight thousand people. We were always ultraconservative in our estimates of crowd size.

How well I remember this evening when I finished preaching and I began to pray en masse for this great crowd of individuals. I say individuals because we never looked at them as just a mass of humanity or a crowd. They were individual people that needed Jesus. I said to them that faith must act. You must do something, you must act, so I told everybody to take a half step toward the platform with your hands raised and praising the Lord as I prayed. Immediately, praise and worship ascended to the Lord that was almost deafening and you could sense the powerful presence of the Lord. I prayed for all of them at one time then stepped back with my head bowed waiting on the Lord to do His work. Though it was only a minute or so, it seemed like an eternity before anyone stepped out or declared they were healed. But then it was like the floodgates were opened as they flocked to testify. It seemed to take people a while before they fully realized they were healed.

So many times the people wouldn't come up that night but would go home to try it out and see if it was still real the next day. It might take them two or three days for them to come up to testify as they wanted to be sure. Sometimes when the blind was healed, they would leave the meeting and run home just to look on their family whom they had never seen before. Then in the next meeting they would testify.

Well, this evening when the people came up to testify, a woman with her small daughter sitting on her hip testified about her daughter being healed. She said that her daughter was born blind and had never seen anything in her life, being about four or five years of age. She testified that her daughter was healed in the meeting last night but she hadn't noticed. The way she realized it was that this morning as she was sitting by the door of her house, cleaning her teeth with a stick and threw the stick away. The little girl ran and picked it up, so she told her to give it to her as it was dirty. She took it out of the child's hand and threw it farther away and the child ran after it again. At this point, she suddenly realized that her daughter had never seen anything in her life so how could she run and pick it up? She was so excited that she repeated the action several times rejoicing in such a miracle. The crowd just roared in praise and thanksgiving to the Lord.

### Miracles yet Lonely

The next day, January 14, Paul spoke in the morning service. I don't know why we each spoke twice in one day except that it just seemed to be the right way to do at the time. Again there was a good number healed, even though our morning meetings were devoted to the basic Bible truths of salvation and living a Christian life. Still the Lord was always present to heal those who in faith reached out to Him. So we naturally took time to pray for the large crowd all at once. The evening service grew to a much larger crowd than the night before. Paul spoke again with another good number of outstanding miracles happening. As usual, there were a great number of people accepting the Lord.

With all the great things happening around us, we still felt so lonely in the afternoon. No doubt the enemy of our soul used it to discourage us. Our thoughts were often on home, the church and our loved ones. So our "morale" seemed to dip so low till we would get some mail which wasn't often because of moving about so much. So today, there wasn't any mail and we were so disappointed. We even wired and called Accra but no one answered.

## Fish Bones

January 15. We still had oatmeal for breakfast, but we also had some eggs and bacon afterwards. This fellow was a very good cook also. He gave us fish at every meal before the main course. The sole that he fixed was very delicious even if it was just the backbone left after filleting them. I don't know what they did with the fillets but we didn't get any of them. I couldn't help but think the first day he did that, "I sure hope this isn't all the meat we get but it was sure great food."

## Presenting a World Vision

I spoke in the morning meeting about having a vision of reaching the world for Christ. I ended up zeroing in on consecration. My, how the people were moved upon and came rushing to the front to kneel and pray. You could see the tears streaming down their cheeks as they came. They really meant business with the Lord. Afterwards, we laid hands and prophesied over two men.

In the afternoon we took a sea bath and a big wave caught me causing me to swallow a gulp of salt water. Yuck! It almost made me sick.

I spoke in the evening meeting and the crowd looked even larger than the night before. The local Radio Station sent their personnel to the meetings and broadcasted the meetings all over the Gold Coast. That was great. However, Rome itself began to get stirred about this thing and sent out letters for the Catholics not to come to the meetings but it didn't stop them. There were a great number healed but not as many as in each of the previous nights. Both of us felt it was hard to preach this evening for some reason. It could have been we were upset about not getting any mail or hearing from anyone and we let our emotions get the best of us. After the service was finished, we did get a wire from Accra. It said that our visas were expired and we must leave the country by the nineteenth of January. This of course saddled us with more frustrations. So the next day, January 16, we sent a fellow to Accra to see what the matter with our mail was and also to send a wire to Dr. Wyatt in Portland.

## Another 200 Filled with the Holy Spirit

Paul preached in the morning meeting on the laying on of hands and we prayed over eight people. The Spirit of prophecy was tremendous over them. One of the eight was Aba, who had been Paul and Max's cook and helper when we first came. It was great to see the women ministered to as well as the men.

Paul spoke again in the evening meeting with a really good number being healed. After this, I had those who had accepted the Lord and wanted to be filled with the Holy Spirit to come forward. We had them get into rows and gave them instructions on how to receive the Holy Spirit. After leading them in a prayer of repentance, we went down each row along with our African Brothers and laid our hands upon them. It was a marvelous thing to be a part of such a thing. Just as soon as our hands would touch them, they would

Paul Downtown Accra

be filled with the Holy Spirit and speak in other tongues as the Holy Spirit gave them utterance. About 200 of them received the Holy Spirit. We had to do it in sections as there were so many that wanted to come but there wasn't any more room. So we had to continue on the next night as time ran out on us. The meetings here were the greatest I had been a part of up to this point, here in the Gold Coast. They certainly didn't want us to leave. What a wonderful people and they treated us so royally.

## Mail Truck Arrived

January 17. We were awakened early with the return of the brother that went to Accra for our mail. What a great day, I had 24 letters. Wow! What that didn't do for our morale! In all of that number of letters was one from Max Wyatt but it still left us in the dark as what we were to do. Our thoughts were that it would be nice to know what they expected of us. Mildred wrote that Donald Murphy was on his way and that I was to go with him to Calabar. We also had another letter saying that he wasn't stopping here in the Gold Coast. So that really left us in the dark. Communication was an enormous problem to us in those days. After reading our multitude of letters we had our infernal oatmeal again for breakfast. Oh joy!

## Inspiration & In-filling

I spoke in the morning service and the scripture really opened up to me. I had never seen such marvelous truth like this before. I preached a solid hour with such a powerful anointing. I must say it was the easiest time I've ever had here in Africa. Oh what fresh inspiration will do for the preacher! We then laid hands on and prayed over seven men and women afterwards. The prophetic was so powerful and life changing.

For lunch, we had peanut soup, rice and foofoo with chicken. It was very good except it was very hot with pepper. They do like their food well seasoned. During the afternoon we were able to take a sea bath and enjoyed it. The waves were really high so it made good surfing.

Paul preached in the evening service and quite a good number were healed. Then I gave the instructions for receiving the Baptism of the Holy Spirit. There were so many who wanted to be filled that we again had to take them in sections because of the lack of space. When we got to the last section, before I could finish giving the instructions, they started speaking in tongues. What a glorious time! All told, more than 300 received the Holy Spirit in that meeting. This made more than 500 people filled with the Holy Spirit in two days. It is so electrifying to be a small part of such a visitation of God to these people. There is just no way to describe the joy that comes with the presence of the Lord filling hearts with His love.

### January 18 - My Twenty-third Birthday!

We arose early for my birthday and packed our stuff as it was moving day. Our cook then served us our daily ration of oatmeal and eggs. We were so thankful that one of our African brothers drove us to Accra in his car and we didn't have to take a lorry. However, Murphy's Law always seemed to catch up to us. We had a flat tire on the way and the spare was really bad but we were able to drive on in.

When we got in, we had a wire waiting for us from Dr. Wyatt that said to "hold all." That was all there was to the wire as nothing more was said. We all simply said to each other, "What in the world does that mean?" Brother James McKeown and Vernon Sanders both thought we should go to Nigeria and were very vocal about it. However, to get away from a confrontation with the two of them, Paul and I went downtown and got the recorder fixed. While we were there, I bought a Jantzen bathing suit of all things. We were so surprised as they were made in Portland and some of the Bible Students worked on them. While we were gone, we discussed what I should do and both of us felt I should stay. That was the way we interpreted Dr. Wyatt's wire of "Hold All."

When we got back to the Missionary house, I told Brother McKeown our decision. Well, he just blew his top! I tell you what, with all the stress that comes with missions; often times people have a short fuse. Come to find out, Dr. Wyatt had sent a letter to Brother McKeown up at Ho explaining the situation but it missed him. Added to that, his former religious affiliation was causing him a lot of trouble so he was very irritable. He then told us that he and a large number of ministers had pulled out of the Apostolic of Wales in Bradford, England a good while before we came and formed the Gold Coast Apostolic Church. This helped us to understand his situation a little.

### A Discouraging Day

On top of that, Brother McKeown had heard that Asan, their maid, told some people that Max told her that he loved her and had committed fornication with her. She also said that Paul was also in on it. We were all totally shocked. This was such a discouraging day and it was my birthday. I felt like throwing up my hands and quitting, but I just couldn't. There was too much at stake.

Of course nothing gets by James McKeown. Being the Scotch/Irish that he was, he immediately got to the bottom of it all. He called Asan in and talked to her very pleasantly, asking her to tell him all about what had happened. She told him that it was after one of the services, with lots of people standing around, talking and laughing very hard. She was standing between Max and Paul. Like many of us Americans, they just put their hand on her shoulder laughing and thought nothing of it. However, she interpreted that in a wrong way. She thought that if a man touched a woman that it was a sign that they loved her and that was fornication. He then explained to her what fornication really was and she said, "No, no it wasn't that."

When Brother McKeown talked to Paul without him knowing he had talked to Asan, he found Paul's story was identical. This put a stop to the rumor immediately. This goes to show how careful we need to be among other cultures. I was glad when this day was over and we could "hit the sack." It was nerve racking to say the least. My, what a birthday!

### Sanders Leaves - I Stay

January 19. We arose a little late and had our usual breakfast. Then we wrote a few letters and went to the immigration office and West Africa Airways Corporation (WAAC). Vernon Sanders and I had reservations to fly to Lagos, Nigeria as our visas for the Gold Coast were expiring as of today. We talked about calling Dr. Wyatt but when we had another talk with Brother McKeown he felt it was all right for me to stay so I did. I really wanted to stay in the Gold Coast as I sensed that things were going to be rough in Nigeria. Vernon Sanders left at 3:15 in the afternoon via WAAC for Lagos, Nigeria. Brother McKeown dropped us at the beach and we took a sea bath. It was really enjoyable. We then went to the Immigration Office and I applied for a two-month visa.

### Visa Granted

January 20. We had corn flakes for breakfast but they were very stale. That kind of food gets stale quickly because of the humidity and heat in the tropics. Actually it is stale when you buy it from the store because it took so long to get there. We went to the immigration office and picked up my passport and they gave me a two-month visa. Oh happy day! Indeed this was a very eventful day. I got some mail from Mildred and a letter from Raymond Hoekstra, telling us what to get for them. We got our letter from Dr. Wyatt with our checks in it. Paul had one for $75 and I had one for $150. We had no idea why the difference. In the afternoon we had a good rest, so I couldn't go to sleep till late that night. Paul was sick with a stomach ache. However, being sick never stopped us. We just went right on ministering the Word of the Lord in spite of the way we felt. We both preached in separate churches in the evening and at each place we had wonderful meetings.

### Bought Land for a Bible School

On January 21st, we had stale corn flakes again for breakfast and wrote a few more letters. At last I caught up on writing letters. This may sound trite but it would take about fourteen days for a letter to get from the Gold Coast to Portland, Oregon. That was using the airmail forms that formed the envelope which you couldn't put anything in them.

Brother McKeown took us downtown to look at the ground they had bought. We had gone when we were here before to help them decide on a piece of property. Actually the Wings of Healing had sent the money to buy the land. They will probably put up a temporary building for the school on this property then later put up a permanent one closer to the middle of town. I've surely learned to love and appreciate Brother McKeown. His heart is truly in this thing.

We took another sea bath, but this time we rented a surf board each and rode the waves in. It was really thrilling. The waves really send you flying to the shore. The McKeown's went and visited some Europeans so Paul and I stayed at home and wrote a few more letters, studied and went to bed early. How strange it seemed not to have a meeting in the evening. We did pack our clothes for our next journey on the morrow.

### Colonial Religion Raises It's Head

January 22. We had our stale corn flakes for breakfast and caught the train for Koforidua at 10:10 in the morning. Koforidua was only 50 miles from Accra. However, it took us three solid hours on the train and was really tiresome. This was kind of the stronghold of the Apostolics of Wales. As so many denominations did in those days, they wanted to establish a colonial type of rule over the Africans but that type of thinking wasn't going over with most of the populace. Prophetically, we saw the end of all colonial rule whether it was secular or religious. We knew deep within our hearts that the churches had to be indigenized and made self controlling.

Brother McKeown showed us a circular letter from their leader, Rosser had sent out. It was filled with so many lies, he told us. They were sending a guy by the name of Sercombe to take his place. The African Brethren told us that this wasn't good and said that this man was absolutely rotten and crooked. They said he was a black marketer during the war in the late forties, yet a missionary at the same time. A good many people in Ashanti seemed to be for him though. I don't know if any of those accusations were true or not as things often get blown out of proportion. People can and do make mistakes on both sides of a situation. I only include this to show the problems that faced us and not to scandalize anyone. As Doc Wyatt had told us, "Rumors can kill you just as much as the real thing." The Apostolic people I have had dealings with were some of the finest people I ever met. Often in religious disputes, little things are so distorted. Besides, the Lord does forgive anyway. The main thing for us is to bring healing to the Body of Christ.

Brother Anaman was completely disgusted with the elders there and he said he just didn't know what to do about the meetings. So they decided to go on with the meetings regardless. It really turned out for the best that they did go on with the meetings. Thousands would have been left out of the Kingdom or would have to live their lives with their disease or affliction.

### Our Purpose – To Minister to the Hurting

That was the situation that we were going into in Koforidua. It did make us wonder if the meeting would be worthwhile with all the supposed opposition. We, of course, had no axe to grind with our Apostolic Brethren as we knew many of them in the States as they had visited and ministered in Portland at the Wings of Healing Temple. We had a great relationship with them. Our policy was to never attack anyone nor even speak about them. Therefore, we did not enter into the controversy. We were there to minister to hurting people and see the lost come to Jesus and that was it. We just preached a simple message about the Lord Jesus with faith and love. Brother Mallet met us at the train station and took us to our room in an African hotel. It wasn't very good, but at least there were electric lights and that was a real plus.

### Greater Crowd than Expected

The meetings were held in a large open area, in the middle of town. We were absolutely amazed at the size of the crowd. Thousands came out, filling the whole area. It was a great service and beyond anyone's expectations. By all the discouraging things that were told to us, we had figured there wouldn't be many people turn out. It was my lot to preach and the crowd was very responsive. There were a great number of people healed, but there wasn't any outstanding miracle because there didn't seem to be any major sicknesses present. However, we did have some competition. They were showing an electoral movie on the other side of the "park" but their crowd was tiny compared to ours.

## First Outstanding Miracle Here

January 23. We started in again with our proverbial oatmeal for breakfast. The morning crowd wasn't very large at the start but at the end it really was good-sized. Paul preached but had a little trouble in preaching yet there were a good number of people healed. Our first outstanding miracle in Koforidua was a woman that was blind. Instantly she could see perfectly. We found it amazing that those white-clouded eyes would turn to normal in the blink of an eye. This was without us doing anything other than preaching faith and praying en masse for the crowd. Miracles like this really excited the city because so many people knew this lady. We never tried to show off any healing. The only way we knew about it was when the people were testifying and the interpreters told us. The people just lined up on their own, to come and testify.

Our dinner of tough beef and mutton liver wasn't too good. The tough beef sure gave our jaws a workout but it was food and tasted good. The mutton liver, well, you guessed it.

Being about 60 miles inland, it really began to get hot during the day. We would just saturate our clothes with perspiration when preaching. We always wore dress slacks with a white shirt and a necktie. It was something they expected of us and we did it joyfully.

I discovered a growth on my leg and it began to really bother me so I had Paul cut it off with my pocket knife. Sometimes you just 'gotta' do what you 'gotta' do! It never gave me any more problems and has never returned. Of course Paul relished doing that! He was such a card!

## An Interpreter Makes or Breaks You

There was a larger crowd in the evening service than the night before. Paul preached and had a tough time because our interpreter wasn't very good. He seemed to lose the punch but in spite of that, there were a large number of outstanding miracles. The Lord is so good to work in spite of our inabilities, failures and shortcomings. For a while it looked like no one was going to come up to testify but then it suddenly broke and people just swarmed up. Many blind, physically crippled and people with heart trouble dominated the type of sicknesses healed. There were always and everywhere those that were delivered from what they called "snakes in their bellies." This was always a curse that was put on them by a juju priest or witch doctor. Whether you believe in such a thing as this doesn't matter but these people did and would simply waste away and die of malnutrition. So to them it was a major thing to have these curses broken when they had spent hundreds of dollars through the years for charms to ward of the evil spirits and curses.

This was a matter of income for the juju priest and witch doctors. So we were fooling with their income as Paul was in Acts 16:16 when he said, "*a certain damsel possessed with a spirit of divination met us, which brought her masters much gain by soothsaying.*" However, we didn't feel any repercussions concerning it as even the juju priest came and accepted the Lord as their Savior and would do away with their juju charms as well.

## After the Struggle – A Great Break Through

January 24. Paul wanted to preach in the morning service so I told him to have at it. He again had trouble and didn't do so well but there

Group of Gold Coast Apostolic Ministers

was a much larger crowd out. He pitched the message toward consecration and many responded by coming forward. It was so moving to see these people crying out to the Lord & offering themselves for His service.

I spoke in the evening service and had a real liberty in the Holy Ghost. This was a great break through for us, as both of us had been struggling with preaching here. The first one healed was a little girl that was a mute (she couldn't speak at all). She was healed instantly when we prayed for the crowd en masse. We wanted to take her picture but while we were doing so the crowd just swarmed up to the platform to come testify. We couldn't control them at all. It was clear out of our hands so there was no way of telling how many were healed. Even with this losing control, no one was injured in any way. They were just having the time of their lives it seemed. All they wanted to do was to testify of their healing.

## Integrity in Handling Money - A Must!

At the close of the meeting, we took an offering and they raised 50 pounds in Gold Coast currency for the expenses of the meetings and our African Ministers. We always paid our own expenses of course and told the people so. We never used one cent of African money on ourselves. In fact we never touched the money except to run our fingers through all those halfpennies and small change. I never saw such a collection of small change in my life. It would fill a large container. Can you imagine the size of the container it would take for fifty pounds of Gold Coast currency in pennies and halfpennies? Our conviction was that offerings in the meetings should take care of the various expenses including the food and stay of the African ministers who came along with us. We didn't want to build a dependency on American money, yet we must not overburden them either.

They had told us, the people were too poor and didn't have much money so we shouldn't take an offering. Our reply was that it is scriptural and it would work in any society. The Biblical promises were not intended just for American or English churches. This is the way to be blessed of the Lord in any society. If we gave the people an opportunity, they would be glad to respond. And of course, they always responded well though it was only pennies and half pennies.

This was so different from the way many missionaries did it. They would take all the money and pay the bills and give it out to the staff. We wanted to teach the Africans to be responsible in finances along with taking of the offering for them. If they were going to carry this gospel then it was imperative they learn how to handle money with integrity. We wanted them to feel equal to us and not build a dependency.

## Oh the Struggle of Preaching!

January 25. Knowing that it was my time to preach in the morning service, I didn't sleep much through the night. I was struggling inside trying to get something to preach on. I don't know what was wrong if anything, but I just couldn't seem to get any inspiration. I felt so dry in my soul. This is certainly one of the toughest places yet to get something to preach on. Finally as the dawn was breaking, I did get a little something to speak on but I felt that I had flopped so hard I'm sure they heard the sound in Portland. Even Paul told me it was terrible.

The problem was that we had a new interpreter and he tried to preach my sermon and just messed things up. I didn't even get to read my text as he took off and read it before me. When I would say a few words, it seemed that he would talk for five minutes. I felt like telling him to stop and let me preach a while. Another part of the problem was that I had a terrible headache. In fact I woke up with it. It seemed to be coming from my eyes or at least the pain centered behind my eyes. However, you can't let something like that stop you. There were many times when we felt so weak that we had to use the pulpit to hold on to, in order to keep from falling.

Paintsil came by for a few hours and what a joy it was to see him. He just came from a town way out in the bush where the chief had placed some Christians in jail for drawing water on Wednesday and Friday. The townspeople said their God was in the pool of water and the chief didn't want to upset him. It was a great opportunity to share the gospel with them because of the problem as Paintsil did of course.

## The Chief Ju Ju Priestess - Delivered, Healed and Filled

Paul preached in the evening service and what a wonderful service we had. A woman came up to testify while he was preaching. Her case reminded me of the woman in the Bible with the issue of blood that pressed through the crowd, touched the hem of the Lord's garment and was healed. She said she was in the hospital with severe stomach trouble that she had been sick with for seven years. She bribed the doctor to let her come to the meeting. She was so weak that she could hardly make it but as she struggled on, she became stronger. When she reached the meeting place and heard a few words of the message, she was instantly made whole. You always stop a meeting for that kind of testimony!

Paul then went on and finished his message and prayed for the whole crowd at once. All kinds of miracles were happening all over the place it seemed. An 86-year-old, elderly lady who practiced juju (witchcraft) with her family and had even killed many people with it (so we were told) came to the meetings. She was also blind but when the devil was cast out of her, she received her sight immediately. Everyone knew her and was afraid of her because she was the chief witch doctor and had held the whole area in bondage. She was among those who were filled with the Holy Spirit that evening. When she testified that she was healed of blindness and could see perfectly, the crowd didn't respond like usual. Then she went on to say that the demon of witchcraft was cast out of her and she had been filled with the Holy Spirit and spoke in tongues. Then the crowd went wild with joy! We couldn't quiet them down for quite some time. They knew her very well and rejoiced more over her being delivered from witchcraft and filled with the Holy Spirit than receiving her eye sight. This freed the town from her dominion by using demonic forces. What a happy day it was for all of them.

It fell my lot to give the instructions on receiving the Holy Spirit before the testimonies. This was something that I really loved to do and the Lord always blessed so mightily in doing it. We then laid our hands on them for the Holy Spirit and more than 300 received the Holy Spirit including the juju Priestess. This town would never be the same as it was really shaken. Brother Mallet and the other African preachers were overjoyed. They said the meetings were much greater than they had anticipated because of the threat of opposition.

We found that if you just love people, even those who oppose you, and minister the grace and mercy of Christ to them, they will be blessed of the Lord as well. When the healings and miracles began to happen, no one could doubt the power and presence of the Lord. This tore down many walls between the groups as they could clearly see it was the Lord working and not just some American preachers working up a lot of emotion and trying to horn in on their area.

### Going to "Crobo" Country

January 26. We didn't sleep much during the night for some reason so consequently both of us were still very tired. We had to arise early and have our breakfast of rice, fish (I couldn't stand it as it smelled like it

112

was rotten) and scrambled eggs cooked in the fish grease. They were to pick us up at 8:00 in the morning but it was 10:00 before they finally arrived. I thought, "If ever we start to go and don't stop before leaving town, the world will surely stop turning." It was only 30 miles but the road was "rougher than a cob!" We arrived at 12:15 in the afternoon. The town was way up in the mountainous jungle at the end of the dirt road. No wonder it took us two and a quarter hours to make it. Of course we didn't have "the foggiest idea" of where we were going.

We were told that this was "Crobo" country whatever that meant. Though our African brothers told us that these people were a lower class of Africans, we didn't see any difference except perhaps they were a bit more primitive. Many people didn't have clothing from their waist up which to us was just a "matter of fact" by this time. Their language sounded similar to the "Ga" in Accra.

They gave us a small mud hut with a thatch roof to stay in. This was the best they had. It was a very small room that looked like a dungeon with one small window in the side with bars on it. The room was wide enough for us to put our army cots side by side, leaving us a very small walkway. We had to turn sideways to walk between them with our luggage at the end.

They had huge scorpions that would fall out of the thatch roof so we had to sleep under a mosquito net and turn our shoes upside down. They told us they were very deadly. Needless to say, it was stifling hot in the room, almost unbearable. If there was any breeze coming in the little window, the mosquito net stopped it from reaching us. Though it was extremely hot, it didn't bother me that much as we were raised using a mosquito net over our beds.

They had erected a huge canopy in the center of town and it was almost filled to capacity for the first evening service. It was my time to speak and the results were very outstanding. While I was preaching, they carried a woman in on a stretcher like apparatus and she was instantly healed while the Word was going forth. When we prayed for the entire crowd at once, a couple of people were healed of what they called 'shaking palsy.' So many others were healed that are too numerous to mention and it took such a long time for them to testify.

Dickson had traveled with us and was our cook here. He was much better than many of our cooks that we had thus far. In fact, he was such an excellent cook, a wonderful man and always easy to get along with.

## Healed While Singing and Worshiping

On January 27, the morning service was to start at 8:30 but it was 9:00 before it got wound up. Though it was so hot with the mosquito net, we slept really well except I dreamed an awful lot. We had a couple of eggs for breakfast and, believe it or not, we didn't have any oatmeal!

In the morning service, it was my time to lead off with a short word while Paul preached the main message. There were a great number of people healed though most of them seemed to be minor diseases. Although, close to half of the people that came for the morning meeting were sick with something. It seemed that everybody had a fever as malaria ran rampant in those days. Quite a number were healed while they were singing and worshiping. This of course thrilled us to the core.

However, Johnny Mallet tried to drag the meeting down to a healing line. He got this idea from Erskine Holt. I told him that we didn't want to get bogged down with laying hands on everybody as we would be there the rest of the day. I went on to explain the laying on of hands was just a point of contact for their faith and that could be anything. I related the story of a Missionary a few years earlier who had prayed for so many that he didn't have the strength to continue. He then told the people that he was going to lay his hands on a tree and all could come by and touch the tree and the Lord would heal them. Many healings took place. I realize this could border on setting up holy places and we would have to be careful as people would distort it. He responded beautifully in the positive. He was a great guy and we loved him dearly.

### Delicious Palm Nut Soup but so Hot

Dickson served us Palm nut soup and rice along with fried chicken for our dinner. It was really delicious but also very hot with red peppers. It burned all the way down and out. Our African Brothers laughed at it and told us that they wanted to see how hot we could eat it. I couldn't help but think of the terrible time I had with my stomach when the ulcer perforated about this time last January and the doctor telling me I could never eat anything with pepper from that time on. My mind went back to that Elim Camp Meeting in Lima, New York with Dr. Wyatt preaching. I came to the meeting with such intense pain in my abdomen but as he ended his sermon, my faith seemed to soar and instantly I was healed. I thought again and said now I am eating food so hot with red pepper that it would have killed me if the Lord hadn't healed me back then. How wonderful to be free from the pain of stomach ulcers!

### Too Shy to Testify

Paul preached in the evening service with many being healed. Many of them were too shy to testify at first. Later they found they were healed and then they came to testify. One boy who was unable to walk and had been carried into the meeting walked out completely healed. This meeting followed suit with the other meetings in the matter of miracles. The lepers, the paraplegics, the blind, the deaf, the mute as well as many internal diseases were healed. What a thrill! It was beyond words to see the Lord doing all these wonders among very primitive people.

On January 28, we had corned beef and coffee for breakfast. It wasn't very appetizing to me as this reminded me of some of our meals in the depression of the 1930's. Canned corn beef was one of them as it was so cheap. Dickson knew we enjoyed the African dishes so he fixed us Peanut Soup for dinner and served it with fried mutton. The soup was excellent, but again hot with peppers. The mutton - Yeah, you're right!

### They Shall Lay Hands Upon the Sick!

I spoke in the morning meeting on the "presence of the Lord." I used this time to show them scripturally how that every believer by faith and with the presence of God could lay hands on the sick. The Scripture says in Mark 16:18, *"they shall lay hands on the sick, and they shall recover."* Who are *"they"* who shall lay hands on the sick? Were they apostles? Or Ministers? Well! It doesn't say specifically. Certainly the Lord was addressing the eleven Apostles after His resurrection but actually He was speaking of those who would believe their words as well. So this could be anybody. The healings would be signs to the world of the power of the gospel of Jesus Christ.

We then had the believer's to come forward and lay their hands upon the sick. It was amazing how such a large number of sick were healed as a result. This caused the people to understand that healing wasn't a ritual performed by a minister but it actually comes by faith - anyone's faith and they could do it as well as us. If we pray for people, we must believe the Lord will heal them.

### More Filled With the Holy Ghost

In the evening meeting, Paul led off and I brought the main message. Again there were a large number of people healed. After this, Paul gave the instructions for receiving the Baptism of the Holy Spirit and led them in a prayer for repentance. We then laid our hands upon them and at least 150 or more were gloriously filled. As usual our standard way of ministering to people for the Baptism of the Holy Spirit was that we would give instructions to them on how to receive the Holy Spirit and build their faith to receive. However the first thing we would do was to deal with the matter of salvation and repentance. Then we would lead them in a prayer of repentance. You could see them break and tears flow down their cheeks every time. It was then that we would lay our hands upon them and always include our African Ministers.

This was the last service in this town so we took the usual offering at the end. It came to 27 pounds, nine Schilling's and 5½ cents. The British pound was running about $2.60 to $1 at the time with the West African money tied to it. The crowd was so thrilled to bring their offerings, dancing all the way down and back.

## An African Toilet

One of the things that broke a lot of barriers was eating African food and also going to an African toilet. Of course there wasn't anything else but the brush which was too far to walk. So really, we had no choice in the matter. The toilet was a kind of communal one, serving that little area of mud huts and was right in the center of an open area. It was very primitive to say the least and not very private. They just had a hole dug in the ground and put palm branches tied to posts as a fence circling it. You could still see through the branches as they were dry. The people watched us go into the bathroom. Fortunately, people couldn't see in, but you could see out very clearly.

## Back to Accra

We awakened at 5:00 in the morning of January 29 and just had a cup of coffee with a piece of bread. We packed our stuff and left at 6:30 a.m. in the back a large Lorrie. It had wooden seats but was better than the little ones. At least there was more room and it wasn't as stifling hot. We arrived at Brother McKeown's in Accra at 10:00 in the morning after a three and a half hour trip. It was such a tiresome journey on that Lorrie though it was only 80 miles.

There was some mail waiting for us but we didn't have time to read it. Brother McKeown wanted us to go see a building they had leased for the Bible School. It was a large two-story building in a compound of 70 yards by 30 yards. The house had running water, a shower and a bathtub and a telephone of all things. The place was very nice and cool being only about 200 yards from the sea shore. A large canopy seating four to five thousand could be erected on the compound to hold large meetings continuous if they so desired.

## New Recruits Arrive

In the afternoon we lay down for a while but didn't sleep because Harold Brown, a fellow student, just came in from Portland. So naturally, we talked and talked. It was so good to see one of our friends. Four of them had left Portland together on the same plane. Three of them hadn't gotten their visas so Paul Mueller and Douglas Wilson had to stay in London. Claire Hutchins stayed in New York as he couldn't get his visa in time either. When will people learn? Because of this Brother McKeown gave us another good talking to but it was to the wrong people.

We took Harold for a sea bath where I really skinned both knees. The waves were quite large and there was a rise on the bottom, so when I was coming in on the surf board my knees drug on the bottom. Paul and I went to the P and B church while Harold and Brother McKeown went to one of the churches in Accra. Brother McKeown always wanted to go with the new guy to see how they would do before he would let them minister alone. Harold spoke and pitched his voice too high and was so hoarse afterwards that he could hardly talk. He was incapacitated to speak for a couple days.

### Trouble in my Spirit

January 30. Things seemed to be troubling me yet I didn't know just what was wrong. There was such an uneasiness in my spirit. So I didn't sleep very well at night as I just rolled and tossed. I wrote to Dr. Wyatt about the school plans to find out for sure what they wanted to do.

We went downtown to get our tickets changed to Lagos and made reservations to leave on Friday, February the fifth. Paul and I also booked our reservations for the United States for March the 17th with the understanding it could be changed if needed. We went on downtown to the Post Office to mail some letters and then to the Kingsway store to get a few needed things.

### Animists Parade

While downtown, there was an Animist parade which was quite typical of them. Two men with staffs in their hands were leading the parade. Following them was a man with a sheep in tow. After this, there was a bunch of men following with a young cow tied down on a trailer. She was "bawling" for all she was worth. A few paces behind the trailer many more people marched to the drum beat of three young men carrying large drums with three men behind pounding them.

Following that were a lot of men and women pounding smaller drums. We asked several bystanders what this was all about. They told us they were going to offer these animals as a sacrifice to their gods. It almost broke my heart because you could see the earnestness in their faces trying to appease their gods. They didn't know that Jesus had already become our sacrifice for sin by giving His life on Calvary.

### Stirred My Heart

This incident so stirred my heart so much that in the evening service at the church I really stirred them up to reach the unreached peoples. I took my text on Judges Chapter 6 and 7 where Gideon defeats the Midianites. Gideon wasn't someone great. He was just a young man, fearful of the adversary, threshing wheat out behind the barn when the Lord arrested him. The Lord even shrunk his fighting force to only three hundred men yet they would rout the enemy. It was a very good service as the people flooded to the front to offer themselves to the Lord. Many tears flowed down their cheeks as the Lord met with His people.

### We Go to Different Churches

On the morning of January 31, I was so weary in my body because I still wasn't sleeping much at night for some reason. We knew there was trouble brewing and we must find out what the problem was at some point. The three of us split up for the morning meetings. Paul preached in one place and Harold in another while I went to another place. There seemed to be a carryover from the last night's service as there was such a Spirit of breaking where I was. Oh, if we can just get the people in the churches stirred up and on fire for the Lord, they will make a big difference in reaching the lost. They will be able to do a much greater work than we can do. For the evening meetings we just changed places so each of us was at a different church. Actually, I went to one place while Paul and Harold went to one place. Both meetings were terrific.

When we arose on February 1, 1954, it was raining like it does in Portland during the fall and winter months. It wasn't a heavy rain but enough to get you wet if you were out for awhile. The Harmattan season was now over and it got hot quickly. After breakfast, we went downtown to take care of some business and get a much-needed haircut.

## A Street Meeting in Labadi

In the evening, one of the young men from the Church went with me to the city of Labadi where we preached right in the middle of the marketplace. It was just an old-fashioned street meeting. A good crowd of people gathered but most of them were idol worshipers. Everyone said that Labadi was a tough place to minister as the people really had a lot of fetish gods and were not interested in the gospel. Up to this time, Missionaries hadn't been able to do much with them. They had fetishes and charms all over their bodies. Their arms and legs were loaded with fetishes and these things cost them a lot of money. It seemed strange but one of the houses was built right in the middle of the gravel street. The street had to go around it on both sides.

After we preached our best, telling them about the Lord Jesus and how He came to save us, they just mocked us and made fun of us. It was quite the experience. But it was all right with us and it didn't intimidate us one little bit. At least they heard the gospel so we didn't let it bother us. To me it was better to do this than all of us going to a church where most of them were already converted. We came to Africa to reach the lost not to minister in local churches. Paul Shaver and Harold Brown went to Merryvilla where it was mostly Christians that gathered. Their report was that it was a good meeting and the people were blessed. That is important too! Why not do both if we have the personnel to do so was my feeling. There was something within me that kept pushing to make the most out of our time. This would cause me a lot of grief and struggles later on in Nigeria because everybody didn't feel this way.

## A Terrible Sense of Uneasiness

On the second of February, we noticed that all of us seemed to have such a feeling of uneasiness as though things were not right. It began to affect all of our sleeping at night. My stomach became very upset as a result. Then the enemy began to bring in thoughts to my mind that the ulcer was coming back and here you are in the heart of Africa with no medical provisions. You said you were healed but look at you now. This immediately brought a tinge of fear to my heart and it felt like my pulse rate doubled instantly. It seemed like I wrestled all night rolling and tossing on my army cot. I prayed and it seemed like heaven was brass and I felt forsaken of the Lord. I kept saying to myself that the Lord has said, *"I will never leave you nor forsake you."* Yet, I was in such a torment in my spirit.

I got up and went into the bathroom so as not to disturb Paul and Harold and lifted my hands and began to worship and praise the Lord. Then I began to take authority over the demonic spirit bothering me. I said, "You lying devil, you are lying to me and in Jesus Name I take authority over you." I felt compelled to hit myself with my fist in the pit of my stomach (not too hard) in the name of the Lord and declare I was still healed. Thank God, I had won the victory and went back and got some sleep before dawn. So when we arose, we just had a simple breakfast of stale corn flakes and coffee and went on our way.

We had been expecting Clair Hutchins to come but there wasn't any word from him. He was waiting in New York till his visa came through. To get our minds off our problems, we went down to the ocean and took a sea bath but the waves were too choppy for surfboard riding. So we didn't stay very long.

On the way back we stopped at the government office where I got a 6-month visa for Nigeria and a two-month re-entry back into the Gold Coast. For his extra ordinary work, I tipped the fellow and he was so appreciative. He thanked me and thanked me. Doesn't it make you feel good after doing something like that?

In the afternoon, we had Palm nut soup for dinner. This was one of my favorite meals in West Africa and it was very delicious. However, our cook again made it really hot with pepper. In fact it brought tears to our eyes when we ate it but I had no discomfort with my digestive system. This was Paul Shaver's birthday. At least it wasn't as stressful as mine was a few weeks before.

### Back to Labadi

In the evening Harold and Paul went to Merryvilla to preach. They said it was a very good meeting. Brother McKeown and I went back to the tough town of Labadi where they had mocked and made fun of us the day before. I spoke from Paul's sermon on Mars Hill at Athens in Acts 17:22-34 using verses 22-23 for my jumping off place. *"Then Paul stood in the midst of Mars' hill, and said, 'You men of Athens, I perceive that in all things you are too superstitious. For as I passed by, and beheld your devotions, I found an altar with this inscription, TO THE UNKNOWN GOD. Whom therefore you ignorantly worship, Him declare I unto you.'"*

I dealt with the fact of the living God being unknown to them and declared Him to them. I told them how God had sent His Son, Jesus into this world as a sacrifice, to pay the price for our redemption. Now He would come into our hearts if we invited Him and we would know it beyond a doubt that we were saved and passed from death to life. They had their juju charms and idols but they could not say they had any personal relationship with either them or their gods. They had no knowledge that they were accepted by their god or if it was doing them any good, protection wise.

This really got their interest and unlike the day before, quite a good number came up to receive Christ as their Savior. However, the children responded the best. What a difference one day made! I guess the people saw that we were not going to be intimidated to the extent that we wouldn't show up again. We found that you have to stand right up and face the opposition in love with the mighty power of the Holy Spirit. Sometimes you just have to go and "beard the lion." They saw that we were not fighting them nor their religion but trying to show them a way of life and they responded accordingly. How easily it would have been for us not to have returned and said, "There's no use returning there because they don't want to receive the gospel." Later on Brother McKeown would plant a church here and it would really grow.

### Looking for Help but no Help Comes!

On the third of February we went to the airport to meet Douglas Wilson and Paul Mueller but their plane hadn't left London yet. Oh the joy and frustrations of the Mission field! We were going to have the new men take the services tonight but since they didn't get in, it was left up to us to do it.

In the afternoon, we had another favorite West African dish for dinner. They call it "ground nut soup" which is simply soup made with peanuts. The only thing is they like it very hot with peppers also. Just like the day before, it brought tears to our eyes as we ate it. The cook just laughed and said she wanted to see how hot we could eat it. Why did they always pull this on us?

### Issue of Touching the Sick

Harold Brown and Paul Shaver went to Labadi, the tough town and Paul preached. They told us it wasn't too good a meeting. Harold had been hoarse for a number of days so he couldn't preach as a result. So it was left up to Paul to do the preaching. Brother McKeown and I went to Merryvilla where I did the preaching and it was a great time in the Lord.

Personally, I really enjoyed ministering with Brother McKeown present. He was a man that loved the Word and never made a person feel inferior but would respond to the preaching very well. He was with you all the way. He told me afterwards that he admired us young Americans because we were not afraid to touch or lay our hands on the Africans regardless of how sick they might be. He asked, "Don't you realize that in touching these sick with all kinds of tropical diseases that you could catch the same thing?" I replied, "We never think of the consequences because we believe that the same God that heals them will also protect us from harm." He seemed to be satisfied with my answer and from then on, he would do as we did in ministering to the sick. When the crowds were not too large, we would lay hands on the sick but with large crowds we didn't dare.

I spoke on 1 Samuel 6:1-14 using verses 10-12 as my text. *"Then the men did so; they took two milk cows and hitched them to the cart, and shut up their calves at home. And they set the ark of the Lord on the cart, and the chest with the gold rats and the images of their tumors. Then the cows headed straight for the road to Beth Shemesh, and went along the highway, lowing as they went, and did not turn aside to the right hand or the left."* I dealt at length about the milk cows that had just calved and had never been broken to pull a cart. They were hitched up to a cart with the Ark of the Covenant on it. This would be a sign to the Philistines that God was in it. The cows went along the road lowing or mooing and never turned to their calves but went straight to the Land of Israel. They were bringing the ark of God back to His people.

I likened the Ark to the presence of God and the sacrifices of the cows to the sacrifices we have to make to bring Christ to others. I tied it in with Psalms 126:6 *"He that goes forth and weeping, bearing precious seed, shall doubtless come again with rejoicing, bringing his sheaves with him."* My purpose was to show them there are sacrifices to be made if the gospel and the presence of the Lord were to be carried to others. For those that are called, it isn't an easy thing to leave family, homes, lands and take the gospel to others who have never heard it. The message really stirred the people and by all counts it was an excellent meeting.

### A Dangerous Situation

We arose early on February 4 and called the airport to find out when our next team would arrive. They told us the plane would be in at 2:30 in the afternoon. Since there wasn't a meeting in the morning, we had a leisurely breakfast of stale cornflakes and coffee and relaxed. With plenty of time before the plane arrived, we went down to the ocean and went surf board riding. The waves were breaking just right but the tide was going out which set up a dangerous situation. One time, I almost got carried out by the tide. I could see workers being transported in wooden boats and thought of trying to get their attention. That was a funny feeling but I fought my way back with all the effort I had. When I was fully exhausted and couldn't paddle anymore, I put my feet down and they touched the bottom. What a blessed sigh went up from my lips and I began to give thanks to the Lord. That taught me a permanent lesson about the ocean.

## Help Finally Arrives

We met the plane when it came in at 2:30 and sure enough Paul Mueller and Douglas Wilson were on board. Douglas Wilson was one of the senior Ministers from the Church and Bible School while Paul Mueller was a student. It was an extremely hot day, especially in the middle of the afternoon. They broke out in a deep sweat as soon as they got out of the plane and stepped onto the pavement. I know it was rough on them as they were dressed in wool suits with overcoats just coming in from Portland and through England in the dead of winter. How nice to see them and get to visit with old friends.

That evening, Brother McKeown, Douglas Wilson and I went to Merryvilla while Paul Shaver, Paul Mueller and Harold Brown went to Osu. Brother Wilson spoke at our meeting while Paul Shaver spoke at the other place. These would be the people who'd be replacing us. Since the guys had been traveling so long, Paul Shaver and I gave up our beds and slept on the cots in the office.

## My Final Night in Ghana

This would be my final night in the Gold Coast. For some reason, I wasn't thrilled about leaving as we had seen so many tremendous things done for the Kingdom of God in the past three months. Multitudes of people would be in heaven as a result of our time spent preaching the gospel. So many hurting people had been touched by the Lord and healed and could now lead a normal life. Children were set free from curses put on them by witch doctors and from childhood diseases and now they could go on to live a normal life. Many African Ministers could now feel like they are equal with any others, regardless of race.

We had hammered home the truth found in Galatians 3:26-29 in almost every meeting, *"For you are all sons of God through faith in Christ Jesus. For as many of you as were baptized into Christ have put on Christ. There is neither Jew nor Greek, there is neither slave nor free, there is neither male nor female; for you are all one in Christ Jesus. And if you are Christ's, then you are Abraham's seed, and heirs according to the promise."* We would always add "There is neither American, English nor African; there is neither Methodist, Pentecostal, Anglican nor Independent for we are all one in Christ. We are brothers and sisters in Christ with no distinctions between us as we belong to one family."

One of our favorite chorus was "Lord make us one. Lord make us one. Lord make us one everywhere." They would join hands and begin to dance all over the place with great joy and grace even though it usually was terribly crowded. In my heart, there was a deep satisfaction, knowing we had done our best. We had proven that Doctor Wyatt's vision could be fulfilled. Both of us had really hit our stride in preaching here in this wonderful land of so many different cultures with so many signs and wonders following. Truly, *the Gospel of the Kingdom"* had been preached among these wonderful people.

## Leaving the Familiar – Going to the Unknown

One thing that bothered me was that I was leaving my dear and closest friend, Paul Shaver. We had worked so closely together for years. We were roommates all through Bible School and would spend each summer working together or preaching together and then held evangelistic meetings all across the United States and Canada. Now it would be up to him to spearhead things in Ghana while I would go back to Nigeria and try to get things broken lose there. There was a lot of fear and trepidation in my heart, not knowing what lay ahead. Yet in my heart, I just knew we were heading into some really tough times because the battle in the Spirit was fierce.

# From Ghana to Nigeria
## Chapter 8

On the fifth of February, we arose early as we had a lot of business to take care of before leaving. We went to West African Airways to get the tickets for Harold Brown and me. Had we known in time we could have waited till Wednesday and gone free of charge to Lagos. We didn't dare stay because Sidney Elton was supposed to meet us in Lagos today. How well I remembered when we first flew into Lagos that no one was there to meet us. At the Immigration Office, we applied for a visa to Nigeria for Paul Mueller, who was to join us in a month or so. Shortly after we arrived in Ghana, I had a craftsman make a lamp for my parents out of the local wood, which I mailed to them.

### Nigeria, Here We Come!

We were late getting to the airport, and had to hurry to catch the plane. Our plane took off at 3:30 in the afternoon and what a plane it was. It looked like an old relic left over from the beginning of World War II. Harold sat in the seat just behind the pilot while I sat on the front seat and had to put my feet on the luggage. Taxing down the runway, the air pipe broke that brought heat from the engine into the cabin. It was so cold when we got up in the air that we thought we would freeze. We were all shivering. The plane arrived at the airport in Lagos at 6:15 p.m., not quite a three-hour flight in that old rattle trap. How wonderful it was to plant our feet on terra firma once again.

It only took us half an hour to go through immigration and customs which wasn't too bad this time. Sidney Elton was waiting for us and took us to the Immigration Office. They were only going to grant us a fourteen-day pass even though we had a six-month visa. They told Sidney Elton he had to put up a $450 cash bond for each one of us. He did and then they granted the visa. This was in spite of the fact we had our return flight tickets and showed them to the immigration authorities. They wanted enough money in their hands to deport us if we caused any problem.

We left the airport at 6:45 that evening and drove the long distance through the dark with a beautiful tropical moon shining brightly. Arriving at Brother Elton's compound in Ilesha at 12:00 midnight, we were weary to the bone. It had been a long, tiring day so we were anxious to "hit the sack." I was greeted with some mail and a box of candy from Mildred, that helped immensely.

### Hit With a Lot of Negatives!

February 6. Though we fell into bed dead tired, I still didn't sleep very well for some reason. I had this gnawing feeling that everything wasn't going right. Both of us were anxious to see our friends and colleagues, Harold Alcock and Vernon Sanders. They were still in bed when we got up but sat up on the side of their beds and talked. They gave us some terrible news that just broke our hearts. They informed us there wasn't going to be a Bible school here in Ilesha because none was wanted. The only school they wanted was the teacher's college but we couldn't have access to it. Things really looked bleak at the moment.

Brown, Sanders, Alcock, Paul

No wonder I had sleepless nights prior to this. At breakfast Sidney Elton began to tell us about all the difficulties of reaching these people with the gospel. One problem was they couldn't be trusted to handle such a major enterprise. He said they were just a half-step from the jungle and most of them had no education. It would take years to bring them to the level they needed to be in order to do what we had envisioned. What He wanted was for twelve American couples to come as resident missionaries to work with him. They would have to spend two or more years studying the language then they could evangelize. This was the idea of many missionaries in those days, but we strongly disagreed with them.

### This Made Harold and me Angry!

We had just come in from such great meetings in Ghana and saw that the Africans could do just as good of a job of it as we could. So we argued vehemently that the Africans can and are doing it. The Nigerians were no different from the people of Gold Coast. If the people of Gold Coast can do it then the Nigerians could do it just as well. It didn't matter how primitive their culture was or what they have been or just came out of. It depends on the Lord and our ability to teach and train them. Just because they were not educated in school didn't mean they were not intelligent. Besides we didn't have a lot of time to work because the Colonial Empires were going to break up soon. It was a "do or die" situation, now nor never. We continued to argue, that the day will come, and that would be very shortly, when we cannot get into some places but the Africans would be able to do so. Consequently they will be able to do much more than we can. Therefore, we must plan accordingly.

I couldn't figure out why this man was so different from what he was when I had left Nigeria for the Gold Coast. I found out later, as I got to know Sidney Elton better that he always plays the devil's advocate at first with everybody. He wasn't about to commit a lot of funds and hard work on people who didn't have a vision for reaching the people. He loved the African people as much as we did and had already done a great work in that region. He was simply testing our faith and resolve unknown to us and we came through with shining colors. One of the things that startled us was that it looked like he had already convinced both Harold Alcock and Vernon Sanders of those things. Maybe this was the reason he was zeroing in on Harold and me. Honestly, I think if we had succumbed to that mentality, we would have been completely neutralized. Thank God that we had the audacity to speak up.

### The Lord had Already Worked it Out!

Before we finished the conversation, a telegram came from the King (Olu) of Warri asking us to come and minister to his people. He was one of the thirteen Chiefs in the House of Chiefs that governed Nigeria under the British. He was the major Chief over the Delta Province. I was absolutely thrilled at this invitation because it meant an open door of ministering the gospel. This was exactly what we needed: a king to invite us. This was what the prophetic word said would happen before we left Portland. When Dr. Wyatt was here back in November, the king had written and wanted us to come to Warri at that time but we had told him we couldn't because of our visa problems. He had even wired and said everything was ready for such and such date, but there was no way we could go at that time.

With this new information, we sat there and discussed what we should do for a couple of hours. Oh, how thrilling that was! We found out there were many more tribes calling for us to come but the African Ministers along with Brother Elton had kept it a secret. It seemed to me that they wanted to keep us in their churches in Yoruba land and not share us with other tribes. It could have been they just wanted to find out if we were really committed. They told us the Ishan tribe was crying for someone to come as they had never heard the gospel plus several others. This was so thrilling and it really lifted our spirits.

Brother Elton thought it was best to go about 200 miles north to one of the tribes there. Morris, one of our interpreters and a fine young man, would go up and make the preparation for us to come. He thought it would take at least six weeks to do it. I wanted us to go to both places by splitting up and going two by two. This way, we could maximize our effort but the older ministers were not buying it. I argued that this was our vision at the beginning with teams going out two by two but they wouldn't have it.

We adjourned the meeting with nothing really decided. Fortunately for us there wasn't any service today. So we had a good time to rest up from all of our labor and travel. I had a letter from my dear friend Dean Burnett with whom we had gone off to bible school together from our home church in Baton Rouge, Louisiana. For dinner in the evening we had bush antelope and it was very good! It was much better than the guinea pig we had in Accra.

## The King of Warri Comes

On February 7th, we were awakened at 5:00 in the morning with Brother Elton pounding on the door of our room. The King of Warri had driven up in his big limousine and had gotten there about 3:00 o'clock in the morning. However, the African Elders wouldn't let him awaken us. They told him that we needed our rest. However, by 5:00 there was no holding him back. He was a crowned King and had on his robe and crown. He came with his driver and policeman over 200 miles just to see us personally. Actually his title was the Olu of Warri. He didn't think his telegram was enough, so he came personally. He insisted he wouldn't leave until we gave him our word when we would come because his people told him not to come back without us coming. We told him we would come in two weeks and for him to send us a couple interpreters to learn our American speech. His reply was that they speak English just as we did so you can come now. I explained that the English spoke with the British English and our American English was different so the interpreters needed to hear us some before we came. He agreed whole heartedly and promised to send two men to learn our American lingo. We asked him to be sure and get us a place to stay and eat since we would be there on that date for two weeks. We stressed the length of time as we had learned we had to do that. If you don't specify the length of time, they'll want you to stay there and not go anywhere else. This would give us many anxious moments later on. We learned that Delta Province was an entirely new area for the gospel and desperately needed someone to come and have follow-up workers as well.

## Nigeria Much Different Than Ghana

I went to a large church in Ilesha with Brother Elton and Morris for the morning service. I spoke on Joshua taking the "Promised Land" and hit man's way of doing things. I stressed that we are to take the kingdom by faith - how we can accomplish much more today than in days gone by. All we needed was for people to arise and believe they can do it. It really brought vision to them and they really became excited about it.

Brother Elton then got up and said a few words and got them to sing and praise the Lord awhile and took an offering. I couldn't help but notice the contrast between here and Ghana. The people didn't come dancing nor were they as responsive as in Ghana. It was like two entirely different civilizations. They sang some more songs and then dismissed the meeting. Afterwards Brother Elton had a long elders meeting. It sure was tiresome waiting as it was extremely hot. I only preached 30 minutes but the services lasted three and a half hours.

## Ife, Our Next Meeting

We went to the city of Ife, which is 20 miles from Brother Elton's compound for a meeting in the evening. It was held in the large Christ Apostolic church instead of in the open air like we were supposed to. Harold Alcock spoke and a few people accepted the Lord but the space was so limited and the crowd was so huge. His text was Proverbs 18:16, *"a man's gift makes room for himself."* In the Yoruba bible it was translated *"a man's offering makes room for him."* Then he preached how the gospel was free which made quite a contradiction. The Yoruba way meant that a person would buy their place in the Kingdom by giving an offering. Harold Alcock was saying it was free so it brought confusion to the people and the anointing lifted immediately.

The Two Women Healed

Fortunately, Brother Elton caught it and explained it to the Interpreter. He explained how the Yoruba in this particular verse was mistranslated. Of course, it hadn't been long since the Bible was translated into the Yoruba language and it still needed refining. A person must be very careful about the nuances of translations especially in other cultures. It broke the flow of the meeting so we ended up praying for lots of people individually. Without the interruption no doubt his message would have borne a lot of fruit.

A woman brought a dead child into the meeting to be prayed for, so we prayed, however, it wasn't restored. This about broke my heart because I knew it was not a big thing for the Lord to do but there didn't seem to be any excitement of faith and no anointing. The prayer line seemed to go on and on for hours as everybody wanted the "Oyebo" (white man) to lay their hands on them. This was so exhausting in that intense heat. I thought that sometimes it seemed to be more in the realm of "magic" to them than what it was supposed to be.

## Two Women Came Two Hundred Miles.

February 8. Things were not going like they had been in Ghana and this alarmed me. You sense that something is wrong but you can't put your finger on it. With all the difficulty that we were having, plus such battles in the spirit, it was affecting all of our sleeping. This in turn was causing me to have an upset stomach. Then the devil would jump on me about the ulcers returning. I kept believing in prayer and believing the Lord nonetheless.

To our surprise, two women came more than 200 miles to Brother Elton's compound for prayer this morning. They had heard about us and all the miracles that happened. You could see there was such a hunger in their hearts as their eyes and faces showed it. We prayed for each one of them individually and the Lord healed them instantly and set them free right there. Oh, how they went away rejoicing because of what the Lord had done for them. You should have seen them skipping along the road because they were so happy. I never cease to be amazed at the love and mercy of the Lord in meeting His people. He will meet them anywhere and at anytime. He is such a good God!

## Back to Ife

We didn't have a morning service so Harold Alcock and Vernon Sanders went to Ife and got their Nigerian driver's license. Just the four of us went back to Ife for the evening meeting as Brother Elton decided he needed some rest. Vernon Sanders drove the car. Driving always posed a danger because the roads were so narrow and the other cars drove so fast. They would come straight at you then swerve at the last second to pass. It was nerve wracking to say the least.

They insisted that I preach. I did but our interpreter wasn't very good. He wasn't interpreting, but was preaching his own message. In spite of that, there were some very remarkable healings but I wasn't satisfied. I always thought we should have had more. In my heart, I was still comparing Nigeria to the Gold Coast meetings. I knew the Lord had much more for the people than what we were seeing. We were not even scratching the surface.

Because communications were so slow and our airline tickets were set to expire March 31, we had to send a wire to Dr. Wyatt in Portland. We needed instructions regarding what they wanted Vernon Sanders and me to do regarding coming home.

## A Chicken Tied to an Idol

We didn't have a morning service on February 9th so Harold Brown and I took a bicycle ride down the dirt road. I needed a diversion because I was still having a problem with an upset stomach with all the uncertainty. This was my first ride on an English bicycle with brakes on the handle bars. I was used to the brakes on the pedal. When I wanted to stop, I squeezed the one for the front wheel and forgot the back one so I went sailing over the handle bars on my face right in front of Ruth Elton, Sidney's daughter. This was really embarrassing but I got up and dusted myself off and went on with Brown for our joy ride.

As we rode down the dirt road, I couldn't help but notice a couple of chickens and a small goat tied to different idols along the side of the road. I asked the Eltons about it and they told me that people do this as an offering and a sacrifice to their gods. The chicken or goat would just stay there and starve to death. I thought, "How cruel." It's all because they do not know that Jesus paid the full sacrifice for their sin. However, they were honest in their approach to God though it was of no value. It made my heart go out to them even more so.

We went into Ilesha and had some short pants made since it was so hot. This was what the British men wore so we decided to try them. They made mine a little too small which made me extremely self-conscious. Having been brought up in the Holiness/Pentecostal type churches, I didn't feel very comfortable wearing short pants anyway. Of course, the British always wore stockings up to their knees which we didn't have.

## Not Well Organized

It seemed to me we were not very well organized here in Nigeria and didn't have a specific plan for what to do. We were not having continued meetings morning and night as we had in Ghana which was so effective. For the night meeting we had to drive back to Ife which was 20 miles in each direction. Again Vernon Sanders did the driving because of having a Nigerian driver's license.

It fell my lot to speak again and quite a number of deaf persons were healed plus other diseases. It wasn't a very large crowd as they had moved the meeting place from the college grounds to a lot beside the Christ Apostolic church. There was only a small crowd that gathered. So I tried to talk with our team to see if we couldn't do better than that. But Alcock and Sanders told me that I was just some little upstart and should just keep quiet as they were the senior ministers. This really cut to the quick. No doubt I was too demanding but I wanted to do more than what we were doing at the time. They really were great guys though. It probably just got to them as these things happen on the mission field.

## Still Struggling

February 10. Because of the lack of preparation before Harold Brown and I arrived, we just had to improvise some things. So this morning we had the meeting in the Okeaye church in Ilesha. It was pitiful as only a handful of people came out. They tied us down, so consequently I was getting the "go bug" again. I felt we were just marking time. Time was too precious, as far as I was concerned to waste it. We must be about our Father's business! I longed for the type of meeting we were used to having and for which we were sent over to accomplish.

I was reminded of John the Baptist when he was in prison and heard about the Lord Jesus having such vast meetings. For him the crowds were gone and it seemed that way with us. But this was our own making because of the lack of preparation. Vernon Sanders and Harold Alcock both spoke and it turned out to be a very good meeting in spite of the smallness of the turnout. In the afternoon Harold Brown and I walked downtown and had our pictures taken to get driver licenses.

For the evening meeting in Ife we drove Brother Elton's "hack" (a little Humber car). The turnout was about the same as the night before. Harold Brown spoke but he had a real problem. He again pitched his voice too high and that didn't leave him with any punch at the end, so the meeting kind of fell flat. Vernon Sanders and Harold Alcock wanted to have a healing line so we paired off at the two gates that led to the platform of the Christ Apostolic Church. Vernon Sanders and I stood at one and the two Harold's stood at the other.

I really didn't care for "healing lines" because they're so massive and seemed almost endless and went on by the hour. Faith didn't seem to be very active so the results were small. It wasn't the fact of laying on of hands as we did that at times but a healing line is different. My feelings were that this was too slow a way and was old order. We had proven for months that by building the people's faith with the Word of God and praying for them all at once there was a greater spiritual excitement and greater things would happen. In the healing line the people would crowd so close to you that you could hardly breathe. The smell was something else in a crowd like that in such hot temperature as everyone was perspiring profusely. It took us such a long time to finish. Harold Alcock began coughing and had to stop. We were so late in getting back to the compound. Besides it was really scary to be on that narrow road in the pitch black of a tropical night with no moon shining.

### A Belly-Flop

February 11. Vernon Sanders and Harold Alcock spoke in the morning meeting at the Okeaye church in Ilesha. I was there while Sanders spoke but left right afterwards as it was so boring to me. One of our interpreters, T. J., and I had to go get some coconuts for Sister Elton as she wanted to make us some coconut pies for dinner. She must not have agreed too much with what was preached as she told both of them they didn't have the anointing or a burden for this people. Actually as we were told later, she got up in the meeting after they had spoken and said a few words but Pastor Paul got up after her and contradicted her. Oh the joys of disagreement on the mission field.

### A Leper To Be One of Our Interpreters

Harold Brown and I went to Ife in the afternoon to get our driver's license. It took us a good hour to get them as the fellow was out that had to sign them. Sometimes things went quite slow. When we got back, the two men had arrived that were sent by the Olu of Warri to be our interpreters. One of them was a leper. This really insulted Brother Elton. He was so upset and just went on and on about how this broke all protocol. After listening to his spiel for so long, I simply told him not to worry about it because the Lord was going to heal him. There was absolutely no doubt on my part that He would and this was just an opportunity to let the Lord show Himself strong to these men as well as to the people we were going to minister to.

There was no time for rest in the afternoon as we had to go back to Ife for service in the evening. Vernon Sanders spoke but it wasn't very inspiring. Anybody can have a bad time preaching so we were not hard on him as all of us had been there and done that. When he finished, we had those who were healed from the last night service to testify. It was so surprising that quite a good number were healed and we were so thankful for that. At least some of the great needs were being met. Again we had a healing line. Harold Alcock, bless his heart, always seemed thrilled about a healing line but Paul Shaver and I saw many thousands more healed without it than with it. Of course with a smaller meeting you can lay hands on people but you wouldn't dare in a huge meeting.

With all due respect to Harold Alcock, he had not been in any of the previous meetings with the huge crowds with miracles flowing like water. So not having seen those things, he did what he knew. He had pastored a good church in Edmonton, Alberta, Canada for years and was among those who began to lay hands and pray for people earlier. This was what he was familiar with. Then too, it's hard for a young minister to tell an older one anything. It's like a son trying to tell his father something. I understood that and I had a lot of respect for him. In fact a year before, Paul Shaver and I held a meeting in his church in Edmonton.

### Such Differences of Opinion

Since we were having such differences of opinions, I asked the fellows on the way back to Ilesha, why not split up and go two by two and not all go to Warri together. We could accomplish twice as much and all of us could have a feeling of greater fulfillment. I told them how that when Max and Erskine were with us, we went two by two. Paul Shaver and I did it with just the two of us for months and we saw greater results. Their answer was a flat out "No" and we were again told we were just a couple Bible School Students and they were seasoned ministers. This bothered me intensely but I kept my mouth shut as I didn't want to be disrespectful to older ministers. It was made harder because I was told by Dr. Wyatt and the Wings of Healing that I was be in charge when I came back to Nigeria. That was why they wanted me to come back. However, Alcock and Sanders were determined that I wasn't.

The original vision of Wings of Healing was that two teachers and two graduate students would go with Doc Wyatt and his team. He would get it started off on a big scale then a teacher and student would pair up and continue the meetings all over the country. Up to this point it had worked out super. Paul Shaver and I paired with Erskine Holt and Max Wyatt and each team carried the great meetings on. Max and Erskine went home and Paul and I continued the meetings and they got larger. Then others would be sent to learn from us how it was done. Paul was to be the lead guy in the Gold Coast and I was to be the one in Nigeria. Somebody must have forgotten to tell Alcock and Sanders though. Don't you love it when you don't have a clear line of authority?

The difficult situations of the mission field will always bring out the worst in a person. When we got back to the compound, I had a letter from Paul Shaver and a couple from Mildred. They were telling us about a division of the faculty at the Bible School. Oh! How this disturbed us! In fact, it bothered all of us a lot. We didn't go to bed till way late and I don't think any of us slept a wink but turned and tossed all night. Division in the ranks like that robs us of our prayer base back home which affects the meetings here. No wonder we were struggling!

## Disunity

We arose on February 12 with heavy hearts being so concerned about what was happening in our home church and the Bible School in Portland. We went on to the service and Harold Brown and I spoke in the Okeaye church in Ilesha. It was a very good service in spite of everything. Ezekiel, our interpreter, also said so plus many others said the same thing. The people said that the young men preached with such power.

In the afternoon Harold Alcock and Vernon Sanders talked to the African Elders about going to Warri next week. They didn't consult with us at all. Harold Brown and my feelings were that we were just a couple of boys, nice to have around to help pray in healing lines. They came back and said the African Elders wanted each of us to go to a separate church next week. Harold Brown and I couldn't agree with the decisions so we just walked away but there were no hard feelings of course. We felt we just didn't have any input.

In the afternoon, Vernon Sanders, Harold Alcock and Sidney Elton went to Ibadan to meet with Chief Ackinyelle, Babalola the prophet and others. Their purpose was to see about getting a Bible School started.

## Finally, a Chance to Do it Our Way!

Harold Brown and I drove to Ife for the meeting in the evening and I spoke with Ezekiel interpreting. It thrilled me so much that Harold and I could finally do the meeting the way we did in Ghana and it worked "slicker than a whistle." Ezekiel was so excited and was with us all the way. He was such a good interpreter as well as a wonderful man. All of us felt that this was the way the meetings should be done.

There were some amazing miracles that took place. A crippled man was physically carried into the service. He didn't sit with the sick but was instantly healed as we prayed en masse for all of them. The man that carried him in seemed to be happier than the one who was healed as he was so excited. Another man that was totally blind was instantly healed. It was so amusing! When he was coming up to testify, a Yoruba minister stopped him and held up two fingers to see if he could see. The man just brushed him aside and said, "of course I can see" and came onto the platform and testified. The crowd got really excited by his testimony. Then the interpreter whom the Olu of Warri had sent, who was a leper, was healed along with many others. This was "the frosting on the cake!" Oh how this thrilled us to no end because it was working as we had seen it work before.

I drove the "Hack" back as well as up. It was terrible, to say the least, on such roads. People just wouldn't dim their lights which made it very difficult to see.

### A Meeting of No Profit

The meeting that the others went to in Ibadan didn't profit anything. The men there were kind of soured on something. Chief Ackinyelle and the others had somehow been turned against us. Brother Elton thought some of Bradford's propaganda was causing Chief Ackinyelle to retract. I'm not surprised as Dr. Wyatt had a lot of trouble with some of the African ministers, especially from the Christ Apostolic group here in trying to get them to see what the Lord was doing. My feelings were that I didn't think any of them saw what the Lord was doing here in Nigeria. In fact Sidney Elton said he didn't think that the majority of them even knew if they were saved.

A Family and Bamboo House in Ilesha

The result of the meeting was that they'll discuss it between themselves and let us know later.

Babalola was brought up to carry on the meetings in Ife. Harold Alcock, Vernon Sanders and Sidney Elton said he didn't see this revival at all but this was coming from others. We must not take what others say and make our decisions on that. My feelings were, "Let us love and reach out to them in spite of their seeming rejection because division hurts us all." The power is in the unity. It's like Mildred's dad used to tell us, "You can catch more flies with honey than with vinegar." I thought this was a good principle to use in this situation.

### A Day of Down Time

February 13. I got up early this morning and washed my hair in cold water as that's all you could do. It was very dusty as a result of going to

Ife each day. There wasn't any meeting today so I cut Brown, Alcock, and Sander's hair. Harold Brown in turn cut mine. I'd cut many young men's hair in Bible College free because the students didn't have much money. However, this was Harold's first time cutting mine, but it didn't look too bad. We took some pictures around the compound then we walked downtown. This was quite a distance to walk. We wore our African shoes (forerunner of flip-flops) and they rubbed blisters on our feet. We tried to take pictures in the market but so many kids would jump in front of the camera. They just wanted to get their picture taken. We loved the kids and they would constantly walk along with us. We got thirsty so we bought four bottles of Krola (like Pepsi Cola) and drank them all.

All the time we were gone, we discussed what we should do next week in going to Warri. On getting back to the compound, we discussed the matter with Harold Alcock and Vernon Sanders. I suggested again that we should go to two different meetings. Alcock and Sanders rather thought we all should be together. I couldn't help but think, "What in the world is wrong with these guys. Are they afraid of going by themselves?" Alcock replied, that we should start the first night and lay hands on people and use a healing line. Oh boy! That really got my ire up so I really bucked him on that and we had quite a discussion to say the least. Harold Brown puzzled me because now he seemed to be on the fence on this issue. At this point, it did look like Harold Brown and I would go to one place while Alcock and Sanders would go to another. I wished, many times that they were not so concerned about a healing line but I guess it's according to your faith. Sadly, there still wasn't any answer from Dr. Wyatt or the office to our telegram of what they wanted us to do.

### Back in the Saddle Again!

On February 14th Harold Brown and Harold Alcock went to the Teacher's Training College for the morning service. Sidney Elton had gotten a young couple from America to start the College several years before to train Teachers for the developing school system. It was indeed a high quality school. Vernon Sanders, Sidney Elton and I went to a small town seven miles out of Ilesha and had a wonderful meeting. Vernon Sanders spoke and did very well, then we asked for those to come up front that wanted to be filled with the Holy Spirit. After instructing them we laid our hands on them for the Baptism of the Holy Spirit and 14 of them received. What a delight that was! We really needed that! It's amazing what others being filled with the Holy Spirit does to the preacher. The same anointing that is upon them is upon you and it refreshes your whole outlook. They asked if two of us could come back for a meeting the next week.

In the evening all of us went to the Teacher's College for the service and Harold Brown spoke. It sure sounded strange to listen to a person preach without an interpreter. Quite a few of the students raised their hands for salvation so we prayed with them individually when they came to the front and the Lord really met them. It was thrilling to see them weep their Way into the Kingdom of God.

After the meeting, I couldn't help but realize that fellowship with the Eltons wasn't the same. They seemed awful quiet and none talkative. I didn't know the reason and didn't feel like I should probe but just let things ride for a while.

### A Good Breakthrough

February 15. All four of us went to Oke Iro Church in Ilesha for the morning meeting where Vernon Sanders and Harold Alcock spoke. It was very good but there were only 50 people there. We went by the Post Office and I had a letter from Mildred. According to it things were looking very good in Portland at the church and school. That certainly brought joy to all of us.

### Another Exciting Time!

For the night meeting, we split into two groups. Harold Alcock and Vernon Sanders went to Ijebu while Sidney Elton, Harold Brown and I went to a town farther into the bush. They took us down a very narrow road that looked more like a path than a dirt road. It was absolutely amazing to see the size of the crowd that had assembled. It numbered about 1200 people and it fell my lot to preach. This was so exciting to me to be ministering again to a crowd at least this size. By all accounts, it was an excellent meeting. Hundreds of people gave their hearts to the Lord and a great number of the sick were healed. We couldn't take a lot of time to let all of them testify because it was getting too dark and there were no electric lights. We went on our way home rejoicing that the Lord had worked so mightily among some wonderful people. Alcock and Sanders were thrilled with their meeting as well. That was also thrilling to me to see them getting into this two by two-thing.

The pressure from home was beginning to get to me so I had a lot of sleepless nights. Consequently, I was feeling sick most of the time. So we wired Dr. Wyatt for instructions of what to do. Because communication was so poor in those days, we hadn't received any word from him. We could certainly understand why with all the upheaval that had gone on.

### Out of Defeat – Victory!

February 16. All four of us went to Oke Iro assembly this morning and Harold Brown and I both spoke. The turnout was very small. I found it very hard to preach as I was so troubled about what was happening in Portland. Though we had heard things were okay, yet in our spirits we knew they were not. My thoughts were, "If only they would let us know something." Vernon Sanders and Sidney Elton each got letters from

Raymond Hoekstra and I got two from Dean Burnett. With these letters we had the other side of the story. I must say it was very different. My first feelings were, "I just can't believe it. Why? What was the reason?"

This made me realize that the Eltons already knew the whole set up and that was why they were so quiet. All Sidney Elton could say was; "Why? Why? Why?" All of us got together and discussed the matter at length. Everyone voiced their opinion of what we should do and agreed that I should go to Portland and try to get things straightened out about our policy on the mission field. I was not in favor of this even though my stomach had been giving me fits. At all of their insistence, we tried to call the B. O. A. C. booking office and get a hold of them but they couldn't hear me. The phone connection was too bad. That ended my going home for a while at least and I was really glad. The plane was to leave the next day at 3:30 p.m. There was no way we could make it in time as it was 200 miles to drive over some narrow, winding roads.

They had left me downtown to make the call and I was in my short pants and African flip flops so I had to walk home alone which was well over a mile. Walking alone, I had a good talk with the Lord about this whole situation. By the time I arrived at the compound, I felt great victory in my soul and my stomach had quit hurting. Harold Alcock and Vernon Sanders went on to the meeting and by their reports had a very good one. Brown had stayed at the compound and he also felt a release in the Spirit as he had been sick as well. Mildred's letters sure helped out as they explained a lot. What a girl! She is tops with me.

### A Small Break Through

February 17. All four of us went to the morning service at Oke Iro in Ilesha where Harold Alcock spoke and did a very good job of it. However the interpreter did a very poor job as he wasn't very experienced. Josiah, who normally was our interpreter, was very good but he had to go to a school meeting so he couldn't interpret. Vernon Sanders then gave the instructions for the Baptism of the Holy Spirit and all of us laid our hands upon them. Though they were few in number, the Lord graciously filled twenty of them with the Holy Spirit. Vernon didn't give them very much instructions so it was a little harder to get them through yet it was a wonderful time and we felt it was very profitable.

### More Trouble Brewing!

On the way to the compound we went by the Post Office. There was a wire from Dr. Wyatt saying, "Letter mailed February 9 with 1500 dollars, also instructions for Cannon and Sanders." The letter came with the check in it but there were no instructions for anyone. We couldn't help but wonder why there were no instructions. We thought, perhaps it will be in another letter.

Alcock got a letter from his wife and one of the Instructors at Bethesda Bible Institute. I didn't like the contents of the instructor's letter as it was so negative. It said "Over half the school had left including Gwen Upfold, Paul Shaver's girl friend. All seemingly are still with Doc - but there is coming a showdown soon." Isn't that, usually, a tool of our enemy, to divide and conquer? He is a master at that.

However, I got a letter from Mildred saying that Paul Grubbs from Memphis had come to minister in the church and the Spirit of the Lord was moving in a greater way. This was great news and I thanked the Lord for it! Paul Shaver and I knew the Grubbs because we had a meeting for them in Memphis back in the summer. For the first time I slept very well, more than in a long time.

Brown, Elton and I started out for Asa Odo in the kit car but it broke a shackle bolt so we went with Sanders and Alcock and then took the Hack on to our village. I spoke on the unknown God and declared Him to them. Brown said it was a wonderful meeting, but I wasn't satisfied. On our way back to the compound we saw where they tied a sacrifice to a tree and also one to their idol. We felt so bad for those little animals as Jesus had already paid the price for sin on Calvary. Oh, if they could only know the truth, it would set them free.

### Good Meetings in Spite of it All

February 18. I awakened weary as I didn't sleep well because of the things we heard about home. It still weighed heavily upon all of us. It reminded me of Nehemiah and Jerusalem. Some friends reported to him, *"And they said unto me, 'The remnant that are left of the captivity there in the province are in great affliction and reproach: the wall of Jerusalem also is broken down, and the gates thereof are burned with fire.'* Then Nehemiah said, *"And it came to pass, when I heard these words, that I sat down and wept, and mourned certain days, and fasted, and prayed before the God of heaven."* Neh. 1:3-4. That's exactly how we felt. However, my stomach was still feeling really good in spite of it all.

All four of us went to the morning service where Sanders led off and I preached the main message. I really enjoyed preaching in this service and the people were so responsive to the Word. There is nothing to describe the emotion of preaching the Word when it flows like a river from the throne of Grace. You don't have to think of what to say as it is right there at the tip your tongue. You can see the transformation of the people right before your very eyes as the Truth sets them free. Then you realize it is neither your style nor your mannerism that brings release but the truth of God's Word penetrating their hearts and minds.

Stopping by the Post Office on our way back to the compound, there was no mail from Doc regarding our instructions as he had said in his last letter. In fact there wasn't any mail period! It made life like a roller coaster, up one minute and down the next but we made the best of it.

For the evening service, Elton, Brown and I went to Asa Odo where a good crowd had turned out. I led off and Brown followed with the main message. The Lord met the people in a remarkable way and the meeting was very good but it was still tough in preaching. Alcock and Sanders went out to Ijebu. They said they had a good meeting but it was tough as well. We didn't let those things bother us as all of us knew very well that the results didn't depend on how difficult it was to preach. You just do your best and leave the results up to the Lord. It reminded me of what the Apostle Paul said to the Corinthians, *"For after that in the wisdom of God the world by wisdom knew not God, it pleased God by the foolishness of preaching to save them that believe."* 1 Cor. 1:21. We did our puny little part and the Lord did the rest.

### A Day Off

February 19. We didn't have any morning or evening service so we just rested for the long difficult journey to Warri. We knew it was going to be a tough ride as we were told it was 225 miles with half of it on winding dirt roads. We would make the trip in Sidney Elton's pickup. It was a 1948 GMC with a wooden box on the back without a door on the rear and no windows. There would be six of us going as Elton wanted to take a young Yoruba fellow with us. I packed everything because they thought it best for me not to have to return to Ilesha but fly directly from Benin to Lagos. There was no road across all those swamp lands to drive from Benin to Lagos in those days. The road from Benin led North through Ilesha then South to Lagos which would have made more than a four hundred-mile trip. However, that wasn't what I wanted to do. I was so excited about going into a new territory and preaching the gospel for the first time to so many new people.

Since we thought this would be my last night in Ilesha, we went downtown and had a Yoruba outfit made up. It cost 1 pound and 15 Schillings, about $2.50 US currency. I also bought a beautiful scarf from Yoruba land for Mildred as they were so colorful. It was not a very eventful day but one we needed, to prepare for what lay ahead. Needless to say, I still was so excited about the coming meetings though we were going into entirely new territory to all of us as well as Sidney Elton. It came a tropical downpour through most of the night with high winds and lots of lightning. Coming from Southern Louisiana it didn't bother me at all but caused me to sleep a lot better.

### A Rough Trip to Warri

On February twentieth, we arose a little early and had "chop" then loaded the truck for Warri. Sanders and Alcock said they wanted the back to start as the first part of the road was a hard surface. They didn't give us a choice but that was all right because we knew with Alcock's coughing problem that he couldn't survive riding in the back when we came to the dirt roads and the dust bellowing in. Besides, they were the older and we wouldn't have had it any other way.

We left Ilesha at 8:30 in the morning with a lot of excitement. But we only got a short distance out of Ilesha when the generator on the truck stopped charging. So we stopped at a mechanic's place by the side of the road and he put another one on. Actually Sidney Elton talked him into renting it to us. This delayed us two hours. The guy had wanted 7 pounds and 10 schillings (close to $20.00 US) for it, so it was a good thing we didn't pay him and only rented it. We had only gone 29 miles down the road when this one went out also. So we had another one put on and went our way.

It seemed such a long time with all the delays but we finally reached the halfway mark. Brown and I went to the back of the pickup and it wasn't very long before we came to the dusty road. If you have ever ridden down a dusty road in the back of a pickup, you know what we were experiencing. The dust comes barreling in like a heavy fog. We could hardly breathe. We had to tie a handkerchief over our faces to keep from breathing the dust though it didn't stop all of it. Besides having to endure all the dust, we had to sit on a wooden board put across from one side of the pickup to the other and lean back against the cab.

The road was narrow and rough as it wove back and forth through the huge rubber trees. Of course we couldn't tell if it was beautiful or not with the thick cloud of dust rolling in. The dirt road was the rest of the way to Benin City where it was oiled from there on. It was a few minutes before 5:00 in the evening when we arrived at one of the estuaries of the Niger River. Actually we got there earlier but we had to get in a long line to wait our turn on the ferry. When Brown, our young Yoruba friend and I got out of the back of the pickup, all the guys just laughed at us. No one could tell which were American or Nigerian as our faces were caked with mud from all the dust and sweating. It didn't bother us with them laughing at us though we sure didn't like the dust caked on our faces.

### Crossing the Niger River

It was beautiful crossing over the Niger River into Sapele. I couldn't help but think this should be a good fishing place but we were on another kind of fishing trip. It was the kind Jesus had spoken about to His apostles, *"Follow Me and I will make you fishers of men."* I thought the crossing was so outstanding that I took some pictures of it. Finally, we arrived in Warri at 6:00 in the evening worn out.

### Met With the King!

The first thing we had to do was to go to the Olu's Palace. His official name was: Erejuwa II, the Olu of Warri. It was a wonderful time of meeting with him and his family. They were all so excited that we had finally gotten there. He sent a young man along with us to show us the English rest house where we were to stay. We all hurriedly cleaned up and went to "chop" in the dining room of the rest house. Our cook had fixed us a fillet of sole and it was "out of this world." The country was exactly like I always thought the jungle would look like. It was very pretty but very, very, damp and humid.

## The Warri Meetings Begin

February 21. Since we were so weary, we slept very well the first part of the night but tossed the latter part. It was extremely damp and foggy in morning. Our cook had prepared us two eggs, sausage, toast, and coffee for each of us. I thought it was quite good.

We had given orders last week that tonight was to be our first service but the Olu had announced service for this morning, so naturally we went. It was held in the open space near the Olu's palace. A couple thousand people were out and Alcock preached since he was the senior minister. It was a good start but we didn't make much of it. When we got back to the rest house, our cook had prepared us a lunch of a cold plate of ham, string beans and tomatoes with potatoes and banana fritters. They were very good. Wow! Were we ever eating very well here! It was much better than we had expected.

The time came for us to go to the evening meeting. We had to drive to the outskirts of town where they had cleared a huge area, at least 600 yards square, in what was a part of the jungle. We were so disappointed that the meeting was not in the middle of town like they had been in most places so they would be accessible to everybody.

The Ju Ju Priests also had set up a big circle of witchcraft stuff right in the middle of the road leading out to the grounds in order to frighten the people away. They stood about eight to nine feet tall because they were on stilts under their garb. On the outer robe they had small skulls and bones tied to it and a hideous mask over their heads with large horns on top. They would run at the people to frighten them and put curses on them. This probably worked some as it didn't look like a very large turnout to us when we arrived.

## An Unusual Service

We parked the truck on the side of the road and walked the 125 yards to the platform and climbed up the rear steps. The platform was on stilts and was about twelve feet square. It was over six feet high with a big board in front and on the sides with the steps going up the back. There was very little standing room on it because it was so crowded with chiefs who were not even Christians. In addition, they made entirely too much noise. Later, there would also be five interpreters who would have to be there and positioned for the various languages. We had an old battery powered public address system with two big horns for speakers that we brought with us. At times, it seemed to have a mind of its own and wouldn't work part of the time. In those times, we learned to project our voices so they could hear us. It was amazing how it worked.

We were so disappointed at the size of the crowd and we had no idea of what we were up against but we would find out later. We figured it would be a huge crowd from all the things we were told. All of us agreed there were about 1600 people out, yet in such a huge area it seemed very small. It was worse than having a small group in a huge church building. They sang their African songs, which none of them were recognizable to us as they were in an entirely different language from what we had been used too. None of us wanted to preach as we were so filled with disappointment. So each one of us kept saying, "I'm not speaking tonight." I would have done it but I went along with the other guys as a kind of joke. Finally we conned Sidney Elton into doing it. He got up with the two major interpreters who had been with us in Ilesha and told a little kindergarten story about Jesus from the gospel of Luke. It wasn't impressive by any means.

Elton was a wise missionary with lots of experience and knew you couldn't give the people a theological discourse. Most of them had never seen or heard of the word "bible." When you used the names of the books of the bible, they may have known people with a name similar but they knew nothing of those in the bible. They didn't even know there was a Jesus who would save them from their sins. So really, you had to speak kind of like you were speaking to first graders or such.

### A Hunchback Boy Healed Instantly!

Though Elton's preaching was not great according to American standards, there were still some good healings. We had some of them to come up and testify. Among those that came up was a lady with a small boy strapped to her back. I would guess the little boy was about four or five years of age with a huge hunch on his back. She came up with those to testify because she wanted prayer for him. So we did and instantly the hunch on his back disappeared. Not realizing that every eye was on everything any of us did. The crowd liked to have "gone wild" as they all were watching very intently! We had her remain in line to testify. While the people were testifying, half the crowd had moved to the back of the platform so they could see the people personally when they came down the steps. After testifying, the mother started to go down the steps when a big black hand from the side grabbed the boy's shirt, tearing it off of him. I happened to be following her with my eyes so as to get some interesting pictures. This frightened the mother and she tried her best to get away from the crowd but they just swarmed her. Of course, this really frightened her even more, so she began running as fast as she could toward town with the little boy still clinging to her back with the whole crowd running after her. That was the end our first meeting. What an end to a meeting! Wow!

All of us just stood there laughing at the scene of the mother running with her little boy on her back and 1600 people running after her. It was a sight to see! All they wanted to do was just to see the little boy's back. They were not trying to hurt anyone. Since all the people were gone, we walked the 125 yards back to the truck and drove off!

When we got back to the rest house, our cook had a pork roast with fried potatoes and cauliflower for supper. It was so good. Right after we ate, the Olu came to see us and we had a wonderful visit. He wanted us to come and hold a few services at his private Chapel for him and his wives. Their custom forbids his wives from coming to the big meetings and also his eyes were bad and he wanted prayer. So we prayed for him.

During supper, Elton told us that the King of a town 22 miles from Ilesha was hanged for cannibalism four or five years earlier. A missionary in eastern Nigeria a few years ago had his cook prepare some meat which he thought was very good. When he inquired further, he found it was human flesh. Oh Yuck! I don't know if those things were really true or not but Elton declared they were. All I know was they sounded horrible.

### Sound of Drums

We couldn't help but notice the sound of drums as we sat around talking. You could hear some close at hand then they would be quiet then you would hear other drums at a distance. This would continue until the sound was only a faint sound. Then the close ones would again sound out starting the process all over again. To us it sounded like they were sending signals out from Warri. This continued all night, stopping when it got daylight. It was difficult to sleep with all that going on. Later, we were told they were sending messages on huge log drums. We certainly didn't have time to investigate to see if it was true or not. Frankly, we were not interested in that as we tried to concentrate solely on Christ and the work He wanted to do.

### More Troubles

February 22. We arose at 8:00 and had a fillet of fish (fresh), fried potatoes, toast and coffee for breakfast. Don't say "yuck" as it was very enjoyable this time. We've surely had it good here thus far but things have a way of changing. There always seems to be "Murphy's Law" on the mission field.

The morning service was held at the same place as the evening meeting. By this time, it was getting very hot for the people but they came out by the hundreds and Sanders spoke. He did a good job and spoke mainly on knowing Jesus Christ as Savior. We knew we had to instill truth in their hearts so they would have a genuine experience with the Lord Jesus. It was rough sitting on the platform in the sun, and extreme heat, let alone teaching. The people were very open to the word.

For lunch, our cook had prepared some kind of liver and kidneys but not like the steak and kidney pie we had in Sunyani, Gold Coast. I was still leery, so I took it kind of slow so as not to disappoint our cook.

### A Rude Awakening!

We had a rude awakening when we discovered that our host never booked the rest house but for only two nights. We wondered, why would they do that when they knew we were planning for two weeks with them? Now, what will we do? It looked like after tonight we won't have a place to stay. Elton came up with a brilliant scripture, *"we shall not all sleep"* which brought a little humor into the situation. This is where a seasoned Missionary comes in handy as he pretty well knows the ropes.

Finally after calling the District Officer, we found out we could all live in the only vacant chalet which had two single beds and a camp bed but there were five of us. However, we found out later that we could have another cabin for the one night which helped for the immediate. It was hard to get some of these local guys to work with us. Of course they didn't know about all the things that needed to be done as this was a totally unreached area and everything was all new to them. Nothing like this had ever been done before in this area.

After service, Elton talked to Babalola about our cabin and discovered he and Josiah both knew they'd only booked it for two nights but didn't tell us. We knew somebody was "pulling our leg."

### The Crowd Grew!

When we went to the evening service at 5:00 there was a large crowd already gathered. This really turned me on! In our estimation, there were about 10,000 people around the little platform. Again we parked the truck on the road and walked the 125 yards to the platform. We were completely surrounded by the people every step of the way. They just wanted to touch us. They were so very friendly and gracious in all of this. They would do their best to get our attention and say, "Oyebo" while patting their head. What they wanted was for us to put our hands on their head as we did the little boy the last evening. Of course we would do it, but we never stopped walking because we never would have made it to the platform.

Because of the number of different tribal languages, we had to use five interpreters now. One of those was in Pigeon English because we didn't have enough interpreters for all the different dialects. The

Itshekiri would speak first, and then the Urhobo and that would be followed by the other three at the same time. We had the crowd kind of separated by language. The Itshekiri and the Urhobo were out front with two of the other languages on the side and Pigeon English at the back. The Itshekiri and Urhobo interpreters were the ones the Olu had sent up to Ilesha to learn our American lingo. One of them was healed of leprosy in the meeting when Harold Brown and I had the service back in Ife.

During the service, Alcock and Sanders went to see one of the Chief's houses where they wanted us to move to. Later they told us it was fair but the fellow thought they were coming to pray for him and his family. They said no they hadn't come to pray but to see what the house looked like for us to live in. So the fellow sent them over to the Olu's. He showed them through his Palace first and said he thought they had come to hold a meeting for his wives. They said they would speak a little and then lay hands of them and pray. That caused quite a little commotion, and the Olu quickly spoke up and said, "No one is supposed to touch the King's wives." This startled them so they spoke a little and prayed en masse for the wives without touching any of them. They got back to the meeting just as I was finishing preaching.

### Tough Going but God!

It was a little difficult preaching as these people had never heard of Jesus. You speak of the book of John but they knew nothing of the bible. I struggled through it trying to find something they understood so as to connect with them and build their faith. You add to all that, these interpreters were doing something they had never done before in interpreting for a minister preaching. It was totally new to them.

Just as I had done in the Gold Coast, I did in this meeting. After finishing preaching, I prayed for all the people at one time and stepped back with my head bowed and eyes closed just waiting on the Lord to do something. It felt like an eternity though it was only a minute at the longest when things began to happen miraculously. This was a good chance for our team to see the Lord work with mighty signs and wonders without a healing line. You could see the stir in sections of the people as different ones were healed. So we invited those that were healed to come up and testify. A young boy was the first to come. He said he could now stand and walk but had never been able to do so in his whole life. One woman was healed of deafness as she went home from last evening's meeting running after the mother with the hunchback boy that had been healed. All of a sudden she said she started to hear and could hear clearly. One little 14-year-old girl testified she was healed of insanity. This insanity was brought about from the curse placed on her by the Ju Ju priest. There were many other wonderful healings of all kinds and descriptions too numerous to mention.

We left the platform amid a lot of jubilation among the people. Just as we came, the crowd escorted us back to the truck with most of them trying to wipe the sweat off us and putting it on them. That sounds terrible, but these people were all from a juju background so it seemed like magic to them.

We had to wait after service two hours before going to the chalet because the truck wouldn't start. The generator had quit working so it never charged the battery. Our cook had prepared us an Irish stew for supper with carrots and coconut pudding for desert and Nescafe coffee. It was real late by the time we finished eating.

The Olu came to see us because he was extremely worried about us leaving. We assured him we didn't want to leave but they had to find accommodations for us if we were to stay. He graciously promised they would do so and went on back home.

## A Chorus Becomes a Theme

February 23. We had scrambled eggs and sausage for breakfast and all of us really enjoyed it. This was the nicest that we've had in Africa to this time. Alcock stayed at the chalet and prayed while Elton and Sanders went to see the Olu. Brown and I took the morning meeting. I spoke on *"He that would be the greatest let him be the servant."* I was trying to show them the true spirit of Christianity was in serving one another. This was the spirit of our Lord in washing the disciples' feet. In all of this we had to weave the doctrine of salvation into it to make sure they were truly "born again." They seemed to get the message quite well. Then I taught them a little chorus that we sang in Ghana. It went like this: "Let the oppressed go free. Let the oppressed go free. There's deliverance in Zion for you and me. Oh, let the oppressed go free." We used motions with our hands and they really enjoyed that. They really took to that chorus and it would become our theme song from then on. Oh, how they danced with great joy as they would sing it. By all signs, it was a really good meeting.

After the morning service we sent the truck to the garage to get the generator fixed. Our cook had prepared fried fish and fried potatoes for lunch and it was very good. Since I had spoken last night and this morning the fellows thought I should stay at the rest house to move our stuff as the fellow was late in moving out of the Number 3 chalet. I had to finish my packing anyway then I could move us into it. They all said it was a great meeting with about 15,000 out with many great miracles happening. It was half again bigger than the night before they said.

What a delight it was to sit down to a boiled beef dinner with lettuce, tomatoes and boiled potatoes. This guy was an excellent cook and had been trained by the British government to cook for their people.

When we finished eating, the Olu came to see us again. It was a time of setting things straight about us continuing to stay. There was no way that he was going to let us leave. He said he would do almost anything to keep us. Since there were only two single beds and a cot in the chalet, Brown and I slept on one of the single beds while Alcock and Sanders had a cot and bed of their own. We felt we should do this out of respect for them, besides we were young and could handle it well. However it was rough with two big guys on a single bed but that is all there was. It reminded me of a time in Bartlesville, Oklahoma when a friend and I held a week of meetings and the two of us had to sleep on a single bed in the hot summertime with no air conditioning.

### Just a Bottle of Water

February 24. After a breakfast of eggs and sausage we went to the meeting. Sanders, Brown and I took the large meeting and I spoke. Alcock and Elton were going to speak to the Olu's wives but when they saw such a huge crowd Alcock got off there with us. We had been noticing the people were bringing bottles of water but we didn't think much of it. Our thoughts were that perhaps in the hot sun they had them for water to drink. However we noticed that when we would pray, they would put the bottles of water on their heads.

At lunch we discussed it while we had a lovely meal of a boiled egg and cold beef and boiled potatoes. We were told they were doing this so the water would absorb the healing virtue when we prayed. Then when they became sick they could drink the water and be healed. Some were going so far as to sell it, kind of like a juju charm. Oh my! How easy it is for people to get off into some kind of heresy.

We finally had a letter from Dr. Wyatt. He said for me to stay until help could be sent. This pleased me to no end as long as we could really stay busy and see multitudes swept into the kingdom of God. I also had two letters from Mildred and that was wonderful as she always kept us up with how things were going at the school and church.

Sanders spoke in the evening meeting and really hit on the matter of the water bottles that the people had been bringing to get blessed. Sheepishly, they took them all down. This was like throwing a wet blanket on things and kind of made the meeting tight. So there wasn't as many healings as there should have been.

### Condemnation Never Builds Faith!

Of course, you can't preach anything that condemns and expect people to exercise their faith. Healing will only work in the brackets of the grace of God. Nobody deserves healing regardless of what they have or haven't done. We had to get people to see that healing is from the Lord, Who is Spirit and not in things. When we accept Him as our Savior,

He will abide with us forever. So when we need healing, its not a magical formula but each of us can pray and God will hear us. So we ask Him, personally to heal us rather than trying to drink some magical formula.

The crowd was way more than 15,000 in the evening service. When we asked for those who wanted to receive Jesus as their Lord and Savior, every hand went up. This was so, partly, because of not having been taught enough about salvation. We found it would take us at least a week of morning and evening teaching to get them to see it clearly.

On the way home to the chalet, we stopped by the Post Office and sent a cable to Paul Shaver in the Gold Coast to see what his plan was for going home. Maybe we could go together because the plane from Accra came to Lagos on its way to London. When we got back to the chalet, our cook had prepared us dinner made up of a boiled egg, chopped beef and boiled potatoes.

Again, the Olu came to see us. He wanted us to go look at a house which he wanted to get for us. So Elton and Alcock went with him to see the house. Of course he wanted us to remain permanently and said if we would, he would build a house for us to live in and turn the ground where the meetings are held over to us. It certainly was a great field and some very good people here also. What a great opportunity!

### Opposition From the Ministry!

February 25. We arose and had our fried eggs and sausage for breakfast. When we arrived for the morning meeting there was a large crowd already gathered. I led them in singing "Let the oppressed go free." Oh, how they loved to sing it and they danced so enthusiastically. Alcock led off with an exhortation with Brown following with the main message. Both of them dealt mainly with "How to be saved." We also ministered to the sick and hopeless as a part of the meeting with an awful lot of them being healed.

After the service we had a meeting with Babalola and the Christ Apostolic Minister that came down from Ilesha. There was opposition coming from the ministers that came with us. These were not local guys, because before we came there were no churches here. These guys seemed to be making a power play so as to get all the converts into their group. So our meeting was to lay everything on the table and find out what was wrong. Our original plans with the Olu were that we would be here for two weeks but now these guys wanted us to leave Sunday night so they could continue the meetings. We knew something was wrong. The meeting ended amicably but we didn't really settle anything.

Our cook had fried fish, fried potatoes and string beans for dinner. The fish here were so fresh and good. Although we were disappointed there wasn't any mail today.

## A Deluge Comes

We went to the evening meeting and just as we drove up, it looked like the "bottom fell out." It just poured down rain like in a monsoon. It was raining and lightning so we stayed in the truck. We didn't think it was wise to get out with all the lightning that was going on. Some of the people left but the greater number stayed and began to sing and pray in the rain without anyone leading them. They were having a great time.

Finally it slacked off just a little so we went to the platform to tell them that the meeting was canceled and told them to please go on home because they were all soaking wet. They quickly replied in broken English and in unison, "We no go home. Oyebo (white man) pray and stop rain." Well, what are you going to do? Are you going to send them on home anyway and admit defeat without trying? Besides, I had preached a few services earlier about Elijah and the prophets of Baal and how he had prayed and fire fell from heaven to consume the sacrifice and all. Then he prayed for rain and the heavens gave forth the rain. Added to this we would say to the huge crowd, "If you don't see God work miracles among you then you don't have to believe a word we say."

So here we were between the proverbial rock and the hard place. We did the only thing we knew to do and that was to pray for the rain to stop. So we prayed and as soon as we said "Amen," it was like you zip open a curtain. Not only did the rain stop instantly but the sun came out in full force with a beautiful blue sky. Just as soon as it stopped raining the people all came running back. In our estimation it was between 10 and 12,000 people standing there in three inches of water soaking wet.

Sidney Elton led off with a short exhortation to encourage and lift their enthusiasm. Then I brought the main message. Oh, were they ever receptive after all that had happened? The Lord did so many wonders among them this night because their faith was so high. Since the people were all wet, we didn't take any time for testimonies. We thought it best for them just to go on home. Besides, it was getting real late and we had no lights. One of the men dismissed the meeting in prayer and all of a sudden it started a huge downpour. It was like when we said "Amen" the sky was zipped back shut and the rains came. Before we could get to the pickup, we were all soaking wet. Yet our hearts were so full of gratitude and thanksgiving to the Lord for doing what He did. Did the Lord stop the rain? I'll let you wrestle with that. However, no one could tell these people that God didn't stop the rain at the "Oyebo's" prayer.

### Lizards, Frogs and Ants

After a lovely supper of roast beef, potatoes, and cauliflower, we sat out in the front of the chalet and watched the huge ants come flying to the light which we had turned on. Since these cabins were built by the

British, they had them wired for electricity. The rains had caused the ants to fly out of their nests and of course they came to the light like the other bugs. When they fell to the ground, they would shed their large wings and begin to crawl off. In just a minute or so, the lizards of every description showed up along with some toad frogs. We watched them devour the ants and get so full they could hardly move. Their stomachs were bulging extensively. Then along came a very small toad. He would flick out his tongue and get one of those huge ants but he had such a hard time swallowing it as it was just too large for his mouth. That didn't stop him as he continued to eat till he couldn't even jump any more. It was all so amusing to us.

## A Troublous Decision at Hand

While we were watching the lizards and toads eating the ants, Elton had a conference with the Olu, Babalola and the Christ Apostolic ministers that came with us. When he returned, he told us they want us to turn all converts over to the Christ Apostolics. They didn't want any other organization to be involved which we thought was awfully narrow. We were supposed to decide what we were going to do tonight. This was very upsetting as we were told that before we came, there were no churches except one little Episcopal and it was in the Olu's palace compound but it was all mixed up with juju.

They told us that this area had been very warlike and hostile and they had burned the last missionaries at the stake some 18 years prior. If this was so, then why make all the fuss? The power of the church is in its unity. We would have a greater blessing with different groups working together in unity than any single group. The job was too great for any one group regardless of their size. So let all the groups come in was our attitude.

## Not Ours But Theirs!

February 26. We had our scrambled eggs and sausage for breakfast then went to the morning meeting. A huge crowd had gathered for the morning meeting. Sanders led off and Alcock brought the main teaching. Both did very well. It was so hot and the sun was so bright, consequently we didn't keep them very long. Regardless of that, they stayed a long time afterwards because they wanted us to pray for them. We did and the Lord met so many of them.

We finally had to leave and go to the Olu's Palace to have our meeting with the pastors, Babalola, and others. It was an open meeting in which we expressed ourselves the best we could, trying to be very understanding and gentle. They likewise did the same and so far things looked very good. We tried to convey to them that we were not here to build something for ourselves. We were only interested in helping to train their people and have them plant churches all over the area. It was thrilling as it looked like we could cooperate with them. Maybe this time we have indeed connected with them. We could only hope so.

## Our Mail Truck Arrived

When we came for lunch there was lots of mail. Of course with just getting mail no one wanted to eat right then, so we postponed it till afterwards. There were several letters from Mildred which had gotten backed up somewhere along the line. She wrote to me every day but they didn't come through every day but in spurts. One letter came from Paul Shaver in the Gold Coast saying he was sick and was returning home on March 17th wanting me to go home with him.

Alcock got a letter from one of the Bible School Instructors and he let me read it but I didn't like what I read by any means. It looked to me like he was trying to poison Alcock's mind. The way I was feeling at the moment was just to let the instructor go. Alcock was so disappointed that Doc had not written to him and said if Doc doesn't write, then he isn't going to write any more either. All of us were terribly depressed this afternoon so we lay on our cots and tried to pray and get a hold of the Lord. You can't imagine the stress of trying to minister in such huge meetings and have such disunity here and at home.

Elton and I were supposed to leave for Ilesha this afternoon but instead we decided to wait and go the next day. We finally had our lunch which consisted of a lovely steak with potatoes and macaroni coupled with jelly fritters. It was very delicious and we enjoyed it in spite of the discouragement that hit us all. I found it so amazing that we could be in such huge meetings with the Lord doing so many supernatural wonders and yet here we are depressed about things back home. We had to do as David did at Ziklag, encourage ourselves in the Lord.

## A Strange Meeting

Parking the truck along the roadside, we walked the 125 plus yards to the little improvised platform. As usual, we were swarmed with excited people. Again, they would take our hands and put them on their heads jabbering in a language that we didn't understand. We tried to show our love for them in any way we could and they reciprocated. The crowd was really huge by any standards. We thought there were about 20,000 out this evening but we hadn't done any mathematics on it yet.

After an exciting song service, Harold Brown spoke and did very well but a strange thing happened. As he was preaching a woman fell down and the whole crowd started running away from the platform toward town as fast as they could run. In just a few seconds the whole crowd had scattered into the bushes. There was nobody left but just us on the platform. It sounded like an earthquake, when all of a sudden that entire huge crowd went running off as fast as they could run. It was a marvel that no one was run over or trampled when they broke and ran. Harold didn't know what to do so he just stood there and prayed while the interpreters translated his prayer.

We could see many of them standing behind the bushes and standing in the brush. In a few minutes all of them came back, looking sheepishly. We found out later about what had happened. Actually a lady fainted because of the extreme heat of the sun and being in the middle of the crowd she fell on the ground. They were saying, "The white man's juju shakes the earth and woman fall down." They were so suspicious of every move we made, especially with the movie cameras as they made a whirring sound. They thought we were using juju with the cameras.

Sidney Elton, Ruth

In spite of all the distractions, there were a huge number healed of such major diseases and ailments. You could name it and it was happening. It was miracle after miracle happening all around. We again invited people to come and testify if the Lord had healed them of anything. There was no way we could have all of them to testify because there were just too many of them. After an hour or so of testimony we closed the meeting in prayer. Often we would have Babalola close in prayer and he would pray in Yoruba. I can almost hear him now as I write this. With an extremely loud voice and with his large mouth wide open, he would say, "Lo de kro, Jesu." This simply meant "In the name of Jesus." The people would repeat it in unison. Then he would say it again, "Lo de kro, Jesu." He would do this three times and then end with, "Lo de kro, Jesu Christi, Olu wa wa." This was, "In the name of Jesus Christ the Lord." He would draw out the last "Wa" for a long time then say a long "Ah-h-h-h-men." Then the crowd would all say "ah-men."

We left the meeting amid all their applause and warm greetings as they sought just to touch us as we walked back to the truck. We relaxed afterwards with steak and kidney made into a potato stew with string beans and chocolate pudding for desert. We sure teased Harold Brown about the meeting in a good-hearted way and he took it very well.

### Back to Ilesha

February 27. We arose early and had breakfast then Elton and I started back to Ilesha. I would much rather to have stayed for the meetings but someone had to take Sidney Elton back home so we could have the truck. No one else wanted to go so it fell my lot and I would make the most of it. Josiah came by and said Babalola was leaving on Monday morning.

We hardly crossed the ferry at Sapele when the generator stopped charging again. Elton drove on to Benin City to get the generator repaired again. The armature was burned-out again. We lost an hour in getting the generator repaired. This made three of them in the last three weeks and they cost us six pounds (about $16) each time to repair it. We got just past the town of Owo and the regulator stuck driving the engine temperature up to 220 degrees. Elton took the cap off the regulator and drove on in and we arrived about 4:15 in the evening.

It was so thrilling in getting back to Ilesha as I had lots of mail. One of Mildred's letters said the Wings of Healing leaders wanted to send her over and for us to get married in Ilesha. They thought it would make a nice missionary appeal. Right then with all the problems, all I could think of was, "No way!" Consequently, I wrote back, "No." I also wrote Max Wyatt a four-page type written letter explaining the set up here and about all the friction going on. I was hoping to get some clarification on the position we were supposed to function in and the chain of command. Whatever it was, we needed to know.

### A Delightful Sunday in Ilesha

February 28. Sunday was most always a delightful time in Ilesha as the Eltons were such wonderful hosts. We kidded them no end about eating on the back of their forks and they would kid us about trying to eat peas with a fork. We had a lovely breakfast of grapefruit, oatmeal, eggs and sausage for breakfast. Brother Elton had planted the grapefruit trees in the compound along with a lot of other fruit trees. They were so good picked fresh from the trees.

Sidney Elton and I went over to the training center for the morning service. He wanted me to speak to them as I was more their age. I did for a few minutes but really struggled. I could hardly do so as it was so strange speaking without an interpreter. With an interpreter, you had a little time to get your choicest thoughts together but without one it was "rapid fire." Regardless, it turned out to be a very good meeting. Some of the students were just weeping as I had them all come and stand in the front as we prayed for them. The Lord did a great work inside many of them that day.

After the meeting, Sister Elton's cook had some bush antelope (duiker), potatoes and carrots for dinner. That was always such a wonderful meal. In the afternoon, Elton met with the pastors of Ilesha and gave them the Warri report. They were absolutely thrilled. Both of us went back to the training center in the evening where he also gave the report of the Warri meeting. I spoke again and climaxed it by asking them would they rather teach 25 or 30 kids or 20,000 people? With a great roar of approval they replied, the larger.

We drove back to the compound and settled in for the night with a great satisfaction that we had done the will of the Lord. It was a good day! However, that bed was something else. It had bumps and low places the full length of the mattress which made it very hard to sleep on. Basically it was simply a cover filled with kapok they had gathered from the trees which would bunch up in spots. Oh well, such is life in Nigeria on the Mission field!

# The Journey Ends
# Chapter 9

On the first of March, we arose early to make the trip back to Warri from the Eltons' place in Ilesha but it was of no avail. We hurried and had breakfast of grapefruit, oatmeal, and scrambled eggs on toast. Everything was ready to go early but the mechanic didn't bring the truck till 9:30. He was supposed to have repaired the generator and regulator but it soon would fail again.

The Elders along with Sidney Elton wanted a young African man to go with me in case I had any problems for which I was very thankful. I was really excited about the trip as we left town bound for Warri with just my young friend and me. He spoke pretty good English so we talked most of the way. It was necessary to fill the gas tank with "petrol" (gasoline) as we left Ilesha at 9:45. However we still had trouble with the generator charging too much but there wasn't anything we could do except pray. Shortly, the regulator started acting up so I took the cap off like Sidney Elton did and it did pretty good. The temperature showed 220 degrees constantly so I figured the gauge must be stuck.

## A Herd of Goats in the Way

As we rounded a sharp curve to the left, a herd of small goats suddenly ran across the road. I mashed the brake pedal but the pickup didn't have much brake to speak of. Honking the horn didn't make them move any faster either. I tried my best to miss them by swerving and did miss the large group but I ran over two little goats in the rear. I started to stop but remembered one of the last things Brother Elton said to me, "If you hit anything don't ever stop. No one owns them anyway and anyone there will try to collect an enormous sum from you though they were not the owners. No one will pick them up right away. They will let them lay there till the sun goes down and then they will make a dash to get them." Though in my heart I wanted to stop, I just drove on as per my instructions. That was tough to do and contrary to my nature. I felt so bad about that!

## Stuck, Really Stuck

About ninety miles out of Ilesha we decided to pull off the road to eat our lunch. Sitting in the shade of a huge tree the sandwiches and flask of hot tea that Sister Elton had fixed were enjoyable. Getting back in the truck, we started to drive off when the two rear wheels sank deep in the soft earth. It was about 12:30 in the afternoon and very hot. After a while some fellows came along and tried to help us. We jacked the wheels up so we could put some branches and sticks under them but this only made us go deeper. Since it was a dirt road just ahead of us, the traffic was very sparse with hardly any lorries coming by. Finally at 2:30, a big truck loaded with men came by and we flagged him down. They didn't have a chain to pull us out so we didn't know what to do. Suddenly a couple of the men said they would get us out if I would give them one pound so I said okay. It was so amusing to watch as I wondered how they would work it. About fifty men got out and picked up the rear of the truck and set it on the road then did the same with the front. This was an amazing task.

I quickly gave the Pound note to those fellows but all the others wanted some as well. I didn't know what to do as I didn't have that much money with me. So I ended up giving the others who complained three shillings each, making a total of 12 shillings and thanked them heartily. It was expensive but we had to hurry to catch the ferry at Sapele by 6:00 that evening because that was the last one for the day. If we missed it then we would have to spend the night in the truck at the ferry. Of course we didn't know how safe that would be either.

### We Must Make the Ferry

Quickly jumping in the pickup, I put the pedal to the metal. To make it, I had to drive 60 miles an hour where 40 was too fast because we had to make the ferry at Sapele. Unfortunately, about five miles from Benin City we had a flat tire on that hot dusty road. Both of us jumped out and changed the tire quickly and went on. On top of that it was necessary to get some petrol in Benin City because we'd used too much trying to get unstuck.

We were following a big truck for many miles and tried to pass him but didn't have enough space. He did everything in the world to keep me from passing but I found a spot and gunned it. Somehow, I just knew we had to get in front of that truck so both of us prayed for the Lord's help. Finally, arriving at the ferry in Sapele at 5:40 p.m. we were the last vehicle they let on the ferry. Whew! How thankful we were! Since we were the last one on, we were the last one off. Driving on to Warri, we arrived about 7:15 that evening at the rest house.

### A Muddy Mess

Since we were staying in the rest house we hurriedly cleaned up as I was absolutely mud from head to toe. The guys all laughed at my friend and me as they couldn't tell us apart with all the mud on us. I couldn't believe our cook had steak and kidney stew for supper with potatoes and peas. But we were very hungry so we quickly devoured it all.

While we were eating the fellows told us about the meetings on Sunday. They said that in the meeting Sunday night there were about 25,000 attending and it was the largest crowd yet. That was such good news to me. Sanders and Alcock said they went to a village seven miles out of town. They left Harold Brown alone at the big meeting. I couldn't believe it! Why would anyone leave 25,000 people and go to a village with only hundreds? I guess they were afraid of the unknown if one person went alone so we can't be too rough on them. Being very, very tired I went straight to bed.

## 4000 Raise their Hands

March 2. We had a good night's rest after being so tired from the trip. For breakfast, our cook prepared scrambled eggs and sausage again. The morning meeting had about 4,000 in attendance. Sanders led off teaching on salvation. When he asked for those wanting to be saved to raise their hand, every one of them did. Then we prayed with them by leading them in a prayer of repentance and acceptance of Christ. You could see the sincerity in their faces as tears began to flow down their cheeks. Afterwards, we asked for those who knew they were saved to raise their hands and the whole lot raised their hands again. I then spoke on "The fig tree and receiving from God by faith." I was trying to lay a foundation of faith in their lives. All of us thought this was an excellent meeting and would have a lot of eternal consequences.

In the afternoon I had to wash my clothes as I was running out of clean things. It was a job as it was extremely hot. Our cook served us liver and onions with potatoes for lunch.

Some men of the Housa people from the North came around and we bargained with them for a while then we tried to talk to them about the Lord. We didn't get anywhere with them so we invited them to the meeting in the evening. Actually, we didn't know enough about Islam and how to approach them. We knew we would never convert them with argument and that is why we invited them to the meetings. We found that when the Muslims saw the miraculous power of the Lord in action they would become believers. Islam hadn't penetrated lower Nigeria very much at the time but in all the meetings, many Muslims accepted the Lord and they were mostly Housa people.

## The Witch Doctors

We loved to stop by the witch doctor's place which they had erected across the street to hinder people from going to the meetings. At first they would run at us and try to put hexes or curses on us and we would just laugh at them. They saw we were not afraid of them and would even pose for us to take their pictures. It had gotten so that we could talk to them and they would listen. I often said to them, "You have power, but only to curse, to hurt and destroy. We have no power to curse or hurt but rather power to heal through Jesus Christ. Healing is better than curses. Come to the meetings and if you don't see our God perform miracles before your eyes you don't have to believe a thing we say. Put your juju up against Jesus Christ and see who the one who blesses is." In a few days they shut down their operation and came to the meeting and accepted the Lord Jesus as their Savior.

## Up Against the Best

Let me say something that we found out about juju and witchcraft. It works mostly on fear but you have to believe in it. They did some powerful things with their curses and juju dolls to people. They did things that I'll never understand. We came up against the best in the business, who had been at it for many years and were feared by all of the townspeople. Our faith, however, rested on the mighty promises of God and therefore we were untouchable. They tried awfully hard to put curses on us but they didn't work and that was what turned them to Jesus. They couldn't do anything against us, yet we were always very friendly and kind to them.

The Lord Jesus said in Mark 16:17-18, "*And these signs shall follow them that believe; In my name shall they cast out devils; .....They shall take up serpents; and if they drink any deadly thing, it shall not hurt them . . .*" We considered juju and witchcraft to be a work of the devil through a person. Of course he was called the old serpent in Revelation 12:9. So when we broke the curses in Jesus' name, we were in a spiritual sense taking up serpents. That was and still is our understanding of those verses. Drinking *"any deadly thing"* was any potion the witch doctors might slip into our food or drink. The Lord also said to His disciples in Luke 10:19, "*I give unto you power to tread on serpents and scorpions, and over all the power of the enemy: and nothing shall by any means hurt you.*" We stood firmly on those promises and the Lord protected us.

## Could Not Be Cursed

That was our mind set as His disciples and we preached it everywhere we went boldly. We fully believed that as the children of God by faith in Jesus Christ, we were as invincible as the children of Israel were when the prophet Balaam tried to curse them in Numbers 23:7-8, " *. . . and Balaam said, Balak the king of Moab hath brought me from Aram .. . saying, Come, curse me Jacob, and come, defy Israel. How shall I curse, whom God hath not cursed? or how shall I defy, whom the LORD hath not defied?*" We fully believed this applied to us as well and constantly confronted the powers of darkness with the Word of the Living God and overcame in every situation.

## Deliverance with a Word

When the people were delivered, they didn't go through with some orgy or contortions. They didn't froth at the mouth, fall down or any such thing. It was so amazing. It was like it was said of the Lord Jesus, "*And they were all amazed, and spake among themselves, saying, What a* word is this! for with authority and power He commands the unclean spirits, and they come out." When we prayed en masse for the crowds of people, we took authority over all the power of the devil in Jesus' name and commanded him to release them. Instantly throughout the crowd you could see people released and set free from the bondage of the devil as the Lord set them free. Such joy filled the people's hearts to overflowing and they "let it all hang out."

## The Anointing

Another thing we held on to was *"the Anointing."* John said in 1 John 2:27, *"But the anointing which you have received from Him abides in you,*

**Vernon Sanders & Man Healed of Leprosy**

*and you do not need that anyone teach you; but as the same anointing teaches you concerning all things, and is true, and is not a lie, and just as it has taught you, you will abide in Him."* This *"Anointing"* was to us the very presence of the Lord Jesus Christ through the Holy Spirit, not only within but upon us that we could actually feel. It gave us a tremendous feeling of authority but we knew the power was not of us. It was God's authority upon us. As David said in 2 Samuel 22:30, *"For by You I have run through a troop: by my God have I leaped over a wall."* We took the verses in Isaiah 10:24-27 spoken about Assyria to be true of God's people today. The principle is the same. Verse 27 says, "It *shall come to pass in that day, that his burden shall be taken away from off your shoulder, and his yoke from off your neck, and the yoke shall be destroyed because of the anointing."* We found this to be absolutely true. The Anointing of the Holy Spirit would destroy the yokes in the lives of people. This we boldly proclaimed and the people received the benefits of it. It really worked.

## Imagine Yourself in Their Place

Put yourself in their shoes for a moment. Just imagine you had never heard anything of the gospel in your whole life nor had your ancestors. Here come some strange men, of a different color than you that stand on a raised platform and tell you about this "Jesus." Living in a society that was filled with supernatural things, though they were on the negative side, yet you fully believed in supernatural things. The first thing you want to see is if "their juju" was stronger than the juju in your area. These "white men" using a big black book they called the bible, tell you that this "Jesus" can forgive you of your sins and heal your body and if you don't see miracles happen you didn't have to believe them. All you have to do is to believe what they are saying. That all sounded reasonable and easy. So you watch very intently and suddenly you see a cripple you have known for years, suddenly stand up and dance. You see those large leprous white spots disappear in the blink of an eye. You see another person whom you knew to be weak and almost helpless. At the prayer they become strong and it lasted. A family member you knew to be absolutely blind and suddenly they can see. Can't you see the tremendous impact this had on these people? They were used to believing in the supernatural so it was no great step for them.

No wonder they came from far and wide to bring their friends and loved ones into those meetings and they were not disappointed. Gradually you begin to realize that there is something more involved here than healing and miracles. You hear them saying, "If you will repent of your sins, this Jesus will forgive you and come to live in your heart. You remember that you prayed for the spirit of your god to come live in your idol and you believed it happened so this is not too big a step for you. However it is a much greater event as He will live within you. You have seen so many miracles that you just cannot explain away so you believe their word and sure enough it happens to you. This revolutionizes a society!

## My Greatest Sermon!

Sanders and Alcock went to Tori, an outlying town, while Brown and I took the large meeting in Warri. The reason we did this was we didn't feel like all of us were needed in the one meeting and we could reach more people by splitting up. There was absolutely no friction about who would take the larger meeting. All of us wanted to be more than fair. The crowd looked like it was way more than 15,000 to both of us and I was supposed to speak. I read the first part of the scripture verse in Romans 16:20, "*And the God of peace shall bruise Satan under your feet shortly.*" Before one of the interpreters could say it, the crowd began stomping their feet. After a few minutes the Itshekiri spoke it and they did it again. Several minutes later the Urhobo spoke it and they were more intensely stomping their feet. Then when the other three spoke it, there was no holding them back. They stomped and stomped their feet in rhythm and it sounded like an earthquake. We tried and tried to get them to stop so I could go on. Finally in desperation, I tried again and they quieted some.

## I Give You Power

So I thought I would give them one last thought. I quoted part of the words of Jesus in Luke 10: 19 "*Behold, I give unto you power. . . . over all the power of the enemy: and nothing shall by any means hurt you.*" The whole crowd just took off stomping again. We went through the same thing again with each of the interpreters. This all took about an hour, so finally we prayed en masse for all of them and suddenly the Lord began to work wonders among them. Paraplegics were leaping up and dancing. The blind were weeping and shouting, "I can see, I can see." Lepers were being healed, the deaf were hearing. You name it and the Lord was sovereignly doing that for those who needed it done. It sounded like pandemonium but the miracles were happening before our very eyes instantly. Oh what joy filled the hearts of the people!

When we could get them quiet enough, we invited them to come and testify. They excitedly swarmed up to tell what the Lord had done for them. There were so many we finally had to cut them off as it was getting too late. What a meeting! To this day, I still think that was my greatest sermon of all time.

Of course in stepping off the platform we were surrounded with so many people. All they wanted to do was show us what they were healed of. They were so excited! I couldn't help but think, "We would be excited too if we had done to us what the Lord had done for them." So we took some time to talk with them and take their picture. I could recognize many of those with the visible ailments as we had seen them daily and had prayed for them individually at times before or after the meeting but this night was their night.

### How Large was the Crowd?

Harold Brown and I discussed how large the crowd was so I "stepped off" the meeting ground. It was 150 yards from the platform to the back of the crowd on each side. In front, it was 125 yards to the road. The road was 25 yards wide, they were 50 yards on the other side of the road. Out back, it was 75 yards in the rear from the platform to the back of the crowd. This put the crowd area at roughly a circle of 300 yards in diameter. I then "stepped off" a square yard and counted the average number of people that stood in it. There were five to six people in it.

### Let's do the Math

Now we don't want to make it sound bigger than it was so let's cut it back to 200 yards square and forget about the 300 yards in diameter. This would give us 40,000 square yards. Let's take the lower number of five per square yard and that would give us 200,000 people. Were there really that many people present? I really don't know, only eternity will tell. As for the distance being right, I had worked for the engineering department of the City of Baton Rouge, Louisiana and worked my way up to an Engineer 1. We were used to stepping off distance in yards as we had to do it so many times. Then at times, to make sure, we would measure it with a steel tape and we were always extremely close.

All I know is that the crowd seemed to be stretched out as far as you could see clearly and they packed as closely as they could. It wasn't like in America where people will not get that close to each other. In our letters home and in my journal, we "guess-timated" the largest crowd was 25,000. This day, we had "guess-timated" it to be about 15,000. Only the Lord knows the truth and it really doesn't matter how large it was. I've always said about the size of a crowd, "We have as many as we have and not one more or less."

## What are Numbers?

My feelings about numbers were that they didn't matter as you had however many you had. Regardless of the size, you came to minister to those who came. We had to turn numbers into the Missionary department so if we erred, we decided we would err on the low side. I was always reminded of David, the king of Israel when he wanted to number the people of Israel and Joab replied that they were all God's people. David got into real trouble with the Lord over that event.

My pastor had drilled into our heads that if you can't preach to one then you can't preach to ten thousand. We found this to be true. However, I still love to preach to a crowd. The more people you have, the greater the prospects of people turning to the Lord. Besides, there is a synergism created in a crowd that you don't have in a small group. Faith seems to inspire faith.

When we got back to the chalet and sat around a table of boiled pork, potatoes and carrots, Harold Brown told Alcock and Sanders about the meeting. They began kidding me about my great theological masterpiece and we had a big laugh. I was only grateful that the Lord sovereignly moved by His Spirit and did things one could only dream of. Yes to me, this was my greatest sermon – just parts of two scriptures!

## Four Days Journey by Dugout

March 3. After a breakfast of scrambled eggs on toast Brown and I went to speak and pray for the Olu's wives. We remembered that we were not supposed to touch the Olu's wives when we prayed for them. They were so appreciative for our coming as they were not allowed to go to the meetings. The Olu let us know that people were coming to the meetings from all over the region. He said, "Some had come four days' journey by dugout canoes from up and down the estuaries of the Niger River to get to the meetings. The first evening and all through that night men had sent out messages by big log drums and they began to come by the thousands." No wonder the meetings kept growing in size.

When we finished ministering to the Olu's wives, we joined Alcock and Sanders at the big meeting already in progress. There were about 5000 people out for the morning service. Sanders spoke a simple message and then prayed en masse for all of them. A great wave of healing swept over the crowd with so many miraculous things happening. He invited those who were healed to give their testimony with so many coming, but we couldn't have them all bear witness. I stood down in the congregation to take pictures and felt like I would burn up because it was so hot. You can't imagine how hot it was in the open sun with thousands of people and a high humidity.

### Finally They Want a Bible School

After a lunch of fish, green beans and potatoes, Babalola and Josiah came over to talk about a Bible School. Now they wanted one, was what they told us clearly. That was good news as that was what we felt would be needed to train young ministers in this area.

At the Post Office on the way back, I sent a cable to Mildred because some of the staff at the Wings of Healing were pressing us to have our wedding over here. I wanted her to know that I didn't feel good about us doing that. I didn't think it would be fair to our families and friends. So I told her I wanted an American wedding then we could return as missionaries. I also asked her to see if Doc wanted us to stay longer than the 17th of March as we still had no word from him.

### Tori Tori Tori

Harold Brown and I went to Tori while Alcock and Sanders took the big meeting in Warri. It was quite amusing as Harold was to lead off. He had told me he would just get up and say a few words then turn it over to me and I would have the main message. He started and preached for 45 minutes then turned to me and said, "Do you want to say a few words." I got up and said just a few words and prayed for the whole crowd.

It never ceased to amaze me how the Lord would begin to work among them in healing and miracles. It seemed so easy on our part and this made us realize it wasn't us but it was a sovereign work of the Holy Spirit. So many wanted to testify of healing or a miracle but there was no way that everyone could do so as it was getting dark and there were no lights. Our guess-stimation of the crowd at Tori was about 2000.

### Crowd Gets Greater in Warri

When we got back to the chalet, our cook had a lovely meal prepared of baked pork, fried potatoes and cabbage for supper. As we ate, Alcock and Sanders told us about the Warri meeting knowing that we were very interested. They said the crowd was as big as the last Sunday night which was about 25,000. Healing and miracles were still happening as they prayed for the whole crowd at once. I couldn't help but think, "They finally see the greater results by praying one prayer instead laying hands on individuals and praying for each one. It works but you have to build their faith first by your preaching or there won't be anything." There was no way you could pray for a crowd like that individually anyway.

## It Was so Hot!

March 4. After a breakfast of scrambled eggs and sausage with toast we went to the morning meeting at the big grounds. There were about 4000 people present when we began and it grew larger as it progressed. Brown spoke and did well ministering mostly about salvation. Our aim was to build a solid foundation of biblical truth about salvation so they would be firmly planted in the faith as it is in Jesus Christ. Only a few were healed for some reason. The sun was extremely hot, almost

Sanders, Alcock, Paul in Market

unbearable. We took some of those who were healed to the Olu's palace where we made a tape of their testimonies since he had electricity. The Olu testified of his healing and salvation on the tape as well.

When we arrived back at our chalet two Jehovah Witnesses met us wanting us to tell them what the Bible teaches. We thought they were in earnest but they just wanted to argue so we told them we didn't want to argue with them and for them to just come to the meetings. They would hear and see things that would revolutionize their lives.

The cook had a delicious meal of steak, macaroni, fried tomatoes and potatoes for lunch. I had to change a tire in the afternoon as it was looking quite bad. At the same time I tried to adjust the brakes but we didn't have a wrench to do so. There wasn't much pedal left.

## Condemnation versus Faith

Brown and I went to Tori again but the service wasn't very good. At first one of the African ministers got up when he saw a baby with some medicine beads around its neck and made the parents take it off. He really "laid the law down" not only to her but to the whole crowd. This seemed to throw a monkey wrench into things. We found you cannot have condemnation and faith at the same time. Condemnation will always destroy faith because faith works only in the brackets of the grace of God.

I then spoke but it was extremely hard and there were not a lot of results. The whole meeting seemed like it was full of confusion. They even started to take the offering before I could ask for testimonies. We had some gospel tracts that we gave out and the people almost swarmed us to get them. This made us realize the value of the printed page and this was something we'd have to use.

The attendance in the big meeting in Warri continued with around 25,000 with Alcock speaking and Sanders leading off. They said it continued on a high note with so many being healed they couldn't have them all to testify. It was so good to see them so excited.

## Good Food - Primitive Cooking

When we got back, we had leg of mutton, cabbage and potatoes for supper and it was very good. While these meals sounded good and we usually enjoyed them, things were not always as they seemed. If you saw how and where they were cooked, then you may not have eaten them. They didn't have pots and pans as we do in our kitchens. In fact, they didn't have a kitchen. They cooked outside on a little charcoal burner in nothing more than tin cans and such. The dishes were washed in a bigger tin can and we were not sure they were always clean. Some of our people wouldn't eat at first and fasted for a few days but if you are going to stay, you have to eat.

## Salvation and Healing

March 5. Before we went to the morning meeting, we had a hearty breakfast of eggs and sausage. Sanders spoke about knowing Jesus Christ as your Savior and gave a call for those who wanted to accept the Lord as their Savior. A great number responded and we prayed with them to make sure they truly received the Lord. The crowd was about the same size as before. He again prayed en masse for the people and a multitude were healed. Afterwards we had people that wanted to testify of a healing or a miracle to come up and testify. There still were so many we had to cut them off as the sun was just too hot. We dismissed them but they didn't hurry to leave. The Lord has sure done great things here and we were so thankful.

## The Hallelujahs Have Come

Back at the chalet we had a lunch of cold ham, salad, potatoes. In the afternoon for something to do as a change of pace, we went to the market. I always loved to walk in the market and meet people on the street. The market was very busy and filled with people buying stuff they needed for their meals. When they saw us, the people ran out of their shops and left their businesses to wave and shout hallelujah with the biggest smiles you ever saw. It was so amazing! Everywhere we went, a crowd would follow us shouting hallelujah, hallelujah! I guess they used that word because we used it so much in our preaching. From then on we were known as the Hallelujahs instead of the Oyebos. This city surely was made God conscious.

## Our Final Meeting in Warri

It was my time to speak in the evening meeting. The crowd was still running about 25,000 which was the same as the last evening. I spoke only about 20 minutes with the five interpreters so that was not a lot to give them. That didn't seem to matter, as again the Lord met His people when we unitedly called upon Him. When we invited them to accept Jesus as Savior thousands raised their hands. We prayed for them and as always, you could see the tears running down their cheeks as they wept their way into the kingdom of God. Then we wanted to allow as many as possible to testify of the wonders the Lord had done for them. It looked like hundreds were coming to testify from all over the audience. The testimonies ran for one whole hour even though each testimony was very short. Finally we had to stop them as it was getting too dark.

## Just Scratching the Surface

This was our final meeting in this wonderful town with such a wonderful people. Even with all that was accomplished; we knew we had only scratched the surface of what needed to be done. Churches would have to be raised up as people would need discipling. Schools would have to be built to educate the children. There must be a Bible School to train ministers. There was a vast amount of labor that would have to be done but this was a start and a good start at that. All of us knew that the longevity of the work depended on how quickly others could come in and raise up the community and local church superstructure.

Our cook had a lovely meal for us of delicious fish, peas and fried potatoes. We were so thankful we were still at the rest house. Actually none of us thought we would be able to stay in it as long as we had, but the Lord was good to us.

The Pastor of the Christ Apostolic Church who came with us asked for the money for our bill for the chalet and food. We gave him 70 pounds in West African currency for the bill so he went and paid it. He wanted us to go to the Eshoko district at some point in time and I whole heartedly agreed. In fact there were a large number of places calling for us to come. However, our immediate plans were already decided for us. Harold Alcock and Vernon Sanders would move over to Sapele while Harold Brown and I would go to Ikoro. Of course none of us knew what lay ahead. If we had, we would have done much differently.

## Never be the Same!

This had been a great time in the Lord with a tremendous break through. This town would never be the same again. We had started on February 21st and ended it on March 5th. In thirteen days of great meetings we were the little instruments in the hand of the Lord that changed the destiny of multiplied thousands of people. Paraplegics could now take their places in the economy of life. The blind could now live an ordinary life. People didn't have to live in fear of the juju priests anymore as many of them were converted. Many on their deathbeds could now look forward to a good life. It would launch this area into the modern world and they would take their place among the nations.

## A Feuding, a Fussing and a Fighting

From what we were told, this area along with Benin City had been a feuding and fighting place. It indeed had been a hostile environment. They told us that eighteen years before we came, they had burned some missionaries at the stake. Others, they tied to the big ant hills and let the ants devour them. I don't know if that was true but it came from reliable people and they never gave us any reason to doubt them. Why should we have been so blessed when others had to pay the supreme sacrifice? I don't have an answer to that. We were simply God's vessels at God's time and He did a sovereign work, shall I say, in spite of us. However, it doesn't matter what a person was, the blood of Jesus, God's only Son, cleanses us from all unrighteousness. I say, "Thank God for Calvary!" Without it, we could have been bloodthirsty savages. Speaking of savages, where could you find more bloodthirsty savages than the Anglos and Saxons that made up the English peoples? The gospel is what changed them and it did the same to these wonderful people.

## Too Much Fresh Pineapple

We had a chance to buy a couple of really ripe pineapples from a fellow that came to our door. So we sat down and ate both of them and then packed our stuff so we could leave first thing in the morning. The guys never realized what it would do to them.

March 6. We arose early but Alcock, Sanders and Brown were kind of sick as they had eaten too much fresh pineapple and it gave them diarrhea. Really, I ate as much or more than they did but didn't get sick because I had taken a dysentery pill before eating it. Erskine Holt had given me some before we left Portland and told me how to use them. So I kidded them awhile about not having faith then I felt guilty and told them what I had done. We had a laughing good time about it all.

## Back to Ilesha

Our breakfast consisted of eggs and sausage and it would be our last meal with this wonderful fellow, our cook. Harold Alcock and Vernon Sanders had to go speak to the Olu's wives first then he would take them to Sapele for their next meeting. We loaded the pickup and left Warri at 8:30 a.m. I had to drive so Harold Brown and Josiah sat in the front while my young Yoruba friend who came back with me rode in the back. I sure felt sorry for him but that was all we could do as he was the youngest. In Africa, age mattered. He didn't mind one bit as he was so thrilled to have been able to make the trip and see things he would never forget.

The generator on the truck again was charging too much so we stopped at the U. A. C. garage and had the regulator adjusted then drove on. It seemed like every time we were to make the trip between Warri and Ilesha, we had generator or regulator problems. Finally we arrived at the compound in Ilesha at 4:45 in the evening. It was a long hot and rough drive and all of us were beat but that didn't stop our excitement of getting mail.

## Lots of Mail

We had lots of mail waiting for us. There were several letters from Mildred. She was wondering just what I was going to do now. I hadn't realized I had written so many different things at different times. It was such an "on again, off again" thing about what we should do. Am I to stay longer? Am I to leave the 17th? The Eltons and all our guys thought it would be neat to have an African wedding and urged us to do so but I never felt good about all of that. Such intense pressure was put on us it seemed from everyone.

## More Difficulties

Sister Elton had such a lovely meal ready for us of fish, peas and fried potatoes. At the table Sidney Elton told us about more difficulties that had arisen. With the transition going on between England and Nigeria getting its independence things were changing rapidly. He said, now the government plans to take over all the schools and kick the proprietors out. This included their Teacher's Training School here in Ilesha as well as all the parochial elementary and high schools run by the missionaries. Things were not looking well at all for the schools.

## Back at the Teacher's Training School

March 7. A little oatmeal, a banana and one egg were all we wanted for breakfast. We just didn't feel much like eating. The morning service was at the Teacher's Training Center where Sidney Elton spoke. He did a very good job of ministering the Word. Of course Brown and I were thrilled that he did the speaking. We were just preached out.

Sister Elton and her cook had a delicious meal of Duiker, potatoes and carrots for dinner when we returned. Being so lifeless and weary, we all had a little nap in the afternoon. Then all of us went to the Teacher's Training Center at 7:00 p.m. and I spoke.

This was the first time in a good while that I had spoken without an interpreter and it sure seemed funny. I asked those who wanted to be filled with the Holy Spirit to come up front and five of them received the Baptism of the Holy Spirit. To me that was always one of the greatest thrills of all. When we got back to the compound, our cook had some cold pork and beets prepared for supper. We ate and hurriedly went to bed.

## Nice to do Nothing for a Change

March 8. Our breakfast was made up of oatmeal, grapefruit and scrambled eggs on toast. Brother Elton wanted me to take the GMC pickup to the mechanic this morning to get the brakes fixed but he was gone. On the way back we stopped so Harold could put some film in to get developed. Our cook prepared liver, potatoes and carrots for dinner. We took a little nap then Harold and I put a puzzle together. It seemed so nice not to have to preach and just to do nothing for a change.

In the evening we were invited over to Brother and Sister Woods', another Missionary couple's house for supper. They had fried chicken, potatoes, beets, cauliflower, cake, ice cream and coffee. I was a little sick at my stomach and couldn't enjoy it too much. There was no mail which was disappointing but expected. We had to wash our clothes as we had to hit the road the next day.

## Bound for Ikoro

March 9. We arose fairly early and had a hearty breakfast of grapefruit, oatmeal, eggs and bacon. We hurriedly packed our things along with all the camping stuff and loaded the pickup. Then we took Sister Elton downtown and got the mail. Wow! I had quite a bit too. However, Harold didn't have any and this made me feel so bad. Sister Elton and her cook had fixed us an early lunch of steak, potatoes and peas which we heartily devoured. Then we left for Ikoro at 1:45 p.m. and arrived at 3:45. It was only a two-hour drive this time.

## Not a Good Feeling

Somehow I didn't have a good feeling about this place. I couldn't help but wonder why we didn't go to the other places that were crying for us to come that didn't have a church. Why couldn't we go on the heels of the Warri Revival to the places around that area? My feelings were, if they had a church, let that church do the evangelism. Let's go to the regions beyond that didn't have a church and raise one up.

Upon arriving, we found out this was an Apostolic of Wales Church and they really wanted us to come. I realized that it would be good to have large outdoor meetings through a local church but we must have unity. Unity seemed to be a thing that was missing among the churches in this region at this particular time.

They put us in the Pastor's house. He lived upstairs in a two-story house. He moved to the bottom level and gave us the top floor for which we were very thankful as we would be able to get a little breeze. Each of us had a room and there was a dining room. So we set up our cots, unpacked the stuff and had some hot tea and visited with the pastor.

## The Meetings Start

The evening service was to start at 7:00 but it was 8:00 before it got under way. Harold spoke and did real well. I was thrilled as he was getting a little more polished. There was a good response to the Word with many being touched and healed. I was so tired and half sick so I went right to bed after the meeting. Sidney Elton stayed here with us.

We had heard there was a little trouble in this area as they wanted a European couple to come or they would go with the Apostolics rather than stay in fellowship with Sidney Elton and his group. This bothered me to no end. My feelings were not to make an issue of things like that but rather keep the unity of the faith in the bond of peace. We didn't need various groups taking sides and isolating themselves. Division has always been a disgrace in the church of God.

## Real Problems Confront Us

March 10. We had our grapefruit and oatmeal for breakfast then went to a business meeting at the church to try to settle the question the Apostolics had raised. Elton spoke a little on the outpouring of God and put the issue on the floor. However, the most influential man present was strongly in line with Bradford but after a little debate the Church said they wanted the revival. They asked me to say a few words about money as we were accused of buying Elton and the Apostolic Church, which didn't have an ounce of truth in it. That part of the meeting took 2 ½ hours but the other business took 2 ½ more hours but we had no part.

Our cook had prepared spam, fried potatoes and peas for lunch. I didn't eat much as I still felt sick. Afterwards, Sidney Elton left for the high country to get the Morrises at 2:15 p.m. and said he would be back on Friday. The meeting was held outside in the open air but the crowd wasn't very large as it wasn't advertised properly. With problems like they were having, it's no wonder. I spoke and there was a good anointing. I hammered away on faith and prayed en masse for them and the Lord really moved by His Spirit. I don't know how many were healed but a good number came and testified. After it was all over, we had leftover spam for supper.

## A Disappointing Turnout

March 11. The morning meeting started at 6:00 which was the earliest we had ever started. Harold spoke and did well but the crowd was very small with only about 125 people out. This was so disappointing but you go on and minister to whoever you have and do the best you can. Afterwards we had our breakfast of grapefruit, oatmeal and scrambled eggs on toast.

It was thrilling when three little girls came up to welcome us and were they ever cute. I just had to take their picture and of course they were delighted. Everybody seemed so wonderfully friendly to us in spite of the religious problems. For lunch we had Palm oil chop but it made Harold sick as it was too rich. I thought it wasn't quite hot enough with pepper to suit my taste but I thoroughly enjoyed it.

In the afternoon, Elton and the Morrises came by on their way back to Ilesha. It was nice to meet these servants of God. Elton promised to come back Sunday morning to get us.

With so much time on our hands we got so restless as there was nothing to do it seemed. We would read our Bibles and pray but still there was lots of time left. We got so lonely at times as we were shut off from the rest of the world. We were bored stiff in between the services!

### A Scorpion Bite Healed

We went to the evening meeting but rain was threatening terribly so we prayed and sure enough it held off till right after the meeting. Harold spoke and quite a few were healed and came up to testify. They carried a woman in that looked like she was in a coma. A huge poisonous scorpion had stung her. So we began to pray and she came to, being healed instantly. Oh, how the crowd rejoiced when they saw that.

### So Small After So Large

March 12. It was terribly hard to get up and get going for the 6:00 morning meeting. I spoke and really enjoyed speaking if no one else did. I just hammered away on salvation and really knowing Jesus. A good number came up to receive the Lord and we prayed for each of them. It was very cool and damp because of the rain storm the evening before.

Our cook prepared us some eggs on toast for breakfast after the meeting. We started on a walk downtown but it rained us out. After a while we did complete the walk "downtown" such as it was in this village. Of course after Warri, this seemed terribly small.

Before lunch we played a game of dots as there was nothing else to do. We had no books or anything to read other than our bibles. We would, of course, read our Bibles by the hour and pray but we still had time on our hands with the meetings so far apart. Needless to say we were bored half to death for lack of activity. We had fish out of a can and fried potatoes for lunch. I got so lonesome in the afternoon I could almost have pulled my hair out. I wrote a letter to Mildred, read my Bible, prayed and slept but still time passed so slowly.

A little later, the chief of the town came to visit us so I took his picture along with his Court and Queen. He even called her "Love." The service was late in starting as it had been cool all day long. When it's a bit cool, the people don't like to get out of their homes and go to an open air meeting. I spoke and there was quite a few healed of all kinds of maladies. In fact only a few were left that were sick. For supper after the service we had potatoes, spam and peas. We went to bed at 10:00 so we could get up in time for the morning meeting.

### Still Bored Half to Death

March 13. We were at the meeting by 6:00 for the morning service and I spoke. There weren't very many out as it was quite cold from the storms. Regardless, it was a very good service. I taught on salvation through Jesus Christ and how you could know you were saved. The people seemed to really appreciate it.

For breakfast we had eggs on toast again. Then we took a walk downtown into the market. It was interesting to see how the Housa People killed their cattle and sold it in the market. Of course flies would cover it, if you didn't keep them shooed off. When we came back, I lay on my cot since there was nothing else to do. Fighting lonesomeness here seemed to be a full time job as it was so long between the services. I couldn't help but think, if only I knew for sure whether I was going home on the 17th or staying! It would have helped considerably.

For lunch we had a delicious meal of steak, potatoes and peas. The steak came from the market where they had slaughtered the cows. No doubt it was some of the fly-covered meat we saw in the market as there was nowhere else to buy it. In fact all of our meats and vegetables came out of the markets most of the time. Peter was a very good cook. Sometimes he just didn't have access to anything better.

We studied, prayed and slept the rest of the day till time to get ready for the evening meeting at 6:00. Harold spoke but there wasn't any response at all. That really makes a person feel discouraged. This was our first encounter with something like this. Though we've had some good meetings, it was very tough here. I couldn't help but think of the other places that had wanted us to come. How much better it would have been to have gone there while "the iron was hot." However, we went where Sidney Elton and his group wanted us to go and this was it. I'm sure it would have been a far different story to have gone to the other towns. At least in them, we wouldn't have had other churches working against us because there wouldn't have been any. After the service we had corned beef, potatoes and peas for supper. After a meeting like that nothing tasted good.

### Ugly Things Behind the Scene

March 14. I didn't sleep very much and awakened early being troubled about the schisms here. We had grapefruit, oatmeal and an egg for breakfast. We went to the service debating who was going to speak this morning. Elton drove up so we went out to see him and convinced him he should speak. He did and it was really good and timely.

After the service they had an elders meeting and it lasted two hours. Elton found out that all of his and our ideas were being leaked out to those opposing. Dan, a prominent man in the Church, knew all about it but didn't tell anyone. Bradford was sure doing a lot of dirty work behind the scenes sowing discord among the members of the local church. No wonder we were having a difficult time here and the attendance being way down. This would be the last meeting here and we were glad to hit the road.

Regardless of the problems, there were a lot of people brought to the Lord and many healed of so many impossible diseases and afflictions. The lady who was brought into the meeting was alive because our God answered prayer. Now they all had a new lease on life. So it was well worth our effort though I still think we would have accomplished much more in unreached villages. That was where my heart was. Like the Apostle Paul, I always wanted to go to the regions beyond.

For lunch we had baked chicken, potatoes and carrots for dinner and then went out to see the chief of Ikoro to tell him goodbye. He was a gracious man and a joy to be with. He gave us a half dozen eggs as a present for coming.

### Finally Directions Come

We left Ikoro at 3:45 in the afternoon for Ilesha and arrived at 5:40. We had lots of mail and three telegrams. The telegrams said it was okay for me to return home on March 17 and also Paul Shaver would be returning from Ghana at the same time.

We hurriedly cleaned up and went to the Teacher's Training Center where Brother Morris spoke. He did a very good job of it. However, his speaking was delayed as it came a cloud burst of rain. Having a tin roof, it was so noisy that you couldn't distinguish his words so we sang until it let up. It was a long song service but we all really enjoyed singing and praising the Lord. When we got back to the compound, our cook had canned salmon, cheese and beats for supper. All of us had a big powwow and discussed the Nigerian situation till real late.

### Troubled In My Spirit

March 15. I didn't sleep much as I was troubled about Bradford's divisive work, so I prayed most of the night. Then I got up really early and had a good time of studying my Bible. How wonderful that the Lord meets us in His Word. For breakfast we had grapefruit, oatmeal and an egg. For relaxation we put a puzzle together. For lunch we had a meal of Duiker, potatoes and carrots.

About 3:30 in the afternoon Harold Alcock and Vernon Sanders came in and had a great report of the meetings in Sapele. They said the crowd had doubled in size and ran about 35 to 40 thousand. That was so thrilling to me as I was hoping by that, they would be launched into greater meetings. However, they didn't give us many particulars as to how many people were saved or healed.

### The Atmosphere Changes

The atmosphere suddenly changed when Alcock and Sanders came in. It seemed to upset everything and everybody. We couldn't help but wonder what in the world was going on. On top of that, I got a confusing wire from Max Wyatt saying for me to stay till after the conference in Accra, Ghana. But it was too late in getting to me and was of no use anyway. The Eltons took the night off and went over to the District Officer's home for supper. Consequently we had cold duiker, canned meat, onions, tomatoes and eggs for supper.

When we were eating, Harold Alcock mentioned about recruits not going home when they want to. I questioned if he was talking about me and he proceeded to give me a good bawling out. I held my peace but couldn't help but wonder what was ailing this man. Did he know something I didn't know? Who was he getting his information from anyway? So I went to bed deeply troubled.

## Conflict Among Us

March 16. We were awakened by Alcock and Sanders knocking on the door. They wanted to get their shaving stuff. All of us got dressed and went to breakfast. We had grapefruit, corn flakes, egg and ham and it was delicious. The fellows went to their rooms but I lingered as Sister Elton wanted to talk with me alone. She wanted to know about the hostile atmosphere between Sidney Elton and Harold Alcock. I simply told her that I didn't know but anyone could certainly tell that the situation was critical.

After I went to my room Alcock came and asked me what kind of a report I was going to take back to the Wings of Healing. I told him it would be a positive report such as I had given in all my correspondence to them and Mildred but I wanted to get to the bottom of the conflicting orders. Things didn't look good and I felt it was my duty to leave and tell Dr. Wyatt just what the set up was and all the problems we were having. After all, I had been ministering almost every day for five months and was just worn out. Besides the wire said Paul Shaver was returning home March 17th and we had come together.

## Such Royal Treatment

Sister Elton and her cook fixed us a real English favorite meal for lunch. It was Yorkshire pudding, roast beef, potatoes and carrots. She did this especially for me as I was leaving and this would be my last big meal with them. I packed all my stuff and I was a little overweight.

Feeling so crushed inside at the problems we were causing each other, I decided to take a walk to a nearby village. As I walked all alone, I talked to the Lord just asking for His help in this situation and for His direction. When I got back, it was suppertime. We had a light meal of sausage and bread.

We all retired to the living room where Sidney Elton, Harold Alcock, Harold Brown and I began to compare notes from Portland. We were amazed that each one of us was sent different stories and instructions. This explained the hostile attitude that had come between some of us. Because of the problems in the church different people in different departments were sending conflicting orders. Mildred was in the inner circle with the Wyatts and got her information straight from them which she sent to me. So all of us including Vernon Sanders decided the only thing for us to do was for me to return home and try to get this thing settled since I had been there the longest. This made me feel a whole lot better. We went to bed at 10:00 and tried to get a little rest.

## Homeward Bound!

March 17. Alcock, Sanders, Elton and I arose at 3:30 and left at 4:00 in the morning for Lagos and arrived at 9:45. That was a rough five and three quarter hour ride. We stopped at the Immigration Office where they gave me a return visa to Nigeria. Sidney Elton couldn't go to Accra, Ghana for the big convention because he didn't have a passport as they had lost his and were looking for it.

All of us looked at some cars with Alcock and Sanders and they ended up buying a little Volkswagen bus for 700 pounds plus insurance. It really looked sharp. This give them their own transportation and free them from having to be at the mercy of a missionary.

It was terribly hot in Lagos especially with my blue wool suit on. The four of us had dinner at the Bristol Hotel. We had their mixed grill that was made up of steak, sausage, liver in an omelet with cabbage and potatoes.

They took me to the airport where I weighed in at 2:15 in the afternoon and wasn't over weight. I had my camera bag on my shoulder and they didn't want to let me by with it. They wanted me to open it but I told them my camera and film was in it but I didn't say anything about the book end I had in it. Also I had one in my over coat plus my Bible but they let me through. We all got on the plane and we left Lagos at 3:45 and arrived at Kano at 6:05 p.m.

## An Extremely Emotional Time

I was thankful I had a window seat, so as our plane was climbing, I could see the African jungle with the villages of mud huts and thatched roofs. My heart felt like it would break. I was overcome with emotion and tears filled my eyes. I couldn't help but weep for all of those who had never heard the wonderful gospel of our Risen Lord. How I would have loved to have stayed and ministered to this wonderful people as their needs were so great but there were so many insurmountable problems that had to be worked out and required me going home at this time. There was no way we could go on with conflicting orders coming from home. This war that had been going on inside of me now for almost three months and it finally broke loose as I wept over those who had never had a chance to hear. I wanted so badly to stay and go to the unreached villages the kings had invited us even in the Muslim North. My eyes and heart were glued to the various villages as we flew over them. There were areas of dense jungles then a clearing filled with mud huts with thatch roofs. Then clearings of the little farms cut out of the jungle. I wept and prayed earnestly that the gospel would reach them before it was too late. I couldn't help think how much more we could accomplish for the Kingdom if there could simply be unity among the churches.

## More Plane Trouble

The country became more arid when we got closer to Kano, Nigeria. Our plane landed and we stayed on the plane as they boarded the new passengers. We took off at 6:45 in the evening which was a little early and got out a half hour or so and turned around and came back. I thought, "Oh boy, here we go again." When we landed, they told us to take our night cases to the airport hotel as they had trouble with the plane. They provided us with a delicious meal of chicken, potatoes, carrots and peas for supper at the hotel. They said we would leave at midnight so we all sat around the airport lobby waiting. When midnight came and the plane still wasn't fixed, they gave us rooms. We were told to arise at 5:30 as we were to leave at 7:00 the next morning.

## A lovely Tour of Kano Free

March 18. I was awakened at 6:30 and hurriedly shaved and dressed and ran to the Hotel lobby only to find out the plane wasn't leaving till 10:00 a.m. So I went to breakfast provided by the Airline. I had fruit juice, eggs and ham for breakfast. The B. O. A. C. Airline took us on an excursion trip downtown to the old city of Kano and what a lovely experience it was. The houses were made of mud. The Masque of Kano was nice looking. We saw the mud wall around the Emir's Palace and various other sites. It was so interesting to visit the vats where they dyed their cloth. We came back at 10:00 only to find lunch to be at the hotel at 12:30 and we were to leave at 2:00 p.m. Finally we left and flew all night.

## So Cold in London!

March 19. As the morning broke, we were flying over the Swiss Alps. The scene was absolutely gorgeous to say the least. What a sight to wake up to. When we landed in London, it was very cold and raining. B. O. A. C. put me in a nice hotel in downtown London since I had missed my flight to New York. The room was very cold because there was no heat in those days. I had my overcoat on but I was still very cold. Just coming in from the tropics and near the equator, I probably felt it more. So I got some hot food and went to my room. It still was so cold, so I got in the bath tub and made the water as hot as I could stand it and just laid in it awhile.

Then I jumped out, dried quickly and jumped into bed under a big thick down comforter and finally got warm. We left the next day in the evening on TWA for New York City, flying all night.

### First Contact with My Family

March 20. We arrived at the Idlewilde Airport (Kennedy now) in New York. I called Mildred first and talked to her. What a joy to talk with my bride to be. Then I called my Mom to let her know I was in New York. She cried when she heard my voice. She always cried when I came home or left. It was always tough hearing my mother cry. I wished her a happy birthday which would be in two days. Then I went to a restaurant and got me a big hamburger with lettuce and tomato. It was the one thing I craved so much during our Africa stay and it was very good. I flew on to Portland on United, flying all night.

### Arrival in Portland

March 21. We arrived in Portland about 8:00 on Sunday morning. Mildred was there to meet me with our close friends, Paul Metcalf and Daleva Harriman. It was so cold and I felt like I was freezing. We had breakfast together and went to the school. We walked into the school foyer just as Doctor and Evelyn Wyatt were leaving for church. They were all smiles and we ran to each other and hugged each one. They seemed so delighted to have me home. I told Doc that I had some things that I needed to talk over with him. He said that would be fine.

### A Final Note:

I was made an assistant pastor to Dr. Wyatt and taught in the Bible School for almost a year. I sat in with Dr. and Mrs. Wyatt meeting with ministers from Lebanon, Europe, Africa, Australia and many other countries wanting teams to come. Mrs. Wyatt told me on several occasions they were so proud of me and the work I had done. They appreciated all of the honesty in handling the money. I had brought back over $1100.00 of the money they had given and sent to me for my personal use. All of us were very frugal in all of our expenses. After all we felt it was God's money.

Paul Shaver returned home from the Gold Coast (Ghana) a week later. He had stayed for the big convention in Accra. A few months later, he married Gwen Upfold, his sweetheart and taught in the Bible School.

Mildred and I were married on May 1, 1954 in Salem, Oregon at Faith Tabernacle in Salem, Oregon, her home church, by her pastor and my dear friend, Max Wyatt. She worked in the Wings of Healing office, pulling money and reading mail. Thousands of requests for prayer came in almost daily. They always removed the letter and put the name of the person and their requested needs for prayer on the outside of the envelope. Those were put in open boxes and taken to the prayer room where a lady in charge saw that they were individually prayed over at least three times before being discarded.

When Harold Alcock Vernon Sanders came back, we talked at length about the work in the Delta Province. They said the meetings in Sapele were twice what the Warri meetings were in everything. The crowds were twice the size and the miracles and salvations were twice the number as well. We compared their pictures of Sapele with ours of Warri and you could easily see that what they were saying was true. It thrilled me to no end to know they had done so well. That was our original vision and it had worked.

### Other Teams Sent

Wings of Healing sent several other teams over in the next few months to both Ghana and Nigeria. Those in Ghana worked with the team Paul Shaver had left behind when he returned home. Harold Alcock and Vernon Sanders traveled and worked with the teams in Nigeria till they returned home. This way the new ones could break into ministering in large meetings and get the swing of things. They went to many of the places that had called for us to come and opened up a number of new regions for the gospel both in Nigeria and Ghana. According to their reports their meetings ran similar to the meetings we had. To me, this was full proof the vision could be transferred to others and they could carry it out.

All of this was only a small beginning to redeem a land. It simply ignited a fire that has been carried to many other lands by the Nationals, themselves. We know that we were only tiny instruments in the hands of an all-powerful Lord. He was the One Who gave the vision and sovereignly carried it out. Certainly, all praise and honor go to Jesus Christ our Risen Lord! I truly feel like Paul when he said to Timothy, *"I thank Christ Jesus our Lord who has enabled me, because He counted me faithful, putting me into the ministry."* 1 Timothy 1:12.

# The Between Years
# Chapter 10

Harold Brown returned home and married his sweetheart and in a few years passed away as a result of Hodgkin Disease. In fact, Harold Alcock, Vernon Sanders and Sidney Elton also died with Hodgkin Disease, the Nigerian variety so we were told by Vernon Sander's daughter years later.

We served faithfully and resigned from our posts at the Wings of Healing in January of 1955 to take the pastorate of a church in Gulfport, Mississippi. So we sold all our stuff and bought a little 4'X4' trailer which we pulled behind our 1950 Olds Eighty-eight.

Mildred was expecting our first child in February 1955. It was an extremely difficult move to make as it was a long way from Portland, Oregon to Gulfport, Mississippi in the dead of winter. Mildred was due to have our baby in about two to three weeks. We did go with her doctor's blessings and orders. Her Mother came along with us as well. All three of us made the trip in good shape and our first child, Philip, was born Feb 3, 1955 in Baton Rouge, Louisiana. An amazing thing was that the doctor didn't charge us one red cent and the hospital really cut their bill to a fraction. Indeed the Lord had taken good care of us. Later, we had two more sons, Thomas and Mark. Both are very active in missions today. All three of our sons have been a delight and we thank the Lord for such wonderful sons. Indeed the Lord has blessed us abundantly.

Harold Alcock went back after awhile and continued to look after the works in the Delta Province of Nigeria till he physically couldn't do so anymore. Years later, he asked Bethesda Missionary Temple in Detroit to take the oversight over the area. They did and sent a number of missionaries who were there for more than ten years and then turned it over to the local brethren.

## Serving in Mexico!

We served a term in Mexico shortly after we were married, working with Nuevo Esperanza Bible School in San Juan de Sabenas, Coahuila. It was moved to Monterey later. We went without any pledged support but believing the Lord would supply our every need and He did. One time we had no food left and no funds, so we prayed together that the Lord would supply our need. I was so impressed of the scripture in Isaiah 65:24, *"And it shall come to pass, that before they call, I will answer; and while they are yet speaking, I will hear."* We went to the Post Office in Rosita and there was a letter from a friend in Orofino, Idaho with a check in it for a hundred and fifty dollars. This made our car payment and provided the necessary things of life. The amazing thing was that a month before, she was praying for us when the Lord spoke to her heart to send the money. The problem was that she didn't know where we were. It took her a while to find our address but the letter arrived on the very day we needed it. We were so thankful that the Lord heard us long before we even called upon His name.

We were helping Bible Students plant churches in unreached villages, off the beaten path, where the gospel had never been preached. Most of these villages didn't even have a road leading to them, only wagon trails. It was amazing what was accomplished by these students. We would take them to villages two by two and leave them for a month or so and they would go from house to house witnessing for the Lord. Someone would invite them to stay with them and feed them just as Jesus had said. They would then have a meeting in the evening which would be the start a local church. On these trips, because there was no place to stay, we slept in the back of the pickup truck under a tarpaulin. We saw whole villages turn to the Lord and in time they built their own church building. Most of our work of church planting was done south of Ciudad Victoria and Matehuala.

## Off to Cuba

Upon leaving Mexico, we were asked to go to Cuba as the civil war had been won by Fidel Castro. He was asking for hundreds of protestant ministers to come and help rebuild the country. Our home church sent me down to look at things and find a place to live in Guantanamo and buy some property to start a Bible School like we had in Mexico. While there, I was able to minister to Castro's troops in many locations and they received me with open arms. Many of them accepted the Lord.

A prominent Banker in Guantanamo took me out to see a piece of property to buy but while there, he took me aside and said, "Reverend, don't buy any land right now as there are things happening in our government that I can't tell you about. Just don't do anything now." I thanked him and went back to the hotel room, wondering what that was all about.

A few days later when we returned from the evening meeting at the church, we noticed armed troops circling downtown in cars. I hurriedly went into my room at the hotel. The next morning, my friend, Pastor Rolando Perez Santana, and I caught the bus to Havana and noticed troops with guns, such as BARs, sticking out the windows of cars. The newspaper said a small plane from the USA had dropped a bomb on Havana & showed the pictures. We wondered what was going on.

We stopped en route in many of the cities to see other missionaries but they had all left for the States and we couldn't help but wonder why. In Havana we had some large meetings with a lot of the troops present and they were all delightful with many of them accepting the Lord as well. There didn't seem to be a problem but you could feel the uneasiness.

### Returning Home!

After several days we went to the airport to return home. When I checked in, they informed me that diplomatic relations had been severed with the USA and I couldn't take any money out of the country. So I gave all I had to Rolando except a quarter and got on the plane. It was one of the last US planes to leave Cuba. Arriving in New Orleans, I called my pastor friend, Charles Green, and told him that I was hungry and only had twenty-five cents in my pocket and had used a dime to call him. He told me to stay there and he would be right there and we would have a meal together. He did, and then I caught my plane on home. Later we found out that Rolando was arrested and thrown into prison in Santiago de Cuba where he spent several years and died of pneumonia.

Later, we planted the Church of New Hope in Muskegon, Michigan and pastored it for twenty-six years. The Lord spoke to both of our hearts, a year earlier, to resign the church and begin traveling in ministry. After presenting it to the church, they voted to have our son, Thomas, to be the senior pastor and I would assist in a time of transition.

During this time of pastoring we had a big outreach to Haiti with Paul and Tressie Sitko of Wheeling, West Virginia. We ministered there several times and helped to finance others working there to establish a Bible School and medical facilities. Out of this pioneer work, Peter and Patricia Gruits came down and with a lot of hard work and lots of prayer, establish Rhema, Inc. They have done a great work in Haiti.

### A Deadly Disease Hits!

In February 1988, I came down with what my family doctor called, "traveling arthritis." I was having a hard time breathing as it seemed to be in my lungs and all my joints ached. We held a meeting at a Church in Indianapolis, Indiana with Paul and Eleanor Stern. When Eleanor saw the difficulty I was having in breathing, she said, "I'm going to call Dr. Bill Hensold, a doctor in our church and see if He will see you." She did and he heartily agreed to see me as we had known him from earlier meetings we had in the Rock Church where the Sterns pastored. Paul invited us to minister for them the next Sunday and we could stay with them. After an extensive examination and a few tests, he determined it was rheumatoid arthritis. Then he got word from the laboratory saying to take more blood samples. This time they took 8-10 vials of my blood and sent it to the lab for 21 tests. The results were that what looked like rheumatoid arthritis had now become full-blown Hodgkin disease. The normal life expectancy at the time was only about a year. Mildred's sister, who had been a missionary to Cuba, had died with Hodgkin disease several years earlier. Dr. Bill said, "Don't worry, we'll pray for you." They did and I felt sure I was in the safe keeping hands of our Lord. Unknown to us at the time, the other four men of our team who went to Warri and Sapele had died with Hodgkin disease, the Nigerian variety.

## We Still Continued to Minister!

We had a Sunday morning and evening meeting in Walker, LA at Revival Temple where our friend, W. S. McMasters was the pastor. Mildred had driven all the way as I was too weak to drive. It was winter so I turned the car heater up to 90 degrees because I felt like I was freezing yet she was roasting. Saturday night, she had to put several pillows under my head because I was having such a difficult time breathing. The next morning, she said, "Dear, you can't go to church and preach this morning, you're too weak." I replied that I had to because the Lord had given me a word for them.

When we walked into the auditorium and I saw the long aisle and the platform having several steps, I cried out to the Lord for help. How could I possibly climb those steps to the platform, but I made it. Being so weak, I remained seated during the singing. It was a very good time of worship, with the congregation really entering into the Lord's presence.

Pastor McMasters then walked to the pulpit and began to sing an old song we used to sing in the depression days. It was written by Charles P. Jones back around 1900. He started with the words of my text that the Lord had burdened my heart with. It is found in Genesis 32:24-28. *"And Jacob was left alone; and there wrestled a man with him until the breaking of the day. And when he saw that he prevailed not against him, he touched the hollow of his thigh; and the hollow of Jacob's thigh was out of joint, as he wrestled with him. And he said, Let me go, for the day breaketh. And he said, I will not let thee go, except thou bless me. And he said unto him, What is thy name? And he said, Jacob. And he said, Thy name shall be called no more Jacob, but Israel: for as a prince hast thou power with God and with men, and hast prevailed."* He started with the second stanza and sang the chorus:

> As Jacob in the days of old,
> I wrestled with the Lord;
> And instant, with a courage bold,
> I stood upon His Word.
> I would not be denied,
> I would not be denied,
> Till Jesus came and made me whole,
> I would not be denied.

## Then he led the third verse and chorus:

> Old Satan said my Lord was gone

And would not hear my prayer;
But praise the Lord, the work is done,
And Christ the Lord is here.
I would not be denied,
I would not be denied,
Till Jesus came and made me whole,
I would not be denied.

So I said to the Lord, *"If he sings that verse again, I'm going to stand up though I feel so weak."* He not only sang it twice but about a half a dozen times and such an awesomeness of the Lord came into the meeting. I stood up on the second time and lifted my hands in praise and suddenly the weakness seemed to drain out of my legs. The presence of the Lord was so mighty that during my preaching some stood up and were filled with the Holy Spirit while I was speaking.

That evening I preached again and it was another powerful service. Afterwards, Pastor McMasters had me step down in front and said he wanted the elders to come and they would pray for me. He knew absolutely nothing of what I was suffering from. They all prayed and then he began to a prophecy. Basically, his word was that the Lord would destroy the infection and remove the inflammation and indicated it would be over a period of time. From that day forth, we began to notice that each day, I was a little better than I was the day before. The color of my skin began to change on a daily basis though it didn't seem like much. I went from an extreme pale color to a robust color. Finally, I walked right out of that valley praising my Lord.

### The Clincher!

We were ministering in a retreat near Lancaster, Pennsylvania with Paul and Eleanor Stern and their son, Philip. Our son Mark was traveling in meetings with Dr. Eldon Wilson in many cities in Mexico, Guatemala, El Salvador, Honduras and had crossed Nicaragua and were in Costa Rica. They were going to fly to Panama where Mark would fly back to the states but that flight wouldn't leave till late the next day. The Noriega revolution had broken out in Panama and the door was closing fast for Americans to get out.

During the night I was awakened by the Lord with a word for Mark. He gave me the name of the airline, the specific flight number and time of departure. So I called Mark and was able to reach him by phone and told him the Lord said he had to be on a certain flight by Pan American Airlines to Panama City with the number of the flight and time and flight into Philadelphia. I told him that he had to be on that flight because the other one would not make it. He said I can't get to the airport in time. He did make it in time and flew into Panama City and his plane was one of the very last ones Noriega let leave. A young lady in the church picked him up and brought him to the retreat where we had two ministers with their sons ministering. It was a great time together.

## The Enemy Attacks!

Mark drove our car home after the meetings were over because I was so weak and could hardly breathe. We stopped at a rest area in Ohio but I stayed in the car. The devil began whispering to me, *"See you thought you were healed but it has come back in full force."* I replied that I had a word of prophecy that said I would be healed. He said, *"How do you know the prophecy is true."* I said that I believed it was true. He replied *"Haven't you heard a lot of so called prophecy that didn't come to pass."* Instantly fear began to grip me and I cried out to the Lord.

The Lord was so gracious and He spoke a scripture to me about Jehoshaphat, King of Judah when several armies were coming against him. Into that hopeless situation, the Lord gave them a word of direction. Part of it was the word He spoke to me that day. It's found in 2 Chronicles 20:20, *"Believe in the LORD your God, so shall ye be established; believe his prophets, so shall ye prosper."* Suddenly I realized that Brother McMasters had given me that word and I had believed it and had been doing much better. So I declared that I knew Brother McMasters was a real man of God and a true prophet and I believe him. I quoted the above scripture declaring that I believed His prophets. In that instant of time, I was on top of things and over the Hodgkin disease.

We continued in meetings all over the country. Meanwhile, Dr. Hensold was trying to get me in to see a Specialist in Muskegon. It took three months before I could get in to see one as they were all so busy. When I finally did see the Specialist, I was feeling great and walking three miles a day. I gave him the full printed report from Dr. Hensold. When he heard I had been in Nigeria, he said I want to do some further testing. He then took many blood samples and had twenty-five tests run. Every one of them came back normal. His exact words were, "Reverend, I don't know what you had but what you had, you don't have any more. You're the healthiest man in the county." I thanked him for his work and went on my way rejoicing.

## Hit With Another Deadly Disease!

A month later, the Specialist wanted me to come in for a routine exam. Probing around all over my body and feeling my throat, he found a lump on my thyroid. He took three biopsies and sent me to the hospital for a sonogram. The technician did one and then he did another one which kind of made me nervous. In a few days, the Specialist called and said he wanted to see me, so Mildred and I went in. His report was that all three of the biopsies and both sonograms showed that I had a large tumor on my thyroid and it was a melanoma. He said that I must have radical thyroid surgery as soon as possible and he was sending me to see an Oncologist.

He then asked how old I was and I told him fifty-seven. He said, "That doesn't help at all. Because at your age, nothing we can do will help and you will be gone before the end of the year. We thought the cancer was all gone but it had localized in your thyroid but you should have it removed anyway." Being so startled, I had to bite my lip to keep from crying before him. This report was so shocking because I had really been feeling great and excited about life. When we got alone, Mildred and I discussed it and both of us wept. We called our married sons, Philip and Thomas and they came over with their wives and joined with Mark, our youngest son, and us in prayer as we all wept before the Lord. I told the church the following Sunday morning and they all gathered at the front and began to pray for me. Again, we all wept before the Lord. It still was so unbelievable!

### God's Word Changes the Outlook!

The following Wednesday, feeling terribly discouraged, I went out in the woods behind our church and sat on an old log and just cried my heart out. I had often gone to this spot to pray and wrestle with many difficult problems one finds in pastoring. I said to the Lord, "I don't think it's fair to be smitten with a deadly disease twice in one year. It was so hard climbing out of that valley of Hodgkin disease and now I'm smitten with a melanoma and told I wouldn't see the next year."

After I had cried all I could cry, the Lord spoke to me and here is what He said, "That doesn't help anything." Suddenly, I realized I was just having a "pity party." At that moment, I realized deep within me that it wasn't a question of how long I lived but what I did with my life while I lived. In eternity, what difference would a year or ten years make, if it wasn't spent building and strengthening the Kingdom of God? Then I said, "Lord, forgive me, I'm getting up from here and with Your help I'm going to do all that I can for Your Kingdom as long as You give me life. I'm not going home and just lie down and die. I don't know if I have six weeks, six months or six years to live but I'm going to do all I can to reach as many people for you and strengthen all I can."

### Radical Surgery!

With a lot of counsel with my family, my colleagues and Dr. Hensold, I went to see the Oncologist. His determination was the same as the Specialist, so he scheduled me for surgery to remove all of my thyroid glands. I will never forget as they were getting me ready in the operating room, a big doctor stood over me and said he was the anesthesiologist and he was going to insert this big pipe in my mouth and they would take over my breathing. I thought, "My God, I've never trusted man in my whole life, I'm looking to You to bring me out of this thing." Immediately, I was out like a light. When I came to, they took me to my room. The Oncologist came bouncing in and seemed very pleased. He said, "Reverend, you still have all the parts that you came in with. I operated and could hardly find the tumor as it had shrunk to less than the size of a peanut. We checked it and it is not a melanoma but an adenoma and it had shrunk so much I could hardly find it, so that was all I removed." He asked how I was feeling and I said fine. So he said I could go home the next day and do whatever I wanted to do.

A week or so later the Specialist wanted me to come in to see how I was doing. Again he examined me and then got his medical books. He opened them to pictures of thyroid tumors and got all the reports out. He said, "Reverend, you had three biopsies and two sonograms and here are the reports. They all showed you had a large tumor that was a melanoma but when they operated, the tumor had shrunk to less than the size of a peanut and it can't do that and it had become an adenoma and it can't do that." I tried to explain it and thanked him.

Someone might say, "Well, you didn't need the surgery and would have been better off if you hadn't." My reply is that I am so thankful I did because then I had proof the cancer was gone. This totally laid it all to rest for me and I'm still free from it.

### My Dad Had a Stroke!

We continued to travel all over the USA ministering in various churches with great results. A little later, my dad had a stroke and was in a nursing home in Baton Rouge, LA. We had another trip in that vicinity, where we ministered in several churches and were able to see him daily for a couple of weeks. He took a turn for the worse and he seemed a bit fearful of dying, yet we all knew that he knew the Lord personally. Asking the Holy Spirit for a word, I told dad that the Lord, whom he would see at death, would be the same one that saved him and he had walked with all these years. Jesus, Himself, would meet him and escort him into his heavenly home. To fortify this, I then quoted John 14:1-3. *"Let not your heart be troubled; you believe in God, believe also in Me. In My Father's house are many mansions; if it were not so, I would have told you. I go to prepare a place for you. And if I go and prepare a place for you, I will come again and receive you to Myself; that where I am, there you may be also."* This was his favorite scripture and he had quoted it to me all my life. That seemed to give him peace as we prayed with him.

It was hard to leave him as we knew it could be the last time we would see him alive. We had to get home and get ready to leave for our scheduled trip to Nigeria. In the ministry, there are many extremely hard decisions one has to make. We remembered that the Lord Jesus had said to a man, *"'Follow Me.' But he said, 'Lord, let me first go and bury my father.' Jesus said to him, 'Let the dead bury their own dead, but you go and preach the kingdom of God.' And another also said, 'Lord, I will follow You, but let me first go and bid them farewell who are at my house.' But Jesus said to him, 'No one, having put his hand to the plow, and looking back, is fit for the kingdom of God.'"* Luke 9:59-62.

Now came the time for us to go back to Nigeria to minister in the churches in the Delta region. This excited both Mildred and me. To think that we would finally be able to see the results of those great meetings in which we were privileged to have a part was exhilarating to say the least. I couldn't help but wonder if we would meet anyone who knew anything about those days. A lot of things can happen in thirty-five years.

## No Follow up Created Problems!

I remembered when Paul and Eleanor Stern had returned from their first term there and what they had told us. Paul said they took a motor launch and went up and down the Niger River ten miles in each direction and found what was called a church in most villages. Many of the people had gone to the meetings which took some of them four days by dugout canoe to get to. When they got back to their villages, they rang the gong and told the others what the Oyebos had said and tried to have service like we did. But how much could they remember without notes or a bible. The problem was that no one had followed up and they just added it to their tribal religion that would complicate things. This is where we had failed to carry out the original vision. That was why we had tried to get a Bible School started before we left. Workers needed to be trained and sent in as soon as possible.

## Preparing to Return to Nigeria!

With great anticipation, we were looking forward to returning to Nigeria. We had booked our flights for November 1, 1989. This would be my first time to visit West Africa since tearfully leaving more than thirty-five years prior. For many years, my heart's desire had been to return but it seemed like this would never be possible. This time Mildred would be going with me. Both of us were really excited!

We would be joined by longtime friends, Paul and Eleanor Stern, pastors of the Rock Church in Danville, Illinois. It had been "touch and go" for a while whether we could go because of insufficient funds. Once we were convinced it was the time for us to go, the Lord miraculously supplied the funds from outside sources without us asking anyone.

The day before we left was extremely busy as there were so many things that needed to be done. Since we had been pastoring a church in Muskegon Michigan for more than 26 years, we really wanted to attend our regular Tuesday morning prayer meeting. It was a great time of prayer as our intercessors really cried out to the Lord in praying for us. Then one of the funeral homes called and wanted me to take a funeral the next day but Thomas, our second son, took it as he had led the lady to the Lord and the family really wanted him anyway.

## One Opportunity to Return

There had been only one opportunity to possibly return to Nigeria. In 1959 our home church sent us up to Detroit, Michigan to the Bethesda Missionary Temple for one of their conventions. W. H. Marshall, pastor of Bethel Temple in Baton Rouge, Louisiana, wanted us to talk with Pastors M. D. Beall and James L. Beall, the pastors of Bethesda, about going back to Nigeria as missionaries. Harold Alcock, one of our Nigerian team, had separated from the Wings of Healing much earlier and had been trying to oversee the works in the Warri and Sapele areas and could no longer physically do so. Consequently, he had asked the Bealls if they could take it over. James Beall had made a trip to look at the work and see what was required and they had decided to send several missionaries. Since we had known the Bealls for several years, perhaps they would be interested in having us go.

At lunch, we discussed the situation. My vision was to do as we had done under Dr. Wyatt and open up new regions, then others could follow. To do this we would spend six months or so each year during the dry seasons holding large meetings to open the areas to the gospel, then return home. Along with this we would send permanent missionaries to help establish churches, schools and drill water wells. However, their vision was different. It was to send couples over for four year stints and then return home as other missionary groups had been doing for years. Since our visions did not agree, we went on our way home after a wonderful convention and a good time together with dear friends.

A couple of years later, we went to Muskegon, Michigan and planted the Church of New Hope. A little later, Bethesda sent Paul and Eleanor Stern and their family over to the Delta Region along with several others and they settled close to Orea Abraka, which was not far from Warri and Sapele. The Sterns spent ten years working in the region and did a great work. Though we couldn't go, we helped to support them and others while they were on the field.

# Chapter 11

What a day November 1, 1989 was! Mildred and I would finally be boarding a plane to return to Nigeria for the first time since tearfully leaving more than thirty-five years before. We would be joined at the airport in Chicago by longtime friends, Paul and Eleanor Stern, pastors of the Rock Church in Danville, Illinois.

### Finally, We're On Our Way!

Our oldest son, Philip and his wife took us to the O'Hara airport in Chicago in our car and we arrived at 11:15 a.m. Just as we checked in, Paul and Eleanor arrived. They checked in and then we had lunch together. We boarded TWA at 1:25 p.m. but left an hour later. This reminded me so much of my first trip and all the troubles we had. I couldn't help but wonder if this would be the same.

Because of our late start, it had us worried about catching our next flight in New York, but fortunately we had a good tailwind and our pilot made up most of the time. We got off the plane and headed to Lufthansa in the rain, not knowing where to go in the Kennedy airport. We felt like the guy in the commercial, running through the airport but we made it to Lufthansa with 25 minutes to spare. They were just loading but didn't know if our luggage would make the flight. This gave us some anxious moments because it was the last flight that night. We left at 6:41 p.m., only 11 minutes late but arrived on time in Frankfort, Germany.

### Meeting Old Friends

We changed clothes in the Frankfurt airport and then met Jan and Meis Barendse, a local pastor and friend of the Sterns and us. He had parked on the lower parking lot and couldn't get on the upper drive so we waited for an hour and finally he came. He took us downtown where we walked quite a bit in several gorgeous old sections of Frankfort and had a piece of Black Forest cake for breakfast. Jan and Meis took us to their apartment where we visited for a while. They told us that Reinhardt Bonnke had just been in Warri and had crowds of 143,000 people. Also, Bonnke had just been in meetings in Frankfurt as well. I thought all of that was very interesting.

### Murphy's Law Again!

We checked back in at the airport and waited for our plane to go to Nigeria and found it was delayed an hour and 20 minutes. Finally we boarded the plane being rudely pushed around by people getting on and found our seat. This time each couple had a window seat. About a half hour later, the captain came on and said they had trouble with the air conditioner belt and they would have it fixed in about a half hour and we would be on our way. Well, in a half hour the stewardess said they were still having trouble getting it fixed and if they couldn't, in another half hour we would have to leave the plane. It always seems that when you go to the mission field, Murphy's Law will take effect.

In a half hour we had to go back to the waiting room which was too small and didn't have enough seats. Fortunately, Paul and Eleanor had gotten off before us and had two seats for us. What a relief as my back was killing me and my left leg was hurting from the knee down and Mildred's legs looked like balloons. They said we would have to wait till they brought another plane and refueled it and put the food and luggage aboard. They finally gave us a small apple juice, cheese, a large salty pretzel and a tiny chocolate candy roll that had a really strong flavor.

Finally they came around and gave us new gate passes and in a few minutes we were pushing and shoving like cattle trying to get out. This time we had to walk down a long flight of stairs and to the tarmac in a pouring down rain. We ran to the double buses and got seats.

Wouldn't you know it; we were the last ones in the back so we were the last ones off? By this time it was raining very hard and we had to wait for all of those ahead of us to put their luggage overhead and get into their seats. I remarked to the stewardess, "I can't believe that you would load us out here in the rain." She replied, "I'm sorry." So I replied, "Young Lady, it's not your fault." I couldn't help but wonder if it was a plane to New York or London would they load them in the rain?

After sitting there for what seemed like another hour we finally took off at 6:00 in the evening, four hours late. They offered to send a telex, so Paul sent one to Ron Childs, our missionary friend who was to meet us in Lagos, which he never got. The flight took off in a rainstorm but otherwise it was quite smooth. We were so disappointed that we couldn't see the Mediterranean Sea and the Sahara Desert in the daytime. I saw it years ago but Mildred hadn't and I wanted her to see it.

### Finally In Lagos, Nigeria!

We landed in Lagos about 12:30 that night and taxied for about 15 minutes, finally arriving at the terminal. Again, it was push and shove all the way in unloading. We made it to about the front third of the line, but by the time the soldier looked at our passports, we were only three couples from the last. People kept coming in and getting people out and taking them on in. After standing for so long on the side of the glass bin, we finally turned our passports in and showed our return tickets and then waited some more. They checked each passport carefully to see if we had been in South Africa, which we never had. Finally they let us get our baggage but we could hardly get up to the turnstile as it was so crowded. Then there was another long line to get through the customs.

Thankfully, Ron and Jerry Childs were there to meet us. They were dressed in their Nigerian clothes. We were ever so grateful as it took us two hours in that terrible heat to get checked out. It was 2:30 in the morning when we finally cleared out of the airport. Thank God, Ron had us a motel secured. We showered with no hot water but it felt so good to get cleaned up. We fell into bed for a wonderful few hours of sleep.

## Up and Ready to Go!

The next morning we awakened about 8:30 and had breakfast together then loaded Ron's Toyota 4X4 wagon and drove to Benin City. I was so amazed at the vast difference in things from 1954. The highway was a modern four-lane road, straight across the big swamp and jungle area between Lagos and Benin City. In 1954, we had to drive hundreds of miles around. The road used to go up to Ibadon and Ilesha then back down to Benin City with the last half of it just a dirt road. Along the way we filled up with diesel and got a Fanta Orange and some fried plantain strips and some bananas. They tasted so good.

Ron took us by Benson Idahosa's Miracle Center at the airport in Benin City. It was very large, seating thousands. We then were taken to the new church that seats 11,000 and to the Bible School and then to Ron's house. They gave us a corn muffin and some water and then we were on our way to Warri. Ron stopped on the way and we had a lovely lunch with them in Benin City at The Ranch.

## What a Difference!

I couldn't help but notice the absence of the big trees along with the jungle and the banana trees. They told us that many of the rubber trees were cut down as they only produce so long. There was a four-lane bridge over the Ethiope River and the other estuary of the Niger in Sapele. We used to have to cross on a small ferry that closed at 6:30 in the evening. What a delightful difference. The highway skirted Sapele to the north so we didn't see any of the city. Soon we got our first glimpse of Warri and oh what a change it was. It had grown from a sleepy little town to a bustling oil and steel city with a huge population.

We drove by the Church of God Mission Church (Benson Idahosa's group) that had between 2000 and 4000 members and on to what was called *"The City of God"* building. This was a huge complex of buildings built by J. O. C. Mosheshe, a Nigerian Christian businessman. We drove to the auditorium and a few men were there and we noticed a sign about some of the meetings that were going on there.

We were informed that Michael Okah, who was our host pastor and who grew up under the ministry of Paul and Eleanor, was not expecting us for another day. Somehow the arrangements got mixed up, which happens often in missions. So they took us to the Mosheshe Mansion at the City of God. Brother Mosheshe was quite the businessman as he owned several companies such as, fishing, dredging, etc. He really seemed to have a heart for God. He welcomed us graciously and had his waiter give us a cold drink as we sat on the front porch of the mansion.

They called Beauty Okah, Michael's wife, and she came very shortly and was so glad to see us all. She just hugged Paul and Eleanor and was so thrilled to see them again. We were introduced and we hugged her. We waited all afternoon for Michael and he finally was able to meet us at 6:30 which was after dark. It was such a delight to meet both of them.

The mansion was quite the place! Such huge porches filled with the most gorgeous overstuffed furniture. While we were waiting, it came a tropical rainstorm. It was gorgeous afterwards as you could see the afterglow of the storm.

Brother Mosheshe had his driver take us on his little bus to a motel that Michael had secured for us. He and Beauty went with us. It was a long, long way on the other side of the city, over by the big steel mill. Come to find out, they were not expecting us either till the next day. They did have some rooms available but no clean sheets. There was lipstick on the pillow case, dirty spots on the sheet and no top sheet just the bedspread and only one towel and the bathroom was dirty.

We did have a lovely dinner with Michael and Beauty and were able to visit and had a wonderful time. Paul gave them a check from a church in Amberler, Pennsylvania for $1200 on a car for them. They were both amazed and thrilled. Praise God for his blessing! We returned to our rooms about nine, showered in cold water that barely dribbled and fell into bed. How wonderful it was to just get into a prone position. I slept on the dirty side and Mildred put the towel over her pillow.

### A Few Problems!

Michael came early the next morning and had breakfast with us. It was interesting because we were just going to have juice or fruit and some oatmeal but they didn't have any. We did have a lovely breakfast but afterwards it left the taste of fish. Michael went in and talked to the people in the office and they gave us another room. However, there were several things wrong with this room. The closet pole was missing so there was no way to hang up our clothes. It had a TV but it didn't work.

Afterwards, we went out on the patio to read and write. It was amusing to watch the lizards play so we didn't get much accomplished. They ran under Mildred's chair and she about had a fit. They were big with an orange or red head and tail with a grayish brown middle. Paul came and told us the maid was moving us to another room so we took our luggage to it. This time we had a clean top sheet. One of our problems was, we had no drinkable water. So we brushed our teeth in the only soft-drink they had, either Coke or Fanta orange – so Fanta Orange won out.

Michael came about five in the evening and we worked out our schedule. We would all go to Michael's church in the morning and Paul would be the speaker. We discovered there were some immense problems in the churches in the area. They were as divided as they are in America and yet all of them came together for the Bonnke meetings. We knew the Lord had us there for a reason and we would find out soon.

### Our First Meeting!

Our first Sunday came on November 5th and we were up early. Michael picked us up in the Mosheshe Estate bus at 9:30 a.m. The church was filled to capacity and they were standing outside, looking in the Windows and doors. This was their annual Thanksgiving service and many people brought their Thanksgiving offering. The Mosheshe family brought their offering first and then the Okahs with other groups and ministers following. They brought big pans of yams, avocados, paw paws (papayas), and even a live miniature goat with its feet tied with a string. It came in bleating and it kind of broke our hearts because we knew it was going to be dinner for some family. Paul preached and did a great job. We prayed for the sick and there

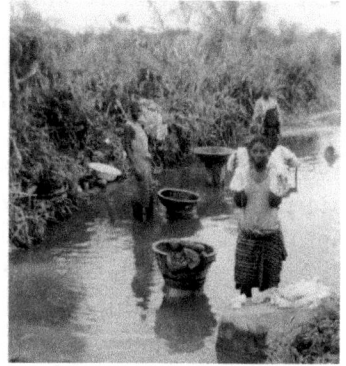
Washing Clothes in 1954

was a great move of the Holy Spirit with many being healed but it was too late to have testimonies after all of that. This was our first service in Africa and all of us were very pleased with it.

Afterwards, Michael took us to the Palm Grove restaurant and hotel for dinner. It was real nice. He insisted that he would pay for the meal. He had spoken to the church how they were not "a gimme people" in the sense of wanting people to give to them. They wanted to give and take care of their guests. They were not always looking for a handout. This was so thrilling to me as those were things we had insisted on years ago. We wanted them to feel like they were our equal in everything we did and part of that was sharing in expenses.

On the way to dinner we saw the huge steel mill and it was a monster! Warri had grown so much in 35 years that it was unbelievable. Of course, nothing was the same. It had become a huge industrial city with oil fields and shipping port with all kinds of related industries.

### Amazing Things!

One of the things that amazed me was that I hadn't seen a leper anywhere. How well I remember there were so many of them 35 years ago. Also, I didn't see many crippled people either and yet there were thousands, years ago. No doubt there were many things that contributed to this. One thing was the standard of living was vastly improved. Most of the people were well-dressed and lived in fairly nice homes. Whereas before, there were so many mud huts with thatched roofs. You never saw anyone naked or half naked anymore, not even the little children. They had a water system and therefore you didn't see the women at the river washing their clothes. The rivers were no longer running soapy. What a change had taken place in those years. It was thrilling!

Another thing we noticed was that most of the shops were closed on Sunday. We were told that was because most of them go to church. They said there were 257 Full Gospel Churches (Pentecostal) in Warri and they all had cooperated in the Bonnke meetings. I noticed one billboard advertizing an American Evangelist's meetings that were coming. It seems that everybody wants to come to Warri because you can always preach to a crowd as the local churches have done such a fantastic job of evangelizing. It made me wonder why it was that every "Tom, Dick and Harry" wanted to come here and minister where most are saved and not into the "bush," as we used to call it, that has not been reached yet. Could it be, we want the prestige of ministering in Africa and not have to endure the hardships? Only eternity will tell.

We had dinner with Ezekiel and Brother Mosheshe's wife. Ezekiel is a brother to J. O. C. Mosheshe and part of the Mosheshe business group. Mrs. Mosheshe was a very lovely, intelligent and well-traveled person. It was so thrilling to see Nigerians prosper. She also was quite the golfer. We showed them our family pictures and they seemed thrilled.

Paul gave Michael a bunch of his books he brought over and I gave him a bundle of our church bulletin inserts with good articles in them. He seemed very pleased. Eleanor said that she wanted to move back here so badly. They called her mama and Paul daddy. They really loved the two of them.

I was scheduled to speak in the 9:30 AM service the next day and was given the subject "What to do about discouragement." It's interesting that the services were in English with no interpreters, yet we had to use five interpreters here in Warri in 1954. So I studied and prayed for a good while until I was confident we were in God's timing. There came such a confidence in my own heart that we were here in the will of God!

### First Opportunity to Preach!

On Monday, November 6, we were up early as the service was supposed to start at 9:00 o'clock. However, the bus didn't come till 9:15 and it took us 45 minutes to cross the city because the city was so large. We arrived at 10 o'clock and then the meeting started. It was made up of all ministers. When we started, there were only about 45 ministers present. There would've been more but another minister from the USA was also holding a seminar at the City of God. We met him at the airport in Lagos, going through immigration and customs. We also met the head of the group he came to visit, Bishop God Do Well. I had mentioned to him that I was one of the original ministers in 1954 at the Olu's meeting and to my joy, he remembered it. He was the first one we met that had been in the original meetings. That was really a thrill.

We had a great time of worship and many other ministers came in during that time. The place was then filled to capacity with a couple hundred ministers present. It was so neat to see Michael introduce Paul and Eleanor as his spiritual father and mother. When Paul spoke to them in Urhobo, they really got excited. You could see their great love and respect for the Sterns. Paul introduced us and Mildred spoke a little and I followed as the main speaker for the morning.

## My Message!

The topic given to me was "How to deal with discouragement and frustration and going around in circles." I used Luke 13:31-33 for my text. *"The same day there came certain of the Pharisees, saying unto Him, Get thee out, and depart hence: for Herod will kill thee. And He said unto them, Go ye, and tell that fox, Behold, I cast out devils, and I do cures today and tomorrow, and the third day I shall be perfected. Nevertheless I must walk today, and tomorrow, and the day following: for it cannot be that a prophet perish out of Jerusalem."* The ministry was about Jesus and His resurrection and ascension and how He went through tough places and He will carry us through them as well. Jesus faced the greatest discouragements and faced them head-on. Let us follow in His steps.

My heart and soul were so filled with the subject of the death, burial, resurrection and ascension of our Lord as it was those truths that brought me out of the Hodgkin disease and the melanoma on my thyroid. It had only been about a year since I came out of that valley but those truths still meant so much to me and still do to this day. How well, I remember the intense hunger I had for anything on this subject. I read the biblical accounts eight times during the time when I was so weak, and then I looked for books on our Lord's resurrection and ascension. I discovered there were innumerable books on His death but only a few on His resurrection and even fewer on His ascension. Most of those dealt only with the proof of each but they helped. I had two old books in my library by William Milligan that revolutionized my thinking and brought life to me. They were: The Resurrection of Our Lord and The Ascension of Our Lord. The Lord used the truths in these books to instill faith in my heart as *"faith comes by hearing and hearing by the Word of God."*

### Our Daddy Has Come Home!

During my time of ministering the Word, I mentioned the initial meetings in 1954 and commended them on their progress both naturally and spiritually. When I finished they all jumped to their feet, clapping their hands, whistling and shouting together in unison. They chanted, "Our Daddy has come home! Our Daddy has come home!" This just went on and on for a good while.

After the service Gabriel, who was head of the Christ Gospel Churches, sat down with me and told me that he was one of our interpreters and that Joseph Okoradudu in Sapele was also one. What a thrill! Just to think that I actually saw again the two wonderful men whom the Olu had sent to Ilesha to learn our American lingo. One of them was a leper when he came and at first Sidney Elton was so upset about it but the Lord had healed him. These were two of the five who were our original interpreters in the huge meetings in Warri and Sapele.

### What a Testimony!

Also we met Wilson Ovwoh, a pastor in Orea Abraka where the Sterns had made their base. His mother had been deathly ill in 1954 and came to the meetings because she had heard of some white men (Oyebos) working miracles. Her husband was a medicine man and had not been able to help her. She came home from the meeting completely well. He left the family and was gone for a few days then came back home and saw his wife was still well. So he said to his wife, "The white man's prayers were stronger than his medicine and black magic." So he threw it all away and said I'm going to serve Jesus Christ and came to the meetings and was really converted. He lived for many years and was a watchman for the Sterns all the time they were in Nigeria and especially during the Biafrian war. Many times he slept on their front porch. He had just died a short time before we arrived but his wife was still living. At the time, she was the oldest person in the delta region. Her age was between 120 and 130 years they told us.

What a tremendous meeting it was that morning! The power and presence of the Lord was mighty. We prayed for many that were sick or had been discouraged and they were blessed by the Holy Spirit's anointing. It was so good to bask in the sunshine of the Lord's presence.

They took us to lunch at a restaurant at the airport. It seemed so strange that the runway wasn't fenced where the planes take off. It was even connected to the road. It was a lovely restaurant but we still couldn't drink the water so we had a soft drink. On the way to the City of God where they moved us, we bought a few bananas and a pineapple. Michael and Beauty had us stop by their home and gave us some oranges as well. It was a nice second-story apartment. It seemed so strange that the porch, doors and windows all had iron bars all the way around.

Those who had air conditioners, which they didn't have, also had bars around them. This probably was to keep thieves out.

The night service was to start at six o'clock but it started at 6:45. The place was packed out. The building must have been more than 200 feet long so we could hardly see the back rows because of the poor light. Again Michael introduced us and Mildred and I spoke a few minutes. Again, they erupted in the chant, "Our Daddy has come home." Paul and Eleanor sang a couple of songs and Eleanor spoke a little and Paul preached. When he spoke to them in Urhobo, the place again just went wild with excitement.

Again it was so beautiful to see their love for the Sterns. When Paul told them he was made an Urhobo chief, again they shouted for joy. Even Prince Mosheshe shouted. He was a Spirit filled Episcopalian that had built the City of God. Paul spoke about the blues that can come after a big meeting. He used Elijah for an example. It was good and very well received. We prayed for the people afterwards and the Lord met so many of them.

### A Nigerian Lesson in Giving!

Prince Mosheshe told us that through the day on Sunday, he had visited four churches in Warri and gave plentifully in their Thanksgiving offerings. He and his family had given in Michael's church the day before. He said he needed the money to complete the new auditorium but just wanted to bless others. Then he told us that some Bulgarian businessmen met with him and worked out a business deal. He showed them the new auditorium and they said they were going to ship all the white marble to cover the outside and send men to install it for free. He said it would have cost him $5 million Naira (Nigerian money) to buy and install it. Well you can't out give God!

### Baby Born as a Result of Meetings!

After the service, we met a young man who was 35 years of age and the business manager of a company that sold and raised baby chicks. He had won the prize for being the best manager of the country. The prize was a trip to the largest chick houses in the USA. Also, he was a graduate of Michael's Bible College, Christ the Rock. He told us that five years before he was born, his mother had another son. Because he was the apple of her eye, her husband poisoned him. When he discovered she was going to have another baby, he poisoned her but she came to our meeting in 1954 and God healed her and a little later, she delivered this young man.

### Tuesday, November 7, 1989

We arose at 7:15 and had a nice breakfast at Ezekiel and Josephina Mosheshe's house. They had a lovely home on the Mosheshe compound. We went to the morning service about 9:45 and Paul spoke first and I followed. It was about finances and missions, so we unloaded on them the principles of giving and praying. I used Philippians 4:19 and gave a friend's little saying. Gladi Dearden used this in our church and it meant a lot to us, *"My God"* – that's personal; *"shall"* – that's certain; *"supply all your needs"* – that's adequate; *"according to His riches in glory"* – that's fathomless; *"by Christ Jesus."* They really seem to appreciate our testimonies. I told them that when they come to the US don't come to get money but come to give the word of the Lord and minister. God also wanted to send some of them to other nations to preach his word.

Two pastors were there this morning who were in our original meetings in 1954. Edmund Dolar was one and he was in a high position in the Christ's Gospel Churches, the one Sterns had started. He was saved in our meetings and arranged a meeting with the key men in his area and we will be preaching to them. The other one was Johnson Menajoren and he also was saved in our meetings in 1954 and was the pastor of Christ's Gospel Church in Warri. We counseled several pastors after the morning service and then went back to Josephina's house for a lovely dinner.

We went to the night service at 7:10 even though it was announced to start at 6:00. There was a good time of worship and Eleanor did a great job of preaching. She spoke on the Lord's Prayer and praying. She and Paul then sang some new choruses to them with Eleanor playing the piano. It was such a good night though the crowd was down by a third because many of the churches had services of their own this night. We got to our room about 11 and showered in cold water as there still was no hot water. It really "shivers your timbers" but makes you feel good afterwards.

### Wednesday, November 8, 1989.

We went to the service at 9:45 but there were not a lot of people out in the beginning. However, many others came shortly. Mildred spoke and did real well with me following. I spoke about David *"foresaw the Lord always before him and because he was at his right hand he would not be moved."* We need to always see the Lord before us and with Him with us we cannot be moved or lose out. Michael had some testimonies afterwards with many of them speaking of what this seminar meant to them. Another man spoke of being in our meetings in Ibadon and Ilesha in 1954 and how they were such a tremendous move of God.

### A Comparison of Meetings!

Wilson Ovwoh talked with me afterwards, comparing the recent Bonnke meetings and the one in 1954. I was very interested to know from those who were there about our meetings back then. He said, "Your meeting in 1954 were much larger and had a greater move of God and was the beginning of all the Pentecostal churches here. With no advertising, no billboards, radio or TV, thousands upon thousands came and the Lord met them. Bonnke spent many thousands of Naira on TV, radio and plastered the city with billboards and still it was the churches that brought the turn out." It was so interesting to me to hear about the comparison from someone who had been in both meetings. The lasting results were what I was looking for as that is the real test of all meetings.

We asked them if they would take us by the site where Reinhardt Bonnke held his meeting. In comparing the size of the crowd, his meetings were about 175 yards in diameter each way with buildings all around and the Nigerians said the crowd was over 200,000. We were told in Frankfort that it was about 143,000 people. Our meetings in 1954 actually measured over 300 yards in each direction with five to six people per square yard. None of this makes a bit of difference and is actually meaningless. As I've always said, you have as many as you have and no more. For my own satisfaction I just wanted to know how realistic were our guess-timation of the crowd size back then. It looked like we were way off in size of the crowd.

Paul went home early as he wasn't feeling good at all. The heat was really getting to him and Eleanor. He also had a white streak down the right side of his nose and red blotches on the right side of his face and chin which looked like the beginning of an infection. However, Mildred and I did fine, though she usually can't take the heat as well as I could. It was terribly hot, but we felt good.

We had lunch with a brother that had four wives and he said the Holy Spirit had convicted him of it. He had 20 kids and was only 49 years of age. Problems like this are something missionaries have often faced and it's not an easy task to get them settled.

We went over and had a prayer meeting in the Stern's room for the service in the evening. Mosheshe was scheduled to speak but Michael told us to be ready because he might not make it back from Lagos in time. So each of us went prepared but I knew in my heart I would not be the one speaking. Mosheshe did make it back and spoke on love and did very well. We laid hands on him and his wife afterwards and there was a good anointing and prophecy over both of them.

After the meeting we gathered in our room and had peanut butter and jelly sandwiches and water. We had to be very careful that everything was sealed because we had a terrible problem with tiny little ants. I also killed a cockroach about 1½ inches long, a real monster. We tried to keep our suitcases closed to keep out all the bugs that crawled around. Lizards were all over the place, so they must have had lots of food. One of them barked at me the day before. Oh how I hated to take a cold shower but had to as it was such a scorcher of a day.

### Thursday, November 9, 1989

We rose early and Michael came and we walked over to the mansion together. Lady Mosheshe met us with her daughter and welcomed us. She served us such a lovely breakfast. It was a beautiful setting with Royal Albert China.

Paul's nose still had a white streak and it had turned hard and looked like it would turn into blisters. He thought it was an allergy and others thought it was a bug bite. Mildred told him he had an infection and should use some triple-antibiotic salve she had but he didn't think so.

After a lovely visit with the Mosheshes, his bus took us to the main market in Warri by the river. This was quite an experience. It had low roofs with small aisles wandering all over. Paul, Michael and I got lost from the women and it looked like we would never find them but all Michael had to do was to ask which way the "Oyebos" went. To me that was funny as they were still using the same word for our pale colored skin as in the 50's. Eleanor was looking for some cloth to make her a dress but all of it was very expensive, 240 Naira for 6 yards.

At 6:00 that evening, I went to the Bible school and spoke about the inevitability of the resurrection of Jesus. They had between 40 and 60 students. It was terribly hot but they were all so very attentive. I then went back to our room and sent Paul over. He still was quite sick with diarrhea and had a fever from the place on his nose.

I walked over to the City of God building for the convention of the Christ Missionary Crusaders Church. It was a huge meeting and I tried to just slip in the back but that wasn't possible with my pale skin. Bishop God Do Well invited me up to greet the people and introduced me as the one who originally brought the Pentecostal message to the Delta region and the father of it all. What a thrill to see the many thousands in this group that sprang out of those meetings. They had such a lovely choir and were such good singers. They really worshiped in the spirit and it was all on television. Oh how I praised the Lord for all of that. Every group thus far traced their beginnings back to those meetings in 1954.

Paul came home from the school not feeling well so he went straight to bed. Eleanor came over and we had our peanut butter and jelly sandwich and water. We went to bed at 10:30 that evening with such a thrill in my heart to see how the churches had grown during those years.

### Friday, November 10, 1989.

We arose early and went over to the mansion by car as it was pouring down rain. Paul was feeling worse and his nose and face looked very bad. We left about 9:15 to go to Orea Abraka on Mosheshe's bus. It was a beautiful drive with very dense jungles and beautiful palm trees with areas of Cassava bushes. They get three things from the cassava root;

starch when they boil it, then they get garie which is like foo foo and tapioca.

We filled up with gas at $.42 a liter and journeyed to Orea Abraka. This is where Paul and Eleanor with their family and the families of Louis Mudrak and Bruce Stallwood lived for nine years. These were the missionary couples that Bethesda Missionary Temple had sent out. We went to the church they built in 1965 and an elderly lady was there praying. She remembered the Stearns and said she was in the meetings in 1954 and was healed and saved in them. She said that I was like God, meaning a man of God. She was sick and just asking the Lord to heal her so we prayed for her and the Lord again met her in a wonderful way. She went on her way rejoicing.

We had stopped in Eku at the Baptist Hospital and met some of the Stern's friends. He saw the doctor and he said it was a superficial infection. So he gave him some triple antibiotic salve and penicillin to take. Paul was feeling better after that.

Wilson Ovwoh and a couple of the sisters from the church went with us to Amia, the village of his mother. We turned off the main road and had to go 7 miles to the village of Amia. The road was very bad and it took us a whole hour to make it. We had to cross a couple of black looking rivers and go through a huge swamp. They said there are all kinds of snakes and even crocodiles in them. It was quite dense with all kinds of trees, vines and bamboo growing all over.

### We Meet a Lady Healed in 1954

We finally made it by 1:00 in the afternoon and went to the village meeting room where all the chiefs and elders were gathered because they had heard we were coming. While there, they brought out Wilson's mother, Mrs. Ovwoh to meet us. They didn't know how old she was but said she was between 120 and 130 years of age. She was still quite lively being the oldest one in the village. Her eyesight was still good as she easily recognized Paul and Eleanor at first sight. It was such a joy for Mildred and me to hug her. This was the lady that was healed in the Warri meetings in 1954 whose husband had been a medicine man. They have four sons pastoring good churches plus the pastor in Orea Abraka was her relative as well. I couldn't help but think, "What a tremendous multiplication of the 1954 meetings."

We had let a pastor off on the way that had been a cripple but was healed in the meetings of 1954 also. He said, "Oh Brother, you have the power of God in you. Everybody still talks about those meetings. What a tremendous impartation it has made. It has literally changed the culture of these people." That was exactly what the British government accused us of in 1954.

### Burning the Juju Charms!

During the meetings in Sapele in 1954, the fellows had the people to bring their juju charms and idols to burn them. It made a huge pile which represented a lot of money they had paid for them. They set fire to them and burned them up to the cheers of all the people. Later the District Officer called them in and told them they had to stop preaching Christ because they were changing the culture of the people. He said the Historical Society in Lagos heard about it and was protesting it. Our guys told him that they could not stop preaching Christ but they would have the people send the stuff to them. That was fine with the District Officer.

### Must Follow Certain Customs

There were certain things that we had to do in meeting the tribal leaders because it was the custom of these people as they were a different tribe and language. They offered us a seat first and Michael went through the ceremony of honoring the elders. They gave us some Fanta orange, Sprite and Coke (warm of course). They had a certain ceremony in welcoming us so they gave us a drink and a piece of coconut to chew on. We didn't eat the coconut because we were not used to the bacteria they live with. We talked a bit and then Paul spoke and then we had prayer. According to protocol, we asked their permission to leave which they granted.

It was 2:30 when we left and we had to drop off the family back in Orea Abraka and then go on to our rooms. On the way, Paul said to Michael, "It's going to rain." Michael said, "Oh no it's just the Harmattan building up." Well after a few miles, it poured down rain, so we really kidded Michael saying, "Is not rain, but is Harmattan." He and all of us laughed heartedly. We had such a great time with Michael.

We made it back by 4:30 as Moses our driver really drove fast. We apologized to Madame Mosheshe for being late for dinner and she was very gracious. She said, "It did not bother me, it only was bad for you to make you really hungry." The supper was excellent. We then went to our rooms and showered and retired about 8:30 that evening.

### Saturday, November 11, 1989

To us, it was very funny about breakfast at the mansion. The cooks asked us what we would like for breakfast the next day. Paul told them we would like French toast so we had French bread toasted with garlic butter on it and honey and coffee. Some things don't translate very well.

After we walked back to our room, Michael came and asked if we would go pray for a lady and a baby in the hospital. So Mildred, Eleanor and I went with him. The Lord really met both of them. We also prayed for a young lady who had typhoid fever. The doctor, who was the owner of the hospital, was so impressed at the answer to prayer that he stood and talked with us for almost an hour.

We then went to the graduation dinner for the graduates of Christ the Rock Bible College which was at the Mosheshe Mansion. There were about 60 graduates. What a wonderful group. They served dinner buffet style and it was all Nigerian food which pleased us to no end. There was pounded yam, egiese soup, rice with a smoked flavor and red pepper, chicken and beef grilled (smoked) and pawpaws. The egiese soup was made of egg, melon rind, smoked sausage, cow's ponch (tripe) and God only knows what else. It was so delicious till I saw the cow's stomach lining and then all of a sudden I lost my appetite. So much for that.

Bishop God Do Well and his wife along with Ron Hunter had dinner with us later. Mosheshe had it upstairs in his big room with overstuffed chairs and couches lining both sides. It was air conditioned which was nice. We talked for two hours with them about their vision and compared our vision to it. They were so very similar. They had an open door to the Bulgarians; in fact some of them were in our service. Doors have opened to them in the Vatican, Portugal, the Soviet Union and other Eastern Bloc countries. Mosheshe wanted to provide a place in Warri for the unity of the Church. So he was building a big auditorium he called Paradise, which would seat 10,000 people.

That evening we went over and had our meeting with the Bible college graduates and students. Both Paul and I spoke. I spoke about God reconciling man to Himself, not imputing their trespasses to them and has committed unto us the word of reconciliation. So we must do as He did. We must not be offended at their ways and sins but just set the good food of the word before them. We must pray the Lord would thrust forth laborers into his harvest. They received it with open hearts.

We then went as a group to Paradise Hall where the Christ Missionary Crusader Church group was having their convention. Mildred and I along with Paul and Eleanor all spoke a little and the crowd really rejoiced in our testimonies. It was a high spot for them and us. There must have been more than 2000 people present but it was extremely hot. It felt like preaching and worshiping in a sauna. Oh how the people loved us! They called both Paul and me "daddy." To them, it was a term of endearment because we were instrumental in their salvation. As we were leaving Bishop God Do Well put his arms around me and said, "I love you so much." I told him I felt the same about him. What a dear man! We came home and hopped into the cold shower then to bed very weary.

### Sunday, November 12, 1989

We walked over to the mansion at eight o'clock but the cook wasn't there. Finally he came and cooked our breakfast. There were two Bulgarians there but they seemed very nervous and wouldn't eat with us. The bus came and took us to Christ the Rock Church for the 10:30 service. The church was full but it was extremely hot. During the song service they put up an electric fan for us. That was great as I had forgotten a handkerchief. Mildred, Eleanor and I spoke a little then Paul followed. There were prophecies and a great move of the Holy Spirit.

At 5:30 we went to Bishop God Do Well's for supper but he wasn't there yet. Finally he came about 6:30 and they served us a soft-drink and some native dancers entertained us. They had on their native dress and used a square box they pounded on with a stick and a larger square box with three prongs over a hole which they played and rapped. This was exactly the same kind of instruments they had back in 1954. Eleanor asked Michael if that was carnal. He said, "Is not carnal, that's the way we worshiped before anyone came to teach us a different way to worship." They continued on through the suppertime. We went inside and had a wonderful dinner.

We left at 8:30 p.m. and went to the Urhobo Center to be with Wilson Ovwoh in service. They had been waiting since 7:00 but they still went through the whole service. I spoke a few minutes on Abraham in Romans four while Paul had the main message. When Wilson asked for those who wanted prayer to come, of course they all came, so we prayed for all of them. We got back to our room about 11:00 – dead tired and hot so we had a cold shower and went to bed.

### Monday, November 13, 1989

We were up and dressed by seven o'clock. We didn't know about breakfast so I walked over to the mansion just to get a thermos of hot water. Prince Mosheshe Jr. picked me up at the gate and took me with him. He was such a nice person, a real quality individual. We had laid hands and prophesied over him the first Sunday at Christ the Rock Church. Madame Mosheshe asked us to come back to breakfast at 9:00 which we did. We met a Greek man from Monaco and conversed with him and also with the two Bulgarians. It was very interesting. They said we could visit Bulgaria now and get a visa at the airport. It was a wonderful time together. This was my first time ever to knowingly shake hands with a Bulgarian. Mosheshe was ecstatic and wanted to talk with us the next morning.

### Meeting the Olu's Son!

Michael and Beauty came at 10:30 with some of the church leaders and took us to see the Olu of Warri in his mansion. On the way we stopped and took pictures where the open field was where we had our meetings in 1954. They had a school on that land and the forest was all gone now. We drove up the street where the witch doctors had set up their camp and then to the Olu's house. We were there at 10:55 and were taken into his upstairs living room. He was a lawyer with a degree from Oxford we were told. He gave that up when his father died to take his place as the Olu. We were told to address him as "Your Royal Highness."

He came out to meet us a half hour later. He was a handsome, big man dressed in his native dress with orange beads on his wrist and ankle and sat on his throne. Michael introduced all of us and we spoke in our turn. He seemed to be so pleased to see me especially. In 1954, he was 13 years of age and was in secondary school. He said there were so many miracles in those meetings and that was the beginning of the Pentecostal churches in this region. He said he personally saw so many miracles that happened. We talked a bit about the meetings. I can't express the joy in my heart in talking with him.

The Olu's waiter served us a soft drink and tea and we prayed for him at his request. He was a Spirit filled man as was his father. Beauty said they could never get in to see the Olu and it was only because he wanted to see me again. We took some pictures and journeyed back to the city of God to pack as we had to move.

The brethren from Christ's Gospel Churches took us to the Idama hotel where we had lunch and then were on our way to Sapele by 3:00 p.m. We went to Gabriel's home and met many of the Christ's Gospel Church ministers. They got after Paul for not letting them know sooner that we were coming. Paul answered and said that we didn't know till the first of October for sure because we didn't have the money to come till then and they accepted that.

They went over our schedule and it was a whopper with two meetings tomorrow. The one in the morning was 45 minutes out of Warri and the one in the evening was in Warri. They were wonderful men that dearly loved the Lord. You could see their great love for Mama and Papa Stern.

I spoke a little and they seemed to be enthralled as they looked at me. One said, "You are the man who worked so many miracles in 1954 and was the first to minister in this region and what a great harvest has been reaped. All the Pentecostal churches come from those meetings."

We then went to see Joseph Okoradudu who was also one of our interpreters and took a picture of him and Gabriel and I together. He was quite elderly and unable to pastor anymore. He had a lovely family and one daughter who was a nurse. Gabriel had a lovely family also and all were very nice looking.

It was dark but we went by Hotel Bendel where we would stay Wednesday through Sunday. Paul's nose had cleared up but he was really sick for a while, giving us a lot of concern. We went on back to Warri and to the Idama hotel. We tried to shower but the water wouldn't come out of the shower head if you raised it higher than the tub rim. Oh what lumpy beds!

### Tuesday, November 14, 1989

What a night! No sleep on the lumpy bed. Mildred's had a big hole in it, the pillows stunk and we itched all night. How wonderful that daylight still comes. We had breakfast then we met Mosheshe at 9:45 and talked for an hour about what he wanted. I had the strongest feeling that he had expected something more from us and somehow we'd lost ground with him. This made me feel bad.

Then Captain Ermousele and our driver came and took us to Agbaro for service and we arrived about 11:30. The village was having a juju festival with groups parading with clubs and guns. Thank the Lord we had turned into the church before they got to us. It was a good meeting with Paul speaking. We prayed for the people and laid hands on many of them. There were some great needs, especially a crippled boy. It was a great day in that village because the Lord met so many of them. They really received us well and took some pictures of us with the choir. It was so precious that the children wanted to shake our hands. You would have six or a dozen hands, all at one time trying to shake your hand. We really loved them and they could sense it.

### Met the First Man at 1954 Meetings

We left about 1:45 and came back to the Idama Motel and had dinner. The chief cook was the first cook of Bruce Stallwood, a Bethesda Missionary, and he really fixed us a terrific meal. We only had a half hour to rest and get ready for the night meeting. It started at 5:00 and was in the Christ Gospel Church in Warri which was in the back of the 1954 meeting ground. The pastor told the congregation that he was converted there and was the first person on the ground and saw hundreds of people healed. They spoke with such glowing tones of those days. They had a nice choir at both churches and they did very well. They had such a lovely protocol.

I finally got to preach and spoke on Hebrews 11:33 *"by faith they obtained promises."* It felt like old times. The anointing was really heavy but my interpreter was not near as good as some or it could have been me. The problem was that he interpreted into "pidgin English" and I found myself listening to him and then I didn't have anything to say. It's better when you don't pay any attention to your interpreter.

After church again all the kids just had to shake our hands. What little dolls they were. Children are the same the world over. On the way out a father gave me a note asking to pray for his sick child in the hospital. I stopped right then with the throng of people around me and everyone that could reach me put their hands on my arms or touched me some way as I prayed. They were so simple in their faith. I would to God Americans were that simple. We sure could learn from them!

Back at the motel, we went to Stern's room and Captain got us some mineral water and a soft-drink. It was good and cold. The captain was very efficient. He had been a captain in the Nigerian army for years and fought in the war, especially in the battle of Calabar. We shared some bananas and oranges with them and went to our room. There was no water for a shower – only if you're a snail. It's almost hilarious trying to shower in a stream of water like a pencil but we tried it anyway.

### Wednesday, November 15, 1989

We were up early as Mildred was up several times during the night with diarrhea. Something had really upset her. We left at 8:45 and went to the City of God to get some of our clothes. We saw Michael and he said we were supposed to go to Aba next Monday through Wednesday. Paul was to respond by telephone but that was impossible because the lines had been down for almost a week between Warri and Benin. We went to the Bendel Hotel which was a little better, at least the air conditioner had a cover and there were overhead fans. The beds were also lumpy and Mildred's seemed like it hit bottom.

The morning service at Christ's Gospel Church was a regional meeting. We had about 40 ministers from various Pentecostal backgrounds. Gabriel's daughter sang a song with the choir and did such a lovely job. His sons, Elias and John, were also bright and handsome young men. Gabriel was one of our interpreters here and at Warri. It was so thrilling to find out some of the pastors children had become lawyers, doctors, nurses and have really climbed the ladder of success. Paul spoke and I followed by encouraging them not to live in the past but look to the future in God. He is the same today as He was back then. Then we prayed for the sick and the Lord met many of them.

Afterwards, we had dinner with several of the pastors and their wives at the hotel. We then went to our rooms and lay down for a half-hour then went back to the church. Eleanor and Mildred spoke to the women while Paul and I spoke to the pastors. I spoke on Jesus ascended to the throne in order to finish his work. Therefore, He will work today from His throne. We went back to our rooms and had a shower by catching cold water in a bowl and pouring it over us. It felt good anyway.

### Thursday, November 16, 1989

We were up early as I wanted to study as I was to preach this morning. Eno, our driver came at 9:00 and we left for Korkori, which was about an hour's drive. On the way we were stopped by the Federal police. They looked us over but since the Captain was with us they told us that armed robbers were working that part of the country. Korkori was a much more primitive area and the church was way down a street that was over grown with weeds.

There was a huge crowd which made it extremely hot inside the building. We were so thankful for the two fans they had blowing right on us. You can't imagine the smell of hundreds of sweating bodies in the building. There was a good spirit of worship in the service. Paul spoke and had me pray at the end and the Lord really met His people.

On the way home the federal police again stopped us and told us that an armed gang had already commandeered two cars in the area. Eno really drove fast, like 120 K. That's fast on these narrow, rough roads with a drop off at the edge of the tarmac. Wow!

We went to our rooms and had a soft drink and then to the restaurant at 2:00 P.M. We ordered and it took a full hour to get our food. Then it was back to our rooms for a short nap but I had to study. Eno came about 4:45 and took us to Jesse Town across the Ethiope River. It was a combined service with many different churches present and many pastors. I spoke on *"the throne of God encircled with a rainbow."* It was about God, how He always looks at us through His covenant and works accordingly. Then we had the pastor's line up down the aisle and hold their hands up and we all prayed with Gabriel interpreting. The presence of the Lord really came into that place. It was ever so hot! I was soaked with sweat and it even made a puddle on the floor as it dripped from my elbow. The meeting was in the town hall and it was packed though it was a large building.

We came back to our rooms and I changed shirts and we went over to the restaurant and celebrated the Captain's 45th birthday with his wife. He has been so good to us so we wanted to treat them so we bought the dinner. Between them they ate three orders of pounded yams and three kinds of soup. One was egusie and one was palm nut with a big fish head in it and the other was some other nut. They take the pounded yam in their fingers and roll it, then dip it in their soup and put it in their mouth. It almost turned my stomach to the see the captain eat his fish head. It was a haddock but it was a big thing to them. We also sang happy birthday to him at the church.

### Friday, November 17, 1989

We were up and dressed by 7:00. We had slept well till about 3:30 when there was such a noise of big guns that awakened us. I opened the door and you could hear machine guns and rifles as well as mortars and big guns firing. We knew there were some soldiers staying here but we didn't know what to think. We found out when Captain Ermousele and Gabriel came that the Army and Navy were having what they called "activities" (maneuvers).

We talked with Captain Ermousele about his vision. He brought another minister friend to see us who had been a pastor for 20 years. He said he left the group because they were so stringent. There seemed to be such upheaval with ministers leaving one group and going to another.

We left about 10:00 for Benin and went to the headquarters of Benson Idahosa. Benson just drove up and took us into his office on the second floor. He gave us some coke and Fanta to drink. He was on the phone 15 minutes then came and sat and talked about 10 minutes. I asked about Ruth Elton, our friend Sidney Elton's daughter. He said she is all right and would send someone to get her to come down to see how she is doing. He wanted us to preach in his churches. We would leave from Warri on Sunday morning and be back for the Mothers of Nations Crusade in Warri in the evening.

By the time service started at 4:45, we were beat. They had planned the meeting to run till 8:30 but we got them to shorten it. Their choir sang beautifully and looked so lovely.

The trip back to Sapele was "hair-raising" as we had a different car and driver from the day before. It was Johnson with a Peugeot 505. He didn't want to run the air conditioner because it couldn't go as fast. The windshield was cracked and scratched quite heavily so it really magnified the lights. I've never seen so many trucks, cars and motorcycles without taillights. People also walked so close to the edge of the pavement. We got back to the hotel about 8:30 so we went right over and got a quick bite to eat and retired early.

### Saturday, November 18, 1989

We left about 8:45 to go to Orerokepe but first we visited the Bethesda Bible College in Warri and they showed us around the campus. It was very nice. On the campus there was a rabbit and chicken farm and they grew things such as cassava, mangos, bananas with other stuff.

The head of all of the Okpe tribe was in Orerokepe. We went to the village mansion and into the Kings Chambers, where many of the Chiefs had gathered for our visit. We sat down and then the king came in. He was a good man and really wanted me to pray for him as he wasn't feeling well. So Paul and I prayed for him. Then he asked if I would lay my hands on him and Paul quickly did and I joined him. Edmund Dolar told the king that I was the one who was the start of all the "Hallelujah Churches" (Pentecostal) in 1954. That was why he wanted me to lay my hands on him, as he had remembered all those miracles. He said he was about 16 when his father took him to our meetings where he accepted the Lord. He even had a Bible class in his mansion.

Edmund Dolar gave a word of prophecy to the king about the idols of his tribe. The king said he was struggling about what to do with all the idols of his tribe since the king is custodian of all the idols and many of his people were still not converted to Christ. Captain Ermousele told him that a lot of Christian chiefs appoint a chief that believed in idols to be the custodian. The high chief said he would do that. We then went out into the big courtroom and all the ladies wanted us to pray for them and again Paul took the lead and we prayed for them all.

Going back to the school, there was a good-sized crowd that had gathered under a tin roof. It was so hot, so we moved the meeting outside under some trees. I spoke on the waters of Marah and the Lord not putting those diseases on us if we did what he said. I had mentioned about the matter of agreement. I felt that Paul should finish it and he spoke a few minutes and we all prayed. The Lord really came down. We went around and just touched some as we prayed. There were so many who were healed.

### Graduation Time!

In the evening, we went to the town hall for the graduation of the Bethesda Bible College. It was literally packed with hundreds and hundreds of people. The choir couldn't even get in and had to stand where we would stand to speak and then go outside. The high chief and his court were also there. He seemed to enjoy the meetings. He told me that he stood in awe of me for the work we had done in their country. The choir from Warri did an excellent job.

They had so many speeches with all of them being read. One of them was an address by the leaders to the Sterns and us as the founding fathers. Here is a copy of part of it.

It is with great gratitude to God that we welcome you to this nation and the Christ Gospel Churches in particular. If we are to put it in the language of Paul the Apostle, we are "The Fruit of Your Apostleship" here in Nigeria. In fact Christ Gospel Church will constitute some of the stars on your crowns when you get to heaven. Till eternity, we shall ever remain grateful to you for accepting the call and the challenge of God to come over here to Africa, risk your lives and property to give us the gospel of light. Prior to your coming, Africa was known as "The Dark Continent" but today, the glorious light of the gospel has shown in our hearts and now Africa is regarded as the continent of light. Hallelujah!

If ever the history of the evangelization is written, your honorable names and of the team in 1954 will be indelibly written in gold. We regard this journey you have made as one of the missionary journeys made by

Paul and Barnabas. *"And Paul said into Barnabas, let us go again and visit our brethren in every city where we have preached the word of the Lord and see how they do . . . and they went through Syria and Cilicia confirming the churches."* Acts 15:36, 41.

We have over the years devoted ourselves to evangelism/crusades which has resulted in the springing up of churches in a number of places. Examples of these include Christ Gospel Churches in Egboker, Benin City, Eku, Abraka, Imo, Ayaba, Ughelli, Ogorode and Oghara Junction. About 80% of these branches are found in the rural areas. Our major vision has been to reach the unreached for Jesus. In the month of August we launched a powerful and successful evangelistic outreach in the Bini River/Lagos Junction. This area is in the creeks of the Niger Delta. The team had to travel nearly eight hours by hired boat to the shanty, Itshekiri villagers who live in little huts built above the water. Here, there are no roads and usually to go from house to house involves paddling a canoe. We rejoice that these churches are standing firm.

Paul then spoke on Ezekiel 47 and the river of God and Eleanor presented the diplomas. There were 16 graduates – all in caps and gowns. Edmund Dolar's wife was one of them and took top honors. Mildred presented special certificates of the Nigerian Bible Society to several graduates.

Edmund Dolar, the Vice President and Director of Christian Education of the Christ Gospel Churches had addressed the crowd at the graduation. He remarked, "Is it not of utmost significance that the Sterns are even right now in our midst this day as their 'Baby,' Bethesda marks the seventh phase of her experience as an institution of Christian education in Nigeria? Let's give them a round of applause for their worthy contributions toward the spiritual growth of Nigeria! We also wish to draw attention to the presence in our midst of Rev. Paul Cannon and his wife, Mildred Cannon. They are here in Nigeria, along with the Sterns, on a mission of comfort and encouragement to the churches in Nigeria. Since Rev. Cannon disclosed to me that he was the only surviving member of that crew of 'Hallelujah' miracle crusaders that stormed Nigeria in the early fifties, I've come to regard the man with awe. His life is indeed a miracle. I'm pretty sure Rev. Cannon still has enough fire in his bones to frighten away a thousand demons! Please also give Rev. Cannon a round of applause for fruitful pioneering service in Nigeria."

We met Pastor and Mrs. Sagay who pastored a church in Warri. He was a nice quiet man. Captain Ermousele took the offering and encouraged the people to give their best and had a good response. Of course the Sterns and us gave heavily. They had all of the ministers to walk out together but the people kept pushing in ahead. All they wanted to do was to touch us or wipe our perspiration on themselves for healing. That might be repulsive to us but the Lord did meet many of them according to their faith. Many times it is only a point of contact for faith to work.

We drove back to the school where the ladies had some "mineral water," cookies that were hot with pepper, peanuts and some meat on a stick and black-eyed pea cakes. Then back to Sapele and our room. We got off at the office to get our key as when we closed the door that morning we couldn't get back in. So they had a carpenter to come and change the lock. Paul met with Captain and Gabriel a few minutes and told him we didn't need to go to Orea Abraka tomorrow so they wanted us to meet with their executive committee at Gabriel's house.

### Sunday, November 19, 1989

We were rudely awakened at 6:50 with something biting Mildred on the left arm and left a welt. We couldn't find it so we never found out what it was. We went to the Christ's Gospel Church headquarters church in Sapele. Gabriel's daughter led the song service and also sang a special with the choir. The church was really full. We went in our Nigerian clothes as they brought each of us an outfit. They were so pretty and we were very appreciative. However, they were terribly hot especially after the power went off. Thank God it went off just at the end of my preaching. They had a good number of people testify that they had been healed. We had communion after Paul instructed them on it. There were so many who wanted to take it but they ran out of the elements, so a number of us shared what we had with our wife.

I spoke in the morning service about the crisis of the Church in Acts 1:14 and on Acts 3 and 4. How that in a financial crisis Peter said to the crippled man, *"Silver and Gold have I none but such as I have give I unto thee."* Lack of money wasn't their problem. They needed the Lord to work among them. That's why Peter and John were on their way to the Temple to pray when this happened. So I encouraged them to pray as in Acts chapter 4. This was a hard week on us physically because it was so tiring in the extreme heat.

### Monday, November 20, 1989

We had breakfast with our dear friend, Michael Okah. A fellow came in a beat up old taxi to take us to Aba. Mildred was so depleted from lack of potassium that it would not have been good for her to go. Eleanor wanted the two of them to stay and Paul and I go but I wasn't going to leave Mildred in that condition. Paul was going to go with Michael but then decided against it so he wrote a letter and sent it with the driver to tell him the reason we couldn't come. All of us then walked over to the little store and bought a few things and got an "ice cream cone" since it was so terribly hot. Bishop God Do Well came by and insisted that we ride back to the City of God. He was a bit perturbed that Michael would let us do that. We told him that Michael didn't know about it and would have provided something but we didn't want to bother him and besides, we liked to walk.

At 2:00 we went to Michael's for lunch and it was wonderful. They insisted that we return at 6:00 for dinner but Mildred just couldn't go. It was 7:30 when we came back. Michael asked Eleanor to speak. I had to go to the room as diarrhea was working on me, so I went to the meeting and sat back a ways. The fans were on low so there wasn't any breeze. Being really tired and with diarrhea and Mildred also being sick, discouragement began to sweep over my mind. I really felt like going home and forgetting this part of the world but I knew there was a great need, especially with the Church ministers. I determined to seek God and get His answer. At the end of the meeting, I shook hands with the Bulgarians and they were very warm toward me. Madame Mosheshe was there – what a jewel! She was so warm and friendly and asked about Mildred and said to greet her well.

### Tuesday, November 21, 1989

Mildred was feeling some better so we went to Michael's for breakfast at 8:30. When we got back, we met with Mosheshe and Michael. We walked through the new building. It was huge and was supposed to seat 10,000 people. The Bulgarians still said they were going to put in a white marble floor and face the outside and the columns with it for free. That would be more than $1 million and they were to start in a week or so. It was so hot in that big building. I mentioned that the pulpit should be the focal point since our belief is that the word of God should be predominant. He thought that was excellent and was really excited. He said that God surely sent us as he needed direction on some things.

We went to the office of the school and were joined by Ezekiel Mosheshe who was headquartered in London. He was a contractor too. That was how Mosheshe had started and owned the Mosheshe group which was several different businesses. He told us that he did not know why the Lord made him wealthy but now after talking to us, he saw that it was to use his wealth for the kingdom of God. He said that he missed us so badly when we were gone and it's like having family return. Michael said that all his workers including the yard men and cooks really liked us. They said that all the other ministers never paid any attention to them and seem so arrogant but we stopped and talked with them and called them by name. I told Michael that they are people just like anybody else. Why shouldn't we treat them with respect?

In the school office we talked and put on paper just what they would like for us to do. The only things they wanted us to get were free Bibles and literature. I was drenched with perspiration when I came back to our room.

Mildred had gone on ahead of us and she and Eleanor had rearranged the room. I said, "Now you feel like you are at home changing the furniture." We all laughed. We laid down and took a short nap and then it was off to Michael's for dinner.

I spent quite a bit of time reading the book of Acts from my Greek New Testament. I really enjoyed it. It just throws a little different light than the King James Version. I was so glad that Mildred came along as she is such a wonderful wife. I felt bad that she wasn't allotted any time at the Mother's Crusade coming up this weekend but it'll work out.

### Wednesday, November 22, 1989

Mildred was up before 7:00 and we went over to Chief O Duma's for breakfast. He lived just a block or two from Michael's. He had a lovely house with a sunken living room with a beautiful marble terrazzo floor. We had a good discussion about the Muslim north. I told them of what we saw about that area when we first came in 1954. Unless the church gets together and converts the north, the Muslims will come down and overrun all the Christian states. They all agreed. We discussed how that our battle is not just prayer but prayer in the spirit.

Back in our room, I read and prayed and fell off to sleep not knowing who was going to preach in the evening. I wanted to speak really bad but felt like Michael should ask, which he did after lunch. We went out about 7:40 and I spoke on Abraham the Pilgrim from Genesis 12:4-9 and Hebrews 11:9-11. Paul and Eleanor really thanked me for the word of the Lord. Mildred said it was a masterpiece. Of course, I didn't feel like it was much of anything only it was very real to me.

Paul finally got a hold of Ron Childs and found out that they wanted each of us to teach in the Bible College in Benin City an hour each, from 10-12 and 6-8. He wanted us to teach on the laying on of hands and then do it if we feel led of the Holy Spirit. That was exciting to all of us. Actually, they wanted us to go to Benin on Sunday morning but it was too hard to make a two-hour trip there and two hours back and be ready that evening for the Mothers of the Nation Crusade in Warri.

We all sat down and had a very meaningful talk with Michael and Beauty. I told him that if Mildred and I weren't needed at the Crusade then we would go to Benin on Sunday to minister and remain there. We understood it was a ladies meeting but they told us it was for everybody with the women being its leaders. This was the first time it was ever done here. Michael then asked if I could be prepared for Saturday evening if the lady from Ibadon didn't come. I told him, "Sure."

### Thursday, November 23, 1989

We went over to the mansion for breakfast and Mosheshe greeted me well and said he thought it was a powerful word the night before and he really enjoyed it. To me, that was a real compliment.

The four of us left on the City of God bus to go to Eku for Thanksgiving. On the way the engine started to miss and then cut out, so the driver shut off the air conditioning. It took about an hour to get to Eku. We got off at Gene and Jackie Leggs' house and let the driver go. Gene was the administrator of the Baptist Hospital in Eku. They took us to one of the lady's home where we stayed. About 4:45 they came and took us to their beach on the Ethiope River. We had to drive through a really swampy jungle but they had made a road and fixed the beach. Then Gene and the Stearns went swimming but Mildred and I with others sat in lawn chairs and took some pictures. I couldn't help but wonder where the crocodiles were.

For Thanksgiving, the whole compound plus some others gathered under Gene's carport for a big dinner. They had invited several of the African doctors and we explained the custom to them. It was a good time of fellowship with some excellent people and wonderful food. We visited with a number of people and found them extremely interesting.

### Friday, November 24, 1989

The alarm went off at 6:30 but we both were already awake. In fact I don't think I slept a wink as the bed was so hard as they had a sheet of plywood between the mattresses. At daybreak a lovely bird began to sing outside our window and then others joined in. Mildred always loved the singing of the birds. We dressed and went to the Leggs for breakfast. They had Ted and Shirley Wiest, the general manager of Life Flour Mill in Sapele as their guest also. We walked back to our cabin and waited for the bus to come. He came at 8:15 so we loaded up and returned. The engine was still missing and jerking but we made it back to the City of God okay.

We returned to our room and Eleanor came to tell us that Reverend Sagay was there to pick us up and that Michael had not canceled that meeting. We went with Brother Sagay to his school and church. He had a school with 300 secondary students. He introduced us to the children and he had them quote scripture and we gave them a gift that Eleanor had given us to give. We each spoke a few minutes and then went over to

Brother Sagay's house and had a soft-drink. Then he brought us home in his Mercedes car.

Bishop God Do Well was at our room and wanted to take us to see the Niger River but we first had to go to Michael's for dinner. The Bishop and Wilson went with us to Michael's and had dinner with us. It was very good but by then it was too late to go to see the Niger River. So we came home and I took a nap while Mildred studied. She was supposed to speak in the morning.

Michael came after us at 7:20 in the evening and we walked over to the mansion where we met Margaret Idahosa and her entourage. She was a very lovely and beautiful lady. We had prayer and then walked over to the outdoor platform. It was a fair sized crowd, but how do you estimate the number? They had been going since at least 6:00 that evening. Beauty Okah was in charge of the service. The church of God Mission choir sang two songs and their ladies also sang a song. Beauty introduced all of us starting with Mosheshe and he declared the crusade open. They took the offering and with a great fanfare introduced Margaret Idahosa and with a great fanfare paid tribute to Mosheshe and then to Mama Mosheshe and had her speak. Mama Mosheshe read her statement which was excellent. Margaret then spoke and was a very good speaker and a crowd mover. I thought, "She is a rare breed for Nigeria!" She spoke on the Syro-Phoenician woman and it was a good, solid, faith building message. It was the same message we had preached over 40 years ago. She called for sinners to come to Jesus and a great number came forward. Then she prayed in mass for the sick which I thought was so interesting. In fact, it wasn't much different from how we did it in 1954. All of it told me that they really got our message in 1954 for which I was very thankful.

### Saturday, November 25, 1989

Our day began at 7:00. They were to have a morning service but this was a time all over the nation for cleaning up the environment which no one told us about. They have it once a month and no one is allowed on the streets from 7:00-10:00 a.m. They must stay in their compound and clean it up. Mildred was glad because she just couldn't seem to get anything. Wilson Ovwoh wanted to take us to breakfast but couldn't because of the cleanup day.

Paul, Michael and I left for Orombo, a small village outside Warri, a couple miles down a two-track road in Miranda's Peugeot. There was a very good turnout and did the Lord ever move! These people really knew how to worship. The pastor had been a hopeless cripple and was healed in our meetings in 1954. I spoke briefly with Paul having the main message. Afterwards they gave us a big pan of tangerines, one of oranges and grapefruit and one of pineapple and paw paw (papaya). We got back about 1:00 and took a little nap before going to Michael's for dinner.

We came back and I studied as well as Mildred and took a short nap as the extreme heat was so exhausting. We both spoke that night. The crowd was down slightly but it was a good turnout with probably about 1100 to 1200 maybe more, who knows. Mildred spoke about Jesus being the bread of life. I spoke about Deborah. There were a number who came to receive Christ. Then I prayed for healing for all that came forward with about half of them coming forward. We saw one of the Bulgarians come forward and he was so glad to see us.

### Sunday, November 26, 1989

Today, Paul and Eleanor went to Christ the Rock Church and we went to Bishop God Do Well's and the Christ Missionary Crusaders church, the one that had their convention a while back. Bishop God Do Well came at 9:45 according to his word. He had left at seven to go to Benin and came back. He had sent word yesterday with his driver but they didn't get it right. So he said if you are going to be their leader sometimes you have to go yourself. We went with him to his house and he put on his white African dress and then we went to church.

They had the video camera on us when we arrived. We went around and came on the platform from the rear. The church was fairly full at the start. It was a combined service and a wedding. We had to wait a long time for the bride to come, even after the groom and best man came in. The choir sang several songs and a couple solos and finally the bridal party came. The bridesmaid and ring-bearer and flower girl all came down with the mistress of ceremonies walking backwards down the aisle to make sure they came properly. Then after a couple of songs the bride came in. A lady was straightening her gown and train most of the way down. She came and stood next to her groom. They had put four chairs up front and covered them with a white sheet and a pink one and put a white blanket on the floor.

The bishop then proceeded with the ceremony. It was unique to say the least. When he came to the phrase, "If any can show just cause why these cannot be married, let him now speak or forever hold their peace," he said, "Now think about it for three minutes and speak up." No one did so the crowd really applauded. The sweat was pouring down the young groom's face. You should have seen the smile when the three minutes were over. The Bishop then had them hold each other's wrist and say their vows and when they made their vows; they would grip the arms very forcefully. The bishop told them that when he said in the name of the Father, Son and the Holy Spirit, they were to embrace for the first time. So when he ran the count down and said in the name of the Father,

Son and the Holy Spirit the man grabbed her and she grabbed him with a big embrace as the crowd roared with excitement. He then pronounced them man and wife and then had me to preach.

It was 1:15 when I got up to speak and I preached a half hour without an interpreter. They did have a group at the back interpreting to those who didn't understand English. I spoke on the man and wife relationship being like Christ and the Church. I finished with Jesus loving the church so much that He died for her and then explained how to be part of the bride of Christ. Then I gave the altar service and we sang "Ya Re, Jesu, se we Ya Re" and about 100 men and women came to the front right around the bride and groom to receive the Lord. I led them in the sinner's prayer and prayed for them and then prayed for the sick and turned it back to Bishop God Do Well. Then his driver took us to the mansion.

Paul and Eleanor were eating with the Mosheshes and we joined them. Michael and Beauty came later and joined us. Mrs. Mosheshe gave each of us men some cologne and the ladies some bubble bath and a scarf. The Mosheshes walked with us to our gate and we shook his hand. They just raved about my message last night.

Michael came and we walked over to the crusade. It was a little cooler but the turnout was down a little, I don't know why. They had four choirs singing and also the Twins. It was so crowded on the platform that they were right up against our feet. Eleanor spoke on Esther and many came to the altar. Afterwards, my thoughts were, "Well this one is over and we look forward to Benin and then home." That was because I was so concerned about my dad.

### Monday, November 27, 1989

Sleep was slow in coming to both of us. I don't know if it was because the air conditioner wasn't working or if we were just restless because of spiritual things. Anyway we were up at 6:00 feeling drugged out. We piled things in our bags and were ready when Michael came at 7:15 to take us to breakfast. We went back to the City of God and loaded our luggage. We had to go by the mansion and tell the Mosheshes goodbye and thanked her for the beautiful clothes she gave us. The seamstress brought a gown for Mildred and a shirt for me that Mama Mosheshe ordered for us. They were a solid light blue with beautiful needlework. We thanked them for the use of their facilities and the gifts. Mama Mosheshe gave us several books. She was such a giver. It was like she couldn't give us enough. What a difference in when we came and when we left. It was like we were on trial and we proved to be okay.

There were three ladies from Benin that rode with us along with Michael and Beauty. We went in the little bus and this time we had Mosheshe's oldest driver. He really put the pedal to the metal. We left as soon as we picked up Beauty. These roads are something else. It used to be a paved road but much of it was nothing but pot holes with so much of the asphalt gone. We left about 9:15 and got to Benin about 10:45. We found Ron Childs and he had them bring our luggage upstairs on the second floor where he lived. His wife wasn't home but was in Jos. Our room had an old air conditioner and it rattled and banged and didn't cool very well. They had just turned it on so it was still extremely hot.

Ron gave us a Coke and some ice and then we went to the Bible school to teach. Paul taught the first hour from 11 to 12 and I taught from 12 to 1. It was so hot under that tin roofed building that I drenched my clothes, so I changed immediately when I got back. I spoke about the outpouring of the Holy Spirit and the restoration of the gifts. Paul had covered the restoration of the Church. We repeated the same to the night school. He spoke from 6:30 to 7:30 with me taking the next hour.

In the afternoon we had dinner about 2:30 with the Hodges on the fourth floor. They were a couple from Australia where she grew up on the Murray River. Their two smaller children were born in Benin. Their baby was about five months old. It was amusing because there was a stream of ants crawling up both sides of their custard bowl so Mildred wouldn't eat any but I did. She had a bunch of ants in a water glass so she didn't drink anything either. We had a lovely visit with them and they had so many questions about our first meetings in 1954.

Earlier we had met one of Benson Idahosa's main pastors and overseers. When he heard I was the only living member of the team of 1954, he was so thrilled to meet me. He said he was a small boy and didn't go to the meetings but a lot of people from his village went and were healed. He said that was the beginning of the "Hallelujah Churches" (Pentecostal). He mentioned how that they were called "Hallelujah Churches" because so many people were healed when we shouted hallelujah. He described all the seed that has come to the church in Nigeria as being like an ear of corn. That grain planted has produced a big, big harvest. That was so thrilling to hear.

What a joy to minister to the students. When I finished, they gave me a standing ovation and they went on and on clapping. There was much more of the Holy Spirit in the day group than the night, but there also were three times more students in the day than at night. Those at night worked during the day. After the evening class we sat around and visited and retired about 10:15.

### Tuesday, November 28, 1989

We got up early as my bed was very saggy – like sitting up in bed with a really hard kapok pillow. The air-conditioner clunked when the compressor shut off but it finally cooled the room.

It was off to class at 8:00 and I ministered on the laying on of hands and prophecy doctrinally for about 30 minutes. Paul took up with being prepared and how to get ready then we took their questions. We then laid hands on a man who was their Prefect but we didn't know it. I saw him as a pier that jutted out into the ocean but the connection to the land was destroyed, and he was an island that had stood against the storms and waves and he would be one that would go to other lands and be cut off from Nigeria but would be one to establish the church and be an overseer of others. He broke, wept and said it was all true.

Then we had a man and wife come and their prophecy was rich and confirmed his life and ministry. Come to find out, he had been a customs officer that had gotten wealthy through bribes. When he was saved the Lord said give it back to the government. So he built a hospital close to Oweiri and gave it to the government. The Church of God Mission was running it. It was thrilling to see such a flow of the Holy Spirit.

Again I came home drenched. I had left a puddle of sweat on the floor where it ran off my elbow from holding the mike. My handkerchief was so wet that it wouldn't soak another drop. So I changed immediately and Elizabeth, their housekeeper, gave me a drink of ice water. Oh, how refreshing! We had dinner about 2:30 in Ron's house. Then we went downtown to the market and bought the boys some hats and the girls some beads. We came home and visited with Jenny Danielson and had some coffee.

We went back to the night class and repeated the teaching of the morning and laid hands on one couple, a single man and one single woman. It wasn't quite as hot but I changed clothes and we went downtown to a hotel with Andrew and Jenny Danielson, Ron and the Sterns for a bite to eat.

Before the service, we went by to see the Faith Center, Benson Idahosa's church, and its grounds. It was a huge place but typically African. The auditorium would seat between 7000 and 11,000. The weather was extremely hot so we didn't walk around much. We saw the primary and secondary schools, and they had about 1000 students.

We went by what they called "the White House" (Benson Idahosa's house). Was it ever palatial from the outside. Then we drove by his new place that he was building. It was a huge place but all we could see was just a big fence. We were told that people in the church were upset over the new house, saying why does he need a new one. His reply was "I have faith to do so." Still they said they were struggling to complete the buildings for the church. This is where ministers could learn a lesson. Don't put your own desires and conveniences above the people. Unity is still the best policy.

## Wednesday, November 29, 1989

We were up at 6:30 and had breakfast. We put our duds in the bags and all of us went to the classes at 8:00. They sang and worshiped a little and Paul spoke for a few minutes. I followed, explaining that we could make the prophet look good or make him a liar by believing or not believing the prophets. We laid hands on a couple from Zaire and a young man from Calabar and then we prayed for the staff. Paul and Eleanor had a word for a Nigerian lady who lost her husband in a car accident a few years earlier. Her husband was a dentist. Both Paul and I had a word for the school. They gave us a standing ovation when we left. They were such an appreciative people.

Some of the students put our bags in the medical van for our trip to Lagos. They told us it was a new one that Benson Idahosa had purchased though it said given by Kenneth and Gloria Copeland on the back. We gave Doreen, a doctor's wife from the USA, who runs the hospital, enough money for gas and the driver's food and lodging. We left about 10:00 A.M. Her driver drove between 80 and 90 miles an hour most of the way down. We made the trip to Lagos in three hours. The seats were really short and cramped but we made it okay even though there was no air conditioning.

We went by a German couple's home in a suburb of Lagos that were part of Bonnke's team. My! What a beautiful house. It was certainly a palace and built by true craftsmen. I was glad for them. Bonnke seemed to take care of his people.

They were getting ready to drive the equipment truck to Ivory Coast for the next big crusade. They will drive through the Republic of Benin, Ghana, etc. to get there. They said it was a very good road. His wife will drive the land cruiser and he will drive a huge semi truck. This couple had been in Africa for 10 years.

We drove on to the airport after stopping to pick up a cane headboard and two chairs for Doreen. Then we went on to the Stop Over Motel. They had one double room and one suite. It was 390 Naira for the one and 430 for the other. Then we had dinner together.

The Sterns went with Ron and Doreen to shop for some cloth. Mildred was afraid of diarrhea and no place to go so we stayed in our room. Ron and Doreen came by and talked about 15 minutes. Then we bid them goodbye.

## Thursday, November 30, 1989

Wow! Was that bed hard? The air conditioner really got us cold so we shut it off during the early morning. This was the first double bed that we've slept on since leaving home. It sure felt good to be next to my wife! This was the day to begin our journey home but it was a one of mixed emotions. We were anxious to get home as we had gotten no news from home or about my dad. We sure hoped everybody was well and things were okay. I thought every day about our sons and their families and about my dad in the nursing home with a stroke. I sure hoped he was still living. That part was terribly hard to take. I hoped the church was doing okay but I realized that if the Lord doesn't build the house we all labor in vain.

All of us took a taxi and went to a shopping area close to the ocean and bought a few Nigerian souvenirs. Then we checked out of the motel and went to the Lagos Airport. We got there about 6:00 in the evening because we knew it would take a long time to get checked in. The Lagos airport, at the time, had a reputation all of its own. Several people had told us about the chaos of trying to get checked in. In fact we had bought the little book about the Lagos Airport describing its problems. We got in a fairly long line since there were several of them. People kept coming in and getting on the side of our line and would push in ahead of us. It was like cattle – if they got their head just a little in front, they forcibly pushed their way in. Finally, about 9:00, Paul said to them, "We are visitors and guests in your country. Is this the way you treat your guests?" They all looked so embarrassed and sheepishly slowed down.

We finally got to the airline counter about 10:00 and they went through all of our passports and information and it seemed like they did a hundred things. Then we went through Immigration and Customs. Finally we got on the plane about midnight. Can you imagine it took us six hours to go through all of that? Our plane lifted off at 12:30 in the morning for Frankfort, Germany. We found out later that my father passed away at that very time back in Baton Rouge, Louisiana.

### Friday, December 1, 1989

We landed in Frankfort, Germany and Jan Barendse was there to meet us. He took us to a place where we had breakfast and then he told me that my sister Maggie Campbell had called and said that my dad had passed away. That was a tough blow even though we knew he couldn't last very long when we left him earlier and had prayed with him. I've often said that even though you are expecting it, when death comes to a loved one, it's still like a mule kicking you in the chest. Jan took us to some folks home where we had stayed before. Our plans were to have two weeks of meetings in Germany before returning home.

I called my sister, Maggie, and told her that we would try to get our tickets changed so we could be there for the funeral. Then we went to Lufthansa to try and get our tickets changed. They told us there was no way they could change them and we would have to contact our Travel Agent and have them change them. They said they were just as compassionate as anyone but they go by the rules. We called New York and talked to our Travel Agent and they told us there was nothing they could do either. Then we went downtown to Lufthansa's main office and talked to a lady. She was nice but said there was nothing they could do but suggested that we go to the airport the next morning early and look for a smiling, generous face as they are the only ones that can allow it.

### Saturday, December 2, 1989

We got up very early as Jan had a young man drive us into Frankfort in a Mercedes Benz. Paul went with us because he spoke some German as they had lived here a few years before. The young man drove 120 kilometers an hour and even higher on the Autobahn. He let us out and Paul helped us with our baggage. We looked over all the long lines and finally we saw this one guy who looked like he was friendly. We got in that line and when we got up to the counter, Paul told him about our situation with my dad dying and we needed to get home for the funeral. Sure enough, he said we could. So he took our tickets and we weighed in and then bid Paul goodbye. We had to hurry as there was a huge backup at the security place. Things were extremely tight with soldiers and policemen all over the place with automatic weapons. Our hallway led into another hallway with a huge mass of people waiting at the security check point. Fortunately, a couple had mercy on us and let us in. We knew the Lord was making a way for us as we had prayed diligently that we could make it for the funeral. We went through security and then on to our gate and got a seat. We had a snack to eat and bought an English newspaper. The headlines were that the iron curtain wall had been breached and was coming down. There was such a thrill in the air as East Germany was being liberated. You could sense the feeling of excitement in the air.

When it came time to board, they said there was a delay as they had some luggage but the passengers of that luggage weren't there. So they took all the luggage off the plane and put it on the ground between the plane and the ramp. Then they had us go by and point out each of our bags and they loaded them. Two were not claimed. Finally we took off for New York City.

### Sunday, December 3, 1989

Upon our arrival at Kennedy Airport in New York, we went immediately to the TWA counter and got in a short line. When it was our time, a young lady waited on us. I asked her if we could trade our tickets that were to Chicago for ones to New Orleans as my father had died and we wanted to get to the funeral. She tried and then told us there was nothing she could do. So we asked to see her supervisor. The supervisor came and we told her our story and how Lufthansa had let us on. So she poked around on the computer and said, "How does $100 sound for both tickets?" She told us this was the original difference in the fare prices from New York to Chicago and New York to New Orleans. We said that would be great. So she changed it and we later boarded a plane for New Orleans. I called Maggie and they met us in New Orleans.

They picked us up and we went to their home in Livingston Parish, then to the Funeral Home where we saw a lot of the family. It was so hard seeing them and dad for the first time. The family wanted me to preach the funeral and it would be at Revival Temple in Walker. Philip and Thomas, two of our sons had come down for the funeral. We buried Dad beside our Mother in Baton Rouge at the plots they had bought years ago. We then rode home with our sons to Muskegon, Michigan.

## Summing up the Whole Trip.

Being our first time to visit Nigeria in many years, we were so thrilled to see the results of our pioneer efforts in those huge meetings back in 1954. It was staggering to our minds and the work was much greater than anything we had ever envisioned. It made us realize that all of our sacrifices had paid off in a great way. Indeed the Lord had done a marvelous work and continued it through all those years by raising up others to carry it on and to expand His work. We also had the deep satisfaction that we had been used greatly of the Lord on this trip to bless His wonderful people in that land. Indeed the original vision we had, has been fulfilled though we didn't get to have the part we wanted too so badly. Jesus is still Head of the Church and He is the One who builds it and to Him belongs all the glory. We were just little instruments in His Almighty hands. Thank you Jesus for calling me into the ministry and letting me have this small part.

# The Return To Ghana
# Chapter 12

From the day I left Ghana in January of 1954, I had a dream of returning and ministering there again. While pastoring in Muncie, Indiana we had our friend, James McKeown, who was the head of the Ghana Apostolic Churches visit and minister in the church. Those were always great times. We discussed our returning to Ghana and he said he would love that. Our feelings were that since we were not a part of the Wings of Healing anymore, we didn't want to be a cause of division there or anywhere. So we never had the opportunity to return though there was always a dream we would return someday.

My wife and I traveled extensively throughout the United States ministering in various kinds of churches. We also ministered in many churches in Mexico, in the states of Michoacan and Guerraro with Dr. Eldon Wilson for a month at a time each year for several years. We introduced the laying on of hands and prophecy to the churches in fellowship with Vida Abundante in Morelia. Also it was our delight to minister in Nairobi and Mombasa, Kenya in various churches for a month culminating in teaching over a thousand pastors and ministers for a week at 9 hours each day with Paul and Eleanor Stern. This was a conference called by Jewel Matheny of the Clarence Matheny Ministries.

Our youngest son, Mark and his wife, Ellen, had been pioneer missionaries in Mexico for fourteen years and planted the first Evangelical church in Purandiro, Michoacan. They had trained the local workers and then turned the work over to them and they have done a great job of carrying it on. Mark then enrolled in Regent University in their Master's program where he became involved with Dr. Howard Foltz, the Professor of Missiology and Founder of Accelerated International Missions Strategies (AIMS).

## Working with AIMS

Earlier, we had built our retirement home in Louisiana and still traveled in world-wide ministry. During our travels, we would stop and see Mark and Ellen and their children whenever possible. On one of our trips we stopped to be with Mark and Ellen a few days in Virginia Beach and all of us had dinner with Dr. and Mrs. Foltz. We had met Dr. Foltz earlier in New Orleans. In January of 2002, we took the AIMS Associates Training at Regent University and became Certified Associates. Dr. Foltz wanted us to join their staff which would require us to move to Virginia Beach. Because their vision was so similar to ours and we felt it was the leading of the Lord, we went home and sold our beautiful new home. We moved to Virginia Beach in August of 2002 and became the Director of

International Development for AIMS. Shortly after that, Mark was appointed International Director of AIMS. During this time, he and our staff did our Equipping for the Harvest Seminars in many foreign lands, such as Ethiopia, Ukraine, Mexico, Cuba, Argentina, Chili, India, Pakistan, Indonesia, China and Mongolia. They also taught them to The International Pentecostal Holiness Church leaders and the Church of God leaders in Cleveland, Tennessee.

## The Work of AIMS!

At AIMS, we specialized in reaching unreached people's groups (UPGs). Our primary goal was in planting churches where there had never been a church before. We did this by getting the groups there to all work together. Then we would go and teach them the principles of going out and planting local churches among them. We taught them to partner with other groups to reach an area. This was all covered in our "Equipping for the Harvest" Seminars. This way we trained workers in reaching the unreached peoples groups in their country.

Overseas our training was usually three days to a week long where they would first find out who the unreached people groups were in their nation. We took the old adage to a new height, "Give a man a fish and you feed him for a day but teach him how to fish and you can feed him for life." We added, "Teach him how to teach others to fish and you can feed a village for life." Basically we were just expanding our vision we had for Africa in 1953-4 where we trained and empowered the nationals to reach their own people. Like the Apostle Paul, we wanted to go to the regions beyond and to those who had never heard the gospel. The seminars were extremely effective. From the year 2000 to October of 2010, we were instrumental in planting 31,966 local churches where none had existed before. We did not count the planting of churches where another church existed. In the year of 2004 it was my privilege to be a part of the teams that did the seminars in China and Indonesia. Both of these reaped tremendous dividends for the Kingdom.

## Our Return to Ghana

Through AIMS, we had tried to contact The Church of Pentecost in Ghana who had changed their name from Ghana Apostolic Church. This was the group that our friend, James McKeown had started when we went to the Gold Coast in 1953 but to no avail. Then one day Pastor Alfred Nyamichi, head of the House of Faith Churches in Ghana, came to Regent University to meet with Dr. Foltz who had done an Equipping for the Harvest Seminar four years earlier. Dr. Foltz had me meet with him and Pastor Alfred at Founder's Inn. It was a wonderful meeting with them. Pastor Alfred told me that they had planted 1500 churches in one year after the seminar. We worked on plans to do several AIMS seminars in Ghana. This finally took place in the fall of 2004.

## Really Excited!

Needless to say, our whole AIMS staff was excited about my return trip to Ghana after fifty years. As International Director, Mark Cannon headed up the team with Pamella Foster, our African Director. Joining us were two AIMS Associates, Paul Gmitter, pastor of Faith Fellowship in Dexter, NY and Patty Giles, wife of Walter Giles, a Priest of the Episcopal Churches in Carthage, Lowville and Copenhagen, NY. This was Paul's first trip with AIMS and Patty's second one. Dennis Jones, CEO of AIMS and Jason Benedict would also do a business track to train business people in Christian principles. Pastor Alfred Nyamichi of the House of Faith churches was hosting the seminars in Kumasi. He also had tried to get some of the other groups we had worked with in 1953 to be a part but none were interested.

Paul, Patty and I left the airport in Norfolk at 4:10 PM, Thursday, October 21, 2004 and flew to Chicago where we boarded a Northwest Airlines flight to Amsterdam, Netherlands. So far all went well but it didn't last. Again, Murphy's law takes effect! We had a 6 hour layover which turned into a 13 hour layover because they said our plane was given to the route going to Tokyo, Japan and they would have to fly another plane up from South America. This would take at least six hours. I couldn't help but think, "Why is it when I'm on a flight going to Nigeria or Ghana they give our plane to another route?

Mark and Pamella Foster had left a day earlier to meet with some people of the International Pentecostal Holiness Church in London about doing AIMS seminars there. The AIMS' travel agent had scheduled all of our flights to arrive in Accra, Ghana within an hour of each other so we could all be picked up at the airport together. Our plane was scheduled to arrive at 7:30 PM Friday night and theirs an hour later at 8:30.

## We Arrive in Accra, Ghana!

Finally our plane arrived and we flew to Accra, Ghana and we were six hours late. It was 1:30 Saturday morning when we finally arrived. Fortunately Pastor Jonathon and two other brothers were there to meet us and take us through Immigration and Customs. This saved us perhaps hours of time. Thankfully these pastors knew a lot of the workers which made it quicker but it still took us close to two hours. They took us to the home of Nana, a business friend of Dennis Jones, our CEO, where Mark and Pamella were waiting for us.

We got a few hours of rest but had to be up for breakfast at 8:00 in order to meet with the Leadership of The House of Faith. We had to work out the details for our travel to Kumasi for the Seminars and for the meetings on Sunday in the Accra area.

After a lovely breakfast at Nana's house, Pastor Jonathon's driver took us sightseeing. We drove through several streets in Labadi (The outskirts of Accra). This was where James McKeown and I went out and preached on the streets fifty one years ago. Back then it was a rough area with a lot of witchcraft and no churches. When I finished speaking the first night, they mocked me and laughed me to scorn but we showed love and kindness to them anyway. There were no conversions that evening. Most of the people's bodies were loaded with Juju charms which had cost them lots of money. We went out again the next evening and had a huge crowd and this time they were much friendlier. There was a great break through, starting with the children with hundreds turning to the Lord. The Gold Coast Apostolic Church (Changed to Church of Pentecost in 1962) had a large church in the area. It was great to go back and see what tremendous advances the gospel had caused.

Nana the Queen Mother

We visited the Textile Market where some of our staff bought some African shirts and dresses to wear for Sunday morning because it was so hot and we were told to wear ties when we preach the Word. We then met with Pastor Jonathon, Ennis and another brother for about 2 hours setting up the meetings for the next day. It was decided that each of us would go to separate churches. Sunday morning the driver took us to the Central Church of the House of Faith in downtown Accra where each of us was taken to the church where we would minister. Mark spoke in the Central Church with Pamella, Patty, Paul Gmitter and I going to outlying districts. I went to Tema, the industrialized area of Accra by the Atlantic Ocean and we had an excellent meeting. It wasn't a large gathering as it was a relative new church plant. They brought us back to the Central Church and then we had dinner at Nana's house. We had requested Peanut Soup and it was out of this world!

Pamella went to the farthest place so she was the last one to get back. She met and got the picture of the Queen Mother that was saved in our meetings with her whole family as a result of a miracle for her mother in 1953. We were scheduled to leave at 3:00 PM for Kumasi but she didn't get back till 3:00 in the afternoon. When she arrived, we hurriedly ate and loaded our luggage and got on our way by 4:00.

### Pamella Foster's Report of The Queen Mother

On October 24, 2004 I was in Ghana as part of ministry team from AIMS to teach and train national leaders. This was a large gathering which was organized under the leadership of Alfred Nyamichi in the coastal city of Accra. On the weekend before the training started, the team fanned out into towns around Accra in order to preach and minister to the local churches. On that particular Sunday I had the privilege of preaching in a village church with about 150 members.

After the service, we began our drive back to Accra when the driver looked in his review mirror and said excitedly, "Oh, you have to meet the Queen Mother."

"Queen mother," I asked?

"Yes, she is the Queen Mother of her people, and you have to meet her!" He was so excited I could only respond with, "That would be great."

Shortly afterwards, we left the main road and drove into a small village and arrived at a series of small houses, all positioned around a common courtyard. I was escorted into one of the homes and there, sitting in a large chair in the corner of the room was Nana, the Queen Mother, one of the most beautiful women I had ever seen.

Nana was 73 years old and when she saw me enter, she stood and greeted me with a big smile and a warm embrace. As she took her seat, I noticed that there were sofas on either side of her chair and she motioned for me to sit on one of them next to her. Word spread that I was there and soon her daughters and grandchildren filed into the room and took their places on the sofas and the floor. There must have been 20 of them sitting and watching Nana.

She began to share her testimony, something everyone in the room, save me, knew by heart. She told me about a team of young men, who five decades ago, came from America to preach in her area. News was quickly spreading that these men were holding large outdoor meetings, and the most amazing miracles were happening. People were telling of the sick being healed, the blind receiving their sight, and even people who had lost arms or legs saw them grow back!

As the fame of these meetings grew Nana, her mother and grandmother decided to go and see if such miracles were actually occurring. Her grandmother was the spiritual guide, *the* shaman of her village, and her mother was trained to be next in line when her grandmother passed away. Nana's mother was now preparing her daughter to follow in their footsteps. As shamans, these women were responsible to intercede for the people by "feeding" the gods, thus appeasing them. Now, however, they were filled with wonder at hearing the reports of such amazing power.

When they arrived at the outdoor meeting, they spent considerable time pushing their way through the huge crowd so they could be right in front of the preachers. If these stories were true, they wanted to be first hand witnesses to them. They were not disappointed. They were seeing people healed, delivered of demons, the blind were seeing and limbs were being restored to the cripples.

As they saw these miracles multiply they understood that this Spirit was not at all like the spirits they served. Their spirits had no such power, this was unique. It was during that amazing meeting that the three women decided to serve this New Spirit and they accepted Jesus Christ as their Lord and Savior.

Patty's Chalk Art

As Nana continued sharing her story, she looked intently at me and said, "Pamella, because this man who preached, saved me from having to worship the spirits of my mother and grandmother, I will never forget his name; Paul Cannon."

I was stunned to find out that this amazing woman was telling me about *my* Paul Cannon. "Oh my goodness, I know Paul Cannon. I work with him and he is with our team in Accra." She embraced me and we both wept, and wept, rejoicing in God's goodness.

Once we calmed down, Nana looked at me and said, "Please tell Paul Cannon that it was his message that saved me from having to serve the spirits of my ancestors." She then told me that her grandmother and her mother are now with the Lord, and that all of her children and grandchildren are followers of Christ.

As I was preparing to leave, her daughters pleaded with me to pray for their Nana. I was so nervous; they wanted *me* to pray for this amazing woman? So, with trepidation I began to pray for her and to bless her. When I finished I looked up and her children were sobbing and they told me, "You have prayed as if you have known our mother your entire life! Thank you so much."

As I left the village, I was in such awe that God had blessed me with this encounter and He had entrusted me to carry this message to Paul. I truly felt as if I had become a member of one more family. God is so faithful! Pamella Foster.

### On to Kumasi!

The drive to Kumasi was beautiful with all the hills and countryside. We went through Suhum, where we held a large meeting but we by-passed Agogo, Asamankese and Koforidua. It was a narrow two lane road with a lot of chuck holes most of the way and it took us 5 hours to make the trip. It was about 135 miles drive. Just before dark we had a tropical storm go through that dropped tons of rain and was quite windy. They took us to Pastor Alfred Nyamichi's house where they had a lunch prepared for us then on to the Lord Cecil Lodge where we stayed. Mark and Paul Gmitter shared the same room and bed while the rest of us had individual rooms. It cost us $550 each for our room and food which the church had pre-paid. So we reimbursed the church for it. We had breakfast each day at the hotel but our other meals were at Pastor Alfred's house where they hired Pastor Jonathan's sister to be our cook.

We met with the lead pastors at 9:00 Monday morning and a little later Pastor Alfred came. We wanted to do two tracks of our AIMS seminars but they told us that some of the literature didn't get printed as part of the CD that was sent was faulty. Also they said that some of the pastors hadn't received their invitations yet because the mail was so slow. So the start would be postponed to Tuesday at 9:00 AM. Mark and Pamella did a masterful job of negotiations as they kept it on a high plain of love and respect without trying to force things. Pastor Alfred and his leaders decided not to have all the tracks. They dropped the woman's track because most of the women wanted to be in the Business Track. Also they dropped the Advanced Track as there were not very many that wanted to take it. So we combined the two tracks of Equipping into one. Another hindrance was the high cost of a place for the pastors to stay. They usually rented a school building and they could stay there and sleep on the floor but the schools were still in session. Pastor Alfred said that it had been 4 years since Dr. Foltz did the Equipping for the Harvest and wanted everyone to take it. He also apologized to us later for having it at this time of the year rather than in August as they did the time before. That way they would have many more leaders to come from all over Ghana. He said they wanted to have another Equipping for the Harvest next year in August when the schools are closed and they would have over 1000 pastors attending.

Tuesday morning we were all at the Central Church of the House of Faith and set up and ready to go by 9:00. However because of the horrible traffic most of the ministers didn't arrive till 10:00 but they told us we could go to 3:00 or 4:00 in the afternoon. Mark played the video message of Dr. Foltz then introduced all of us and did our starter, "Why We Are Here." There was a great response of the 200 or so men and women ministers to it. I taught the Harvest Connection through the State of the World then Patty Giles taught on Prayer. Then Paul Gmitter, Mark and I finished it up. Mark and Pamella taught our seminar on Final Focus. Paul Gmitter did Church Planting Movements and I did the Biblical Basis of Partnerships and Jason taught on Networking. Dennis Jones spoke to the Pastors on Thursday afternoon and along with Jason, Joel and Neil

(Two Calvary Mission guys from Burkina Faso) did a business track all day Friday and on Saturday morning. We just ran out of time to do all that we had planned and wanted to do. Patty Giles did three chalk art drawings which they thought were "out of this world." The first one, they wanted to use for their church logo. She gave all the drawings to them after she sprayed them with a clear coat.

## Went to Separate Churches!

On Wednesday and Thursday nights each of us went to separate churches in the Kumasi area. I stayed at the Central Church on Wednesday while all the others went to the other churches. On Thursday night Paul Gmitter was at the Central Church while the rest of us went to the outlying churches. I went to a small one in the East Section where Joel had gone the night before. They had a lady pastor and I was so impressed with the respect the people had for her. She was also my interpreter. While speaking the electric power went off but I continued and finished the message. The building was packed out and it was extremely hot. I was dripping wet with perspiration. We all met at Nana's Kumasi house, friend of Dennis Jones. We had a wonderful African meal. Come to find out all of us could have stayed at Nana's but out Facilitator didn't know about it in time and had pre-paid the hotel. He also was in London, England.

The Central Church is located close to the big market where they are building a huge shopping mall. The market is across from the Zoo and entirely fills up the old Prince of Wales Park where we had a great meeting in 1953. Driving by at 5:30 in the evening the sky was filled with huge bats that nested in the big trees at the Zoo. They were as big as crows and are eaten by the mountain people as their main meat.

Friday afternoon we had the ministers to divide up into 4 groups and develop their strategies for the Unreached People Groups. Pastor Alfred and his leaders had decided to adopt three UPGs in Ghana. They were the Bana in the North, the Buam in the East and the Aowin in the Southwest. However, the largest group wanted to be involved in the AIMS China project. In the evening Dennis Jones spoke while Patty did a chalk art of the commissioning. Then we had all those trained to come and stand in groups and we prayed for them. It was a powerful time as the Lord graciously met them all. Mark and Pamella then closed out the training.

The reports from the ministers and Pastor Alfred were that it was a powerful time and they were all very pleased and excited about reaching the unreached. So many of them told me that the training was so beneficial to them and they greatly appreciated it. Ennis, one of our Translators, was a teacher of law at the University in Kumasi and said that he now wants to give his life to missions to reach the unreached because of the training.

Mark, Pamella, Jason and Dennis left Saturday afternoon for Accra and their flights to their destinations. Joel and Neil left for Burkina Faso by bus. Both of them are great guys. That left Patty, Paul Gmitter and I to minister on Sunday morning in various churches. Pastor Alfred had Paul and Patty to go west about 40 miles to a big gold mining city where they ministered in the church. He was going to speak at the Central Church but asked if I would as they were having all of their churches in Kumasi to all come for the special missions meeting. It had been four years since he had spoken to the whole group.

### What a Meeting!

The place was packed out with people dressed in their finest with standing room only. In fact many stood on the outside looking in through the windows. They worshiped for a good while and then danced for a while. It was all very orderly just as it was 50 years ago and beautiful. They would start at the back row on one side with the women and then the men. They would dance down the aisle and across the front and back to their seats. They continued this till everyone had danced. What a lovely people!

Pastor Alfred introduced me and told the crowd that I held meetings all over Ghana and he was one year old at the time. What a joy it was to stand before a sea of black and brown faces again. They were so receptive! There were about three thousand people present with a lot that couldn't even get inside. They wanted me to tell some of the things about our meetings fifty years ago. Rather than just recite history, I wove it into my message.

My message was on Joshua 14:5-15 about Caleb coming to Joshua and saying, *"Give me this mountain . . ."* I felt the Lord had given it especially for them at this time and it included a prophetic word to them which I gave at the conclusion. I drew a parallel between Caleb and myself and the many years in between. Our vision then was to bring the Gold Coast, whether kicking or screaming, into the Kingdom of God. I was only 22 years of age at the time. There were great mountains before us like the culture, the climate; the death rate of children being 7 out of 10 would die before reaching the age of 10.  I told about the great meetings in Wiamoase on Christmas morning and night where over 650 miracles happened and 850 were filled with the Holy Spirit. They really got excited! I told how the Catholics in Tarkwa, the tough gold mining town, marched up and down on the street at our meeting but when the miracles started happening they quit and came and was a part of the meeting with 1000 people coming to the Lord one night. Mentioning the names of many of the cities, like Dunkwa, Suhum, Swedru, Koforidua, Asamankese, Agogo, Cape Coast, Sekondi, Takoradi and Crobo country had them standing on their feet rejoicing.

Then I hit them with the punch line of Joshua 14:12, *"Now therefore give me this mountain . . ."* Explaining that all that happened 50 years ago was nothing compared to what the Lord has for them today. I wanted to inspire their faith so they could carry the gospel to the unreached peoples of the earth. So I hammered home the fact that they have done a great job so far but there are some huge mountains before them. There are giants in the land and great cities with great walls. These are the toughest groups of all times to reach. All that Caleb needed was a yes from God's servant and leader and he would go do it. It didn't matter what the enemy said or did because he believed God. Just as Caleb did what the whole nation couldn't do 45 years before, you will do what we couldn't do 50 years ago. Then I used their slogan which they had in a big banner across the platform, "The Church, a Monument or a Movement!" We don't want to live in the past as a monument! We want to be a Movement that takes the gospel to the ends of the earth. There is a great future ahead when the great harvest of the earth is to be brought into the Heavenly garner. By this time they were in the aisles dancing and praising God. I prayed for them en masse as we did 50 years earlier and the Lord really worked. There was no time for testimonies as Pastor Alfred wanted to receive their Faith Promises for missions. They all came bringing their envelopes dancing down the aisles just as they had done before. It was an amazing thing to watch.

### A Visit to the Past!

Pastor Alfred was so excited about Wiamoase that on Monday morning he had his driver take all of us out to this city along with Pastor Charles who had been there several times. It was only 31 miles from Kumasi but it was a step back in time. It was a beautiful drive up into the mountains with lush tropical growth at the edge of a very narrow road. Just as it was fifty years earlier, the streets of the city were all dirt including the main road in. We saw an elderly man sitting on a porch of a business so we stopped and asked him if he knew anything about the meetings fifty years earlier. He said he was seventy-three now and remembered them very well. There were very large crowds and many miracles. We asked him about the church. He said it was very large when it started and for many years but there was a war between churches and it all when downhill till hardly anything was left and his brother held what was left together. This showed us the reason why this place had not improved much in fifty years as the other places had. He showed us where the meetings were held and we drove up and took some pictures. It was right in the middle of town but is mostly filled in with buildings now. Time was running out as we had to get to the airport by 4:00 to leave for home. It was an exciting time.

I couldn't believe the progress Ghana had made during those years. Much of it is the product of the gospel of our Risen Lord being preached and people turning to Him. On Sundays, the markets don't open till afternoon as most of the people go to church. The people are so bright and intelligent with a great zeal for God. I never saw a happier people as well as so friendly. They took super good care of us.

## In Summation!

Summing up the whole thing, in spite of the problems, the Equipping for the Harvest went great. Mark handled the whole situation exceptionally well. Pamella did a great job as well as Paul and Patty. Patty said this was the greatest mission trip she had ever been on and felt we accomplished more than any trip she had been on. I figured we trained 200 ministers, both men and women. They were really excited about adopting the Bana, the Buams, the Aowins and the Chinese. Alfred said that for the rest of the year, in all their churches, they will teach the AIMS materials that we taught. They will do it in Sunday School in the youth and adult classes. They intend to reach those UPG's and that very soon. In fact, the group which adopted the Aowins has already planted five churches in that region! So they are serious about the long-term goal of reaching these groups through planting churches.

Attakra, Pastor Alfred's driver and an Elder in House of Faith, took us to the airport with Pastor Charles. It was extremely hot between 4:00 and 5:00 PM. The little plane we boarded at 5:00 had sat on the tarmac all day so it was exceptionally hot. It didn't cool off hardly any the whole trip. Arriving in Accra, we had to walk quite a ways to get to the International Terminal where long lines awaited us. We got through all the lines and still had 2 or 3 hours to wait. The rest of the trip home went smoothly. We arrived in Norfolk at 3:15 in the afternoon very weary where Mildred and Jessica Gmitter met us. Paul and Patty then boarded their individual planes for home. Thus ended a very successful mission trip! We were all glad it was finished. I came down with a bad case of Bronchitis from being tired for so long and had to see our family doctor who took care of it.

## A Finishing Note

In December of 2010, we went to Jonesborough, TN to spend Christmas with our son Thomas and Candy, his wife, and their three children. Two days after Christmas, I awakened because I was wheezing and was short of breath. A little later that morning, Tom took me to First Assist in Johnson City. They did an EKG and the doctor said that something abnormal was going on with my heart and suggested we go to

Johnson City Medical Center, one of the top one hundred heart hospitals in the country. It was very near so we went to the ER where they immediately took me to the closest room. After taking an EKG a doctor came in. I looked at him and said, "You're from Nigeria, aren't you." He looked a bit puzzled but replied, "Yes." I then asked what part was he from and he replied, "From Calabar." I then told him about being head of the team that first opened the Delta Province for the gospel in 1954 that survived. He really got excited and began to thank me and thank me for what we had done for his country. He said that he went to the University of Ibadan and because of hearing the gospel, he was converted. Well it just so happened that our first big meeting was at the race track in Ibadan. He went on to explain that if it hadn't been for us bringing the gospel that he would not have been here and be a doctor.

They found I had a heart attack and quickly did a heart cath and discovered I had a 95% blockage in a small artery right at the juncture of the major artery which was 60% blocked. The Cardiologist put in two stints which was very difficult because when he did the small one it closed up the big one. He had to use what he called "kissing balloons" to get the job done. He told me that there was no damage to my heart. They kept me overnight and discharged me the next evening. When my wife asked the doctor what would have happened if we had gone home the next day. He replied that I would not have made it. In fact he told Tom that it was a widow-maker heart attack. When I went to the Cardiologist at home, he told me I was one of the most fortunate men living after that kind of a heart attack.

Reflecting on it afterwards, my family and I began to realize the importance of it all. Here I was 700 miles from home in a hospital facility with a heart attack and the guy that saves my life is an African man who became a doctor because of our having preached the gospel to his people in Nigeria over fifty years prior. All I can say is the Lord is very gracious! As the Scripture says, *"Known unto God are all his works from the beginning of the world."* Acts 15:18. As a friend of ours, Pastor M. D. Beall, used to say, "God is cute."

On January 23rd, the first Sunday after my 80th birthday, Jack Greenwood, the pastor of the church where I'm Mission Director, had me to preach the message that morning. I had just finished my 60th year of preaching on Thanksgiving weekend. In giving the missions report, I told about the event of my heart attack and the Nigerian doctor. It excited the church greatly to see how our Lord provides ahead of time. Who knows, one you lead to Christ may one day save your own life. One never knows.

### All Praise Belongs to Jesus!

To me, the Missionary Trip to Ghana was a trip of a lifetime and it made me realize that what we had done in 1953-54 was even greater than we had ever expected. I've often said that the Lord did it all in spite of us and He did it to redeem a land. The Colonial Empires have fallen but where the Church was placed in the hands of the nationals the nation has made a lot of advances. The church in Africa is in good hands and proves we were right in 1953-4 to train and commit the work to the nationals. Again, I am so thankful that the Lord Jesus Christ let me have a small part in His great work. I feel as the Apostle Paul must have felt when he said in 1 Timothy 1:12, *"And I thank Christ Jesus our Lord who has enabled me, because He counted me faithful, putting me into the ministry."* Truly, all the glory belongs to our Lord Jesus Christ. Praise Him! PEC

# Acknowledgments

First of all, thanks and Praise goes to our Lord Jesus Christ who has done so much for me. He washed my sins away with His precious blood and filled me with the Holy Spirit then thrust me into the ministry and healed me. It was He that opened the way for me to go to Africa and then supplied the funds to do so. He was the One who did all the miracles and made a way where there was no way. Without that, there wouldn't have been anything to write about.

Secondly, thanks goes to my wonderful wife of fifty-eight years who has read the manuscript so many times and given me such encouragement though it all. She found the lost diary which has made this book possible. Thank you for loving me and praying so much for me and going with me wherever the gospel called. You have been a real inspiration to me and thousands of others. Thanks for being a wonderful mother to our three marvelous sons, Philip, Thomas and Mark and a loving grandmother to our ten grandchildren.

A special thanks to our son Thomas who has labored side by side with me for years and is involved so heavily in missions today. He has kept encouraging me to finish the book and helped so much in getting it published. Without his help, it may not have happened at all.

Thanks to Rebecca Chapman who has been such a dear friend to our family and proof read the manuscript. Thanks to Pastors Harry Jensen, Paul Gmitter, Walter Giles and Jack Greenwood for your prayerful support and all our prayer partners for praying for us.

A special thanks to Philip, Andrea, Andrew, T J, Patty, Alycia, Elizabeth, Katie, Emily and Timothy, our grandchildren who kept on asking, "Grandpa is your book done yet."

All scripture references are taken from the King James Version unless otherwise noted throughout the book.